The Five Wounds of Saint Francis

The Five Wounds of Saint Francis

An Historical and Spiritual Investigation

Solanus M. Benfatti, C.F.R.

With a foreword by Fernando Uribe, O.F.M.

TAN Books
Charlotte, North Carolina

Cover art: "Francis Receives the Stigmata," by the Master of the Bardi Saint Francis. Florence, *Galleria degli Uffizi*, tempera on wood, 1240-1250. Used with permission of the *Ministero per i Beni e le Attività Culturali* in Florence. Further reproduction by any means is forbidden.

Cover design: Lauren Rupar

ISBN: 978-0-89555-873-2

Printed and bound in the United States of America.

TAN Books
Charlotte, North Carolina
2011

To Fr. Conrad L. Harkins, O.F.M.,
my first teacher of Franciscanism

Volens autem Dominus ostendere dilectionem quam habebat in eum, posuit in membris eius et latere eius Stigmata dilectissimi Filii sui.

Wanting to show how much love he had for him, the Lord placed in his members and his side the Stigmata of his most beloved Son.

—Anonymus Perusinus

TABLE OF CONTENTS

FOREWORD

There is no doubt that the phenomenon catapulting Francis of Assisi to the highest fame even while he was still alive was his stigmatization, which occurred in September of 1224. One need only recall how the primitive biographical sources describe the immense crowd that accompanied him during his descent from La Verna or the throng of Assisians keeping watch at the Portiuncula the day of his death to see his remains marked with the five Christ-like wounds.

Yet, even if the stigmatization of Francis is recorded by various thirteenth-century sources, they are neither unanimous in their details nor complete in their descriptions. This, together with other factors, contributed to the early development of two different interpretive currents, almost two irreconcilable parties, one in favor of and the other against the historicity of the stigmata of the saint of Assisi. The polemic had a spirited rebirth towards the end of the nineteenth century and has remained alive even unto our own day, some moments being livelier than others, especially in the last two decades.

In general, the phenomenon of stigmatization can be studied from various points of view: pathological, psychological, mystical, theological, and others besides. But surely in the specific case of Francis, the necessary point of departure taking precedence over all others is the historical one. And this is precisely the perspective chosen by Solanus Benfatti for his work.

To this end, the author carries out a new and meticulous analysis of all the data in the medieval sources regarding the stigmata of the Poverello and submits the opinions of modern

scholars of the subject to a calm and serious examination. He makes a careful evaluation, moreover, of the four most representative critical theories and arrives at some convincing conclusions that, given the seriousness of the analyses and the judiciousness of the arguments, offer good assurance of the historicity of Francis's stigmata.

Then, based on the historical facts, the author is able to take up the spiritual meaning of the stigmata. Here he enters the domain of "historical theology" and, applying the modern methods of spiritual theology, successfully establishes the tricky relationship between the objective and the subjective dimensions of the historical analysis.

We are before a highly mature work. It is both conducted with great responsibility and seriousness and circumspect in its judgments and conclusions. For the still current "question" of the stigmata of Francis, it makes a valuable contribution that cannot be ignored.

—Fernando Uribe, O.F.M.

PREFACE

There are two groups of people who meet only rarely, devotees of Saint Francis of Assisi and scholars who study his life. His devotees—a wide ranging group, Christian and non-Christian alike—have no idea that the other group exists. They might see its members without knowing it, of course. When they happen upon the Libreria Francescana Internazionale in the piazza of Santa Maria degli Angeli just below Assisi they find what they need at the shop's entrance and main aisles: beautiful images of the saint and devotional books. Meanwhile, men and women of an altogether other world quietly but tenaciously examine the terse lines of the latest studies lining the bookstore's perimeter. And if the former group briefly forays into the shelves where these works live, the befuddlement is short-lived as attention quickly returns to what is familiar. But if they only knew . . . (Indeed, even in the wider scholarly world of the historical sciences—certainly outside of continental Europe, but probably anywhere outside of Italy—most academics are unaware of the complexity, breadth, and vigor of the world of Francis scholarship.)

And even while many who have dedicated entire careers to studying the Poverello are also devotees of his, the fact remains that the two worlds stand apart, and no one seems to be capable of effectively bridging the two. (I certainly am not.) So much of what is good and exciting in the academic research rarely or so slowly filters its way down to something accessible and useful for the non-specialist. Maybe this is unavoidable. Maybe we will never again see that breed of individual capable of excelling in

both worlds, the Augustines who truly plumbed the depths of both scientific study and sanctity.

It seems to be equally unavoidable, nevertheless, that there be those moments in which certain kinds of ideas do leap across the chasm, or seem to. I mean those times when the scholars are discussing among themselves questions that jar the world of devotion. The scholars are not trying to cause trouble, but only ask honest questions of the sources at their disposal with the best tools they have available. But merely asking the question draws the immediate and rapt attention of everyone else. Yes, sometimes the scholars even find through their honest research that the taboo questioning in the end did not actually yield the feared taboo results. But the damage has been done, because only headlines stick.

My book deals with such a case. The average avid reader of today has by now discovered that those miraculous Christ-like wounds that Francis of Assisi bore on his body were probably not miraculous at all, but perhaps a form of leprosy, which the saint contracted through his generous service of those suffering from that terrible disease. And yet no one has been told in a popular medium that this theory is a mere conjectural construct to answer the question: "if the stigmata were not miraculous, what might they have been?" In other words, there is no positive documentary evidence to support the theory. The historian understands the problem here, but the made-for-television documentary does not. Only headlines stick.

The fuller story of this scholarly debate—the truth or fiction of the miraculous wounds of Francis—is a long one. It began over a century ago, in those same years that scholars of the Bible were first looking critically at Divine Writ. It was hotly debated then, but remained for the most part a discussion contained within the world of scholarly journals. Only recently, with the

revival of the discussion in the early 1990's, were some of the tentative conclusions "leaked," as it were. But this was irresponsible, at least in my opinion, for the debate was unfinished.

It still is unfinished. Or at least I have wished to prolong it. At times I wondered if it were possible to make progress. I admit to having been haunted by the advice of a kind European medievalist of the highest caliber who told me before I began my work in earnest that the field was at a deadlock: the debate would remain forever open, because the medieval source documents had been fully pillaged and would yield no new spoils to resolve the debate. My respect for him alone should have been enough to bring me to set the topic aside, but against my own better judgment I continued anyway, and the present work is my best attempt at a contribution to the debate.

While I await the criticism of the scholars of my field, I will offer my own summary estimation of the state of the question: it seems to me now that the sage scholar who advised me against this work was penetrating indeed in his assessment of the situation. For he boiled the whole problem down to the dating of the tiniest of writing on the tiniest of parchments, meaning the little notes about Francis's stigmatization personally made in red ink by Brother Leo, companion of Francis, on a little parchment received from the saint himself. No scholar doubts that the handwriting on that piece of goatskin, which we still have today, belongs to Leo; the question is rather its dating. I really did not see at first how the dating of those rubrics could be a cardinal piece of evidence. And I certainly had no sense of how to contribute to the debate over that dating. In the end, though, always standing on the shoulders of the great scholars of the field, I believe to have discovered both.

To all such scholars of Francis and Franciscanism, I will be forever grateful.

Particularly, I thank the resident scholars and guest professors

at the Pontifical University "Antonianum," under whom I had the privilege of studying when I first became interested in this subject. To Fr. Pietro Messa, O.F.M., head of the medieval faculty, I am particularly grateful for constant and kind words of encouragement.

I am indebted to Fathers Wiesław Block, O.F.M. Cap., Leonhard Lehmann, O.F.M. Cap., and Joseph Henchey, C.S.S., who read an earlier version of this manuscript and offered invaluable advice.

Many helped me along the way since the time when I first began this writing project. There are numerous benefactors who assisted financially, especially with books. Earnest thanks to those who did excellent proofreading at various stages of this book's life: Bro. Richard Bailey, Cong. Orat., Bro. Paschal Coby, C.F.R., and Bro. Bonaventure Rummell, C.F.R. Thanks to Sara L. Trudeau, S.T.L., who helped me at crucial junctures to understand what was emerging from my research. I owe tremendous gratitude to Taylor Marshall for believing in this project when it was easy for me not to, and for superb editorial suggestions. I am so very thankful for the friendship and artistic inspiration of Thomas and Susan Upshur.

I thank the T.O.R. friars of Holy Spirit Friary at Franciscan University of Steubenville, who provided me a place to study quietly for a time, along with the gracious and welcoming staff at the John Paul II Library on the same campus. Also, to the friars at La Verna, who care for "*il crudo sasso intra Tevero e Arno*" and also cared for me many days one winter while I tried to penetrate the mystery of Francis, *vi ringrazio di cuore*. I thank the supportive library staff at Corrigan Memorial Library (Saint Joseph's Seminary, Dunwoodie), Fr. Steven Boyle and the Norbertines in Rome, and my friend Fr. Fidelis Moscinski, C.F.R. Thanks to the *Centro di documentazione francescana della Basilica e Sacro Convento di San Francesco* in Assisi for kindly and

efficiently supplying me with images of the *Chartula* of Francis and permission to use them.

In a very special way, I express my deepest thanks to Fr. Fernando Uribe, O.F.M., who has always made himself available to me ever since I was his student in Rome. Fr. Uribe is a most unassuming scholar. He goes about his work quietly without attracting the attention that makes headlines. Yet his method of research is so exacting, consistent, painstaking, and, above all, honest, that his labors will undoubtedly pass the test of time, and always provide sure footing for the rest of us to travel on. I am so grateful for his kindness and example.

Finally, words fail to communicate my debt to the Franciscan Friars of the Renewal and the Franciscan Sisters of the Renewal, for they have taught me those things about Francis not found in books, things indeed never said aloud, things that probably cannot be.

LIST OF ABBREVIATIONS

1 Celano	Vita prima S. Francisci / Vita beati Francisci / The Life of Saint Francis by Thomas of Celano
1 Letter to the Faithful	1 Epistola ad fideles / Earlier Exhortation / The First Version of the Letter to the Faithful
2 Celano	Vita secunda S. Francisci / Memoriale in desiderio animae / The Second Life of Saint Francis by Thomas of Celano
2 Letter to the Faithful	2 Epistola ad fideles / Later Admonition and Exhortation / Second Version of the Letter to the Faithful
3 Celano	Tractatus de miraculis beati Francisci / The Treatise on Miracles by Thomas of Celano
4 Celano	Legenda ad usum chori / The Legend for Use in the Choir by Thomas of Celano
Acts of Blessed Francis	Actus beati Francisci et sociorum eius / The Acts of Blessed Francis and His Companions
Admonitions	Verba sancte admonitionis / The Admonitions
AnalFranc	Analecta franciscana sive Chronica aliaque varia documenta ad historiam Fratrum Minorum
AnnalMin	Annales Minorum
ArchFrancHist	Archivum Franciscanum Historicum
BullFranc	Bullarium Franciscanum

CCSL	Corpus Christianorum Series Latina
Jord. Giano Chronicle	Chronica fratris Jordani / The Chronicle of Jordan of Giano
CollFranc	Collectanea Franciscana
Coming to England	Tractatus de Adventu Fratrum Minorum in Angliam / The Chronicle of Brother Thomas of Eccleston or The Coming of the Friars Minor to England
FA:ED I, II, III	Francis of Assisi: Early Documents, 3 vols., The Saint, The Founder, The Prophet
Fioretti	I Fioretti di San Francesco / The Little Flowers of Saint Francis
Florilegium	The group of stories (not known to us in their original form) sent by Leo, Rufino, and Angelo to the Minister General on August 11, 1246
Fontes	Fontes Franciscani
Forma vivendi	Forma vivendi sanctae Clarae / Form of Life Given to St. Clare
FrateFr	Frate Francesco
GreyfrRev	Greyfriars Review
Julian Speyer Vita	Julianus de Spira, Vita S. Francisci / The Life of Saint Francis by Julian of Speyer
Last Will for Poor Ladies	Ultima voluntas scripta sanctae Clarae / The Last Will Written for St. Clare and Her Sisters
Letter of Elias	Epistola encyclica de transitu S. Francisci a fr. Elia tunc ordinis vicario generali ad omnes provincias ordinis missa / Letter on the Passing of Saint Francis by Brother Elias
Letter to Leo	Epistola fratri Leoni / A Letter to Brother Leo

Letter to the Order	Epistola toti Ordini missa / A Letter to the Entire Order
Major Legend	Legenda maior S. Francisci / The Major Legend of Saint Francis by Bonaventure
Major Legend, Miracles	The collection of miracles that close *The Major Legend*
Mira circa nos	The canonization Bull of Francis, *Mira circa nos*, by Gregory IX
MiscFranc	Miscellanea Francescana
MS Little	The collections of episodes (at ff. 104-141) in Oxford Bodleian Library cod. lat. theol. d 23 that are related to the *Florilegium*
PG	Patrologia Graeca
PL	Patrologia Latina
Praises of God	Laudes Dei Altissimi / The Praises of the Most High God
Regula bullata	Regula bullata / The Rule of 1223 / The Later Rule
Regula non bullata	Regula non bullata / The Rule of 1221 / The Earlier Rule
Rubrics of Leo	The autograph "rubrics" made by Leo on the autograph parchment of the *Blessing for Brother Leo*
Scripta	C. Paolazzi's critical edition of the writings of Francis (2009)
Three Companions	Legenda trium sociorum / The Legend of the Three Companions
True Joy	Da vera et perfecta laetitia / True and Perfect Joy

Other abbreviations

bk.	book
cf.	confer
chap.	chapter
cod.	codex
col.	column
esp.	especially
fig.	figure, figures
f., ff.	folio; foli
MS	manuscript
n.	note
no., nos.	number, numbers
p.	page, pages
prol.	prologue
pt.	part
r	recto side
tom.	tomus, tomi
v., vv.	verse, verses
v	verso side
vol., vols.	volume, volumes

Unless otherwise noted, I will cite the biographical Francis sources using the additional verse divisions found in the *Fontes* printing. For the writings of Francis I will use, except when otherwise noted, the text and divisions of *Scripta*. All English translations, when available, will be taken from *Francis of Assisi: Early Documents*, but are always subject to modification.[1] Vulgate quotations will be made from *Biblia sacra vulgatae editionis, Sixti V Pontificis Maximi iussu recognita et Clementis VIII auctoritate edita*. English translations of Italian materials are mine when not otherwise noted.

---

1 Modifications I have made were rarely to correct translation errors but rather to make the text more clearly reflect the original on a literal and syntactical level, which occasionally has been helpful for expository purposes, though sometimes to the detriment of style. In a few places I have had to update the writings of Francis according to the new critical edition, *Scripta*.

CHRONOLOGY OF THE LIFE OF FRANCIS AND RELATED EVENTS

The Youth of Francis (1182-1204)

1182 Francis is born to a successful cloth merchant, Pietro Bernardone.

1202 At a battle between the Assisian "middle class" and Perugian / Assisian nobility, Francis is taken captive and imprisoned for about a year, probably released in light of the November peace agreement of 1203.

The Beginning of His Conversion (1204-1205)

1205 *Spring.* After a long period of convalescence following imprisonment, Francis joins a military expedition headed to Apulia. He returns after a few days, however, having been instructed to do so by the Lord in a dream.

Francis's Life as a Penitent (1205-1208)

1205 Francis begins a period of seeking to understand the Lord's will for him, and perhaps at this time has his decisive encounters with lepers, which he cites in his *Testament* as the turning point in early conversion away from "the world."

Praying before the crucifix in the little and ruined church of San Damiano one day, Francis hears words from the crucifix: "Francis, don't you see that my house is being destroyed? Go, then, and rebuild it for me." He begins to live at the little church and physically rebuild it, leaving the world and joining the ranks of the class known as "penitents."

1206 Francis's father takes him to trial before the bishop because he had sold some of his father's cloth without permission, hoping to use the money for the broken-down church. Francis dramatically returns not only the money gained but also even the clothes he is wearing, announcing as he does so: "Until now I have called Pietro di Bernardone my father. But, because I have proposed to serve God, I . . . say from now on: 'Our Father who are in heaven,' and not 'My father, Pietro di Bernardone.'" Francis leaves Assisi for a brief time. When he returns he dedicates himself to rebuilding churches and probably continues to work at leprosaria.

A Band of Penitents (1208-1209)

1208 *April 16*: Two Assisians, Bernard of Quintavalle and a certain Peter, tell Francis that they want to do what he is doing. Going to the Church of San Nicoló, they open the Gospel book three times and on each opening discover passages about leaving everything behind to follow Jesus and on the manner of doing so. These verses will become the basis of a brief, written "rule of life."

The Initial Oral Approval (1209-1216)

1209 Francis and a small band of followers take their rule (now lost) to Rome, seeking universal approval for their way of life from Pope Innocent III, and receive oral approbation. The friars return to Assisi, their preaching missions begin to have more success, and their numbers increase.

1212 The young Clare of Assisi is received by Francis into the state of penitence at the Portiuncula. After two brief sojourns elsewhere, she soon begins her own way of life at San Damiano with her sister Agnes, a cloistered mode of living distinguished from other such by its radical

choice for poverty. Francis writes for them a "form of life," fragments of which are preserved in Clare's Rule (Chap. 6).

Growth, Mission, Expansion (1217-1219)

1217 The friars' General Chapter sends its first missionaries beyond the Alps and overseas to the near East. The attempts are terribly unsuccessful: the friars are unprepared, do not know the languages, are treated as heretics or fools, and are even beaten and humiliated.

1219 Now the General Chapter chooses to try once again to send out missionaries. Friars go to Germany, Hungary, France, and Spain-Morocco. This time they are better prepared: well-educated clerics have joined them who can preach to clergy in Latin with finesse, and friars who know the vernacular languages can preach to the people. They also now bear papal letters proving their legitimacy. New provinces are established and growth in numbers is tremendous.

Francis chooses as his missionary assignment a trip to the Middle East. He and a companion go to Damietta in Egypt in the midst of the Fifth Crusade. Francis gains an audience with the Sultan of Egypt and preaches the Gospel to him.

Crisis in the Order, Interior Trials, the Rule (1220-1223)

1220 *Summer.* Francis returns to Italy after receiving news that aspects of the Order's legislation are being changed against his vision by the vicars left in charge. Francis goes directly to Pope Honorius III and requests that Cardinal Hugolino of Ostia be given as the Order's "protector"—a special helper, advisor, and advocate.

At a September chapter Francis renounces his formal governance of the Order, appointing a vicar in his stead.

He seems to be struggling to know his role in the Order he founded.

1221 *Spring*: Francis's vicar dies and Elias Bombarone is appointed.

Cardinal Hugolino has probably helped the friars to realize that it is crucial to finalize the written form of the Rule, which has been growing and changing at each General Chapter since 1209. At Pentecost, the Chapter approves a version of the Rule we still can read today (generally referred to as *Regula non bullata*—the rule without a papal bull), but it is not in turn approved by the Holy See, so work on it must continue.

1222 During these years the physical suffering of Francis increases dramatically, especially because of a serious eye disease he has contracted. Likewise, Francis is suffering interiorly from a prolonged "temptation." It is hard to say what this was precisely, but it seems related to the evolution of the Order. One thing is clear: he is hurt that some friars are leaving behind the original simplicity of their vocation to seek ambitious roles instead. The dictated lesson on *True and Perfect Joy* perhaps may be read and understood in this light.

1223 Francis goes to the hermitage friary at Fonte Colombo to work on the Rule, which is presented to the Chapter at Pentecost, certainly modified there in various ways, and approved. *November 29*: Pope Honorius III officially approves the Rule of the Friars Minor, which we call the *Regula bullata*.

Stigmata, Final Illness, Death (1224-1226)

1224 A cleric and talented Master of Theology, Haymo of Faversham, joins the Order at Paris. In September

of that same year, a group of friars, including some well-educated, sets out from Paris to begin an English province. By late October friars from this mission are established in Oxford, the other leading university city of Europe.

September: On the mountain of La Verna, while making the "Lent" of Saint Michael, Francis receives the stigmata, after which he writes the *Praises of God* on one side of a little parchment, with a blessing for his companion Leo on the other.

Winter: Francis begins his last preaching tour, riding on a donkey because of his failing health. He probably passes through Rieti, Siena, and Le Celle di Cortona.

1225 *Spring*: Francis stays for a long period adjacent to the monastery of the Poor Ladies at San Damiano. There he writes the *Canticle of Brother Sun*, a robust and masterfully composed prayer somewhat in the tradition of Daniel 3:29-68. It is directed to the "Most High, powerful, and good Lord," who is praised in and through his creation. There Francis also writes an exhortative canticle addressed to Clare and the Poor Ladies. Both writings are in the vernacular Italian dialect of the region, unlike almost all his other writings, which are written in passable Latin.

Summer: Francis is taken to the Rieti Valley for treatment by a physician at the residence of the papal curia. In the town of Fonte Colombo Francis's eyes are cauterized in an ineffectual attempt to cure his advancing eye disease. Later, Francis's ears are pierced at San Fabiano near Rieti in another futile treatment.

1226 *Spring*: Now Francis goes to Siena for more treatments, where he hemorrhages and vomits blood. He dictates some final words, the so-called "Siena Testament," of

which we have biographical testimonies but no independent manuscript.

May or June: Francis sets out again for Assisi, resting along the way at Le Celle di Cortona, where it is sometimes said that he wrote the longer *Testament*.

July or August: He is taken from Assisi to Bagnara (in the mountains north of Assisi), probably to escape the summer heat.

August or September: When Francis is brought back to Assisi he stays in the bishop's house, but when he knows his death is imminent he asks to be returned to the Portiuncula.

October 4th (after sunset on October 3rd): Francis dies at St. Mary of the Angels, the Portiuncula. The next day his body is taken to San Damiano for the Poor Ladies to see one last time, then to St. George's to be entombed.

After the Death of Francis

1227 *March 19*: Cardinal Hugolino becomes Pope Gregory IX.

Pentecost: The General Chapter elects John Parenti as Minister General.

1228 *July 16*: Pope Gregory IX canonizes Francis at the Church of St. George.

Friar Thomas of Celano is asked by the pope to write the first and official "biography" of Francis.

1229 Before February 25, Thomas finishes the *Life of Saint Francis*, often known as *1 Celano*.

1230 *May 30*: The body of Francis is transferred to the Basilica of Saint Francis (which indicates that the *Basilica inferiore* would have been largely completed by then).

1232 After John Parenti dies, Elias is now elected by the Chapter to serve as Minister General.

1239 *May*: Elias is asked by the Chapter to step down from office. Albert of Pisa, first priest Minister General, is elected in his stead.

1240 Between March 4th of this year and August 22, 1241, the work we now call *The Anonymous of Perugia* is written.

1244 The General Chapter of the Friars Minor, held at Genoa, issues a request that friars who know things about Francis's life not recorded in the official legend write them down and send them to the Minister General.

1246 *August 11*: Companions of Francis and his caretakers at the end of his life, Leo, Rufino, and Angelo, write a letter from Greccio to serve as a cover for a collection of stories about Francis they have written and are forwarding to the Minister General, Crescentius of Iesi.
Soon Thomas of Celano receives this collection of stories among a packet of new materials from Crescentius and begins working on writing a new form of Francis's life.

1247 Thomas dedicated the completed work, which is often called *2 Celano*, to Crescentius while he was still in office (up to July), so the work was completed some time before then.

1257 Regent master of theology at the Parisian study house, Bonaventure of Bagnoregio, is elected as Minister General.

1263 Bonaventure completes a new life of Francis, meant to become the official one and replace the other existing ones.

1271 *November 13*: Leo, companion of Francis, dies.

1311 Some time during this year, probably before the Council of Vienne, a friar at the Sacro Convento in Assisi incorporates passages from the old scrolls of Leo, perhaps kept in a bookcase there since the time Thomas of

Celano used them in 1247, in a compilation of stories of Francis.

1322 Some time between the death of John of La Verna in this year and 1337, the *Acts of Blessed Francis and His Companions* is completed, the work on which *The Little Flowers of St. Francis* (*Fioretti*) is based.

GENERAL INTRODUCTION

I. Reading the Early Writings about Francis

Without pretending that this book is written for a popular audience, I still have the thought that non-specialists might be interested in it. That is why I will begin by trying to introduce in a broader way the basics of the early written materials about Francis of Assisi.[1] His dossier, like his person, is indeed fascinating, which probably accounts for so many non-Franciscan historians devoting considerable attention to it.

1. The "Franciscan Question"

The so-called "Franciscan Question" was and is a historiographical debate about the identification, chronology, interrelationship, and historical value of the early written materials about Francis.[2] I will give a highly abbreviated version of its story.

The seed ground of the debate was tilled in the nineteenth century as scholars began to profit from the first printed editions of numerous hagiographical sources for Francis's life. But the discussion really began in earnest at the turn of the twentieth century and gained particular momentum when the French historian Paul Sabatier discovered a manuscript copy of the *Speculum perfectionis* (Mirror of Perfection). That manuscript styled its contents as the earliest biography of Francis. And since, we now know, elements of that work in fact flow from a later (early fourteenth century) and polemical perspective on Francis, Sabatier's thesis sparked vivacious debates and contributed to the mushrooming of text- and literary-critical studies.[3]

A new urgency created a barrage of scholarly activity in Europe, especially focused on mining medieval manuscript

collections so as to locate every potentially valuable written documentary source for the Assisian's life. What emerged was as dizzyingly abundant as complicated. There were officially sanctioned biographies (*legendae*) and works for liturgical use of the highest literary and rhetorical quality; there were disjointed compilations of unpolished vignettes written in passable but mediocre Latin; there were collections of stories with a polemical edge; there were works edited and translated for popular divulgation, sometimes quaint, sometimes fantastic. The dossier of Francis had it all, and that prolifically (no other medieval hagiographic dossier matches it in size). It had everything except apparent anchor points that scholars could agree on and use to make sense of the whole.

2. Anchor Points: 1 Celano and 2 Celano

With time, however, two texts would finally emerge as fixed points, anchors in an otherwise stormy debate, namely the two major hagiographical portraits of Francis written by Thomas of Celano: the *Vita beati Francisci* (1 Celano)[4] written in 1228-1229, and the *Memoriale in desiderio animae* (2 Celano),[5] written in 1246-1247. Scholars still agree today: the other early texts essential for historical knowledge of Francis of Assisi can all be explained in relation to these two.

For example, a constant and consuming question has always concerned the sources for *2 Celano*. We are happily in a position now to know some certain elements of the answer. A simplified version is this: the sources we have today (at least in some form, complete or incomplete) that Thomas of Celano himself had at his disposal for writing that second life are these: *(1) The Anonymous of Perugia*;[6] (2) some form of what is known to us today as *The Legend of the Three Companions*;[7] and (3) a collection of stories written by his companions, Leo, Rufino, and Angelo.

As for *1 Celano,* the only certain, detached, and extant written sources of Thomas's that we still have are an encyclical letter

written by the then acting Minister General, Elias (*The Letter of Br. Elias*),[8] and some of Francis's own writings.

Adding the so-called *Treatise on Miracles* by Thomas of Celano,[9] we have now listed the essential extant written documents for historical knowledge of the saint from Assisi. All the other documents and stories, with certain minor exceptions, depend on these. Legends such as the *Vita* written by Julian of Speyer rely almost exclusively on *1 Celano*, while the spiritual-theological masterpiece of Bonaventure, the *Legenda maior,* adds precious little historical information, and instead merely reworks the data provided by *2 Celano* (with a few exceptions). Other biographical sources, even later ones, have historical value at times, but remain marginal enough that a concise introduction like this one need not discuss them.

3. The "Two Waves" of Material

It is helpful to look at these materials positioned between the two Celanian poles in terms of belonging to one of two "waves" of material.

a) The canonization and the production of the official legend

The "first wave" of material comes about in connection with the canonization. While we no longer have the canonization process in a detached, integral form, it is plausible that it has been subsumed into the last part of the third book of *1 Celano.* Probably around the time of the canonization itself Thomas was commissioned by the pope to write the official *legenda.* So, the materials that he received or generated in those days, plus the collections of materials likely recorded at the tomb, and any other possible interviews conducted by the Holy See leading up to the canonization would constitute the first wave of written material about Francis.

b) The Chapter of Genoa and the wave of "companion materials"

The "second wave" of written material is that which Thomas of Celano held in his hands as he wrote *2 Celano* in 1246-1247. I said earlier that this material comprises *The Anonymous of Perugia*, *The Legend of the Three Companions*, and a collection of companion stories. I will explain this in more detail.

The friars' General Chapter of 1244, held at Genoa, issued a request that memories of Francis not recorded in the official legend be written and sent in to the Minister General. The responses to that request constitute the second wave of materials at issue here. Locating those materials, however, is not simple, because they were not systematically copied or disseminated in their original form, being meant rather for incorporation into the existing *vita*.

In order to locate and identify this material, we have to begin with *2 Celano* and work backwards via source-critical study, consisting essentially in philological comparison of that document with other existing documents. And, though I have said we have still today at our disposal many of the sources Thomas had for his own use in 1246-1247, it is nevertheless clear that in some cases the current form in which the apparent source document exists is not as it was when Thomas first received it. In the case of *The Anonymous of Perugia*, possible changes do not seem to be many or dramatic. But as for *Three Companions*, it seems that the last two chapters are later additions (among other possible interpolations and changes). Meanwhile, the effort to locate the other collection of companion stories requires its own discussion.

c) The Letter of Greccio and the "*Florilegium*"

The effort to locate the original material consigned to the Minister General in response to the Chapter of Genoa centers especially on the search for a collection of stories that we can call the *Florilegium*.[10] The way we know about this group of

stories is from a letter sent from Greccio on August 11, 1246, and addressed to the then Minister General. The authors are Brothers Leo, Rufino, and Angelo, and their letter purposes to be a cover for material described as a few "flowers" picked from the larger field of potential stories about Francis.[11]

But the problem with the Greccio letter, the authenticity of which no scholar doubts, is that it appears to have come down to us separated from the material it originally accompanied. Instead, the letter is found attached to most manuscripts of a small *legenda* (odd, since at 1:8 the three friars say that they are not writing a legend),[12] which is named in modern times precisely for its codicological association with this letter, the *Legend of the Three Companions.*

If this is true, then where are the real "flowers" written by Leo, Rufino, and Angelo? The basically agreed upon answer to this question, finally reached in recent decades after much toil and vivacious debate, is that a particular, early fourteenth-century manuscript is the single best preserver (though not the only)[13] of a large number of these episodes. Nowadays, we call that manuscript (which is catalogued as Codex 1046 at the Biblioteca Augusta in Perugia) *The Assisi Compilation.*

d) *The Assisi Compilation*[14]

The Assisi Compilation is a hodgepodge of stories compiled and copied by an unknown person[15]—probably a Friar Minor at the Sacro Convento—in 1311.[16] As a compilation, therefore, it obviously does not precede *2 Celano*. Among the mishmash of episodes, however, are a great many that scholars agree are primitive forms of the *Florilegium* episodes that Thomas had at his disposal when he was writing in 1246-1247. In fact, scholars sometimes hold that the apposite groups of episodes in *The Assisi Compilation* might even have been copied directly from the original scrolls of Leo reported to have been in the *armarium* at the

Sacro Convento in the first quarter of the fourteenth century.[17] There are other compilations similar to this one, which in a few cases contain some primitive episodes that *The Assisi Compilation* does not. One of those will be relevant to this book. It is found in a document we normally call *Manuscript "Little,"* and I will introduce it later.

4. Conclusion

With this, we have the more important facts for understanding the gist of the documentation most essential for coming to sound historical knowledge of the biographical details of Francis of Assisi's life. Here I only introduce the bare facts. Important questions about the value of each work will have to be addressed as they come up in the context of my study.

In Part One of this book, I will have to introduce other more minor documents that figure in not so minor ways to the discussion of the stigmata. In Part Three, it will be essential to speak of Francis's own writings, which are by now considered to be the measuring stick against which any hypothesis about Francis's experience must always be finally judged.

II. The Historical-Theological Approach

Since studies on Francis's stigmata have been done from many different methodological and ideological perspectives, I think the greatest service I can make at the outset of my book is to be explicit about my own, for it has every bearing on the procedure and outcome.

This book should be categorized as historical theology. When I use this term I am referring to historiographical work on a theologically relevant topic done from the perspective of a Christian believer. I will try to explain this more.

1. Subjective and Objective Dimensions of History

In the abstract, and at its most basic, the work of the historian is to identify events that have occurred in the past and

describe them. This definition implies a subjective dimension and an objective one.[18]

The work of the historian always bears a significant subjective dimension. This is immediately evident already in the mere choice of which events to study and which to leave aside. Or again, it is evident in the act of describing the events because every act of description is already an interpretation of the data. For, every description necessitates the exercise of making connections with other events and of identifying patterns and themes. This is all interpretive and thus subjective. My view is that this subjective dimension is absolutely and necessarily part of the historian's work and should not be considered a weakness or some kind of unhappy byproduct of the burden of limited human perspective. Historical truth, in my view, is not to be found in some quantifiable, discrete fact plucked out of time by the surgeon-steady hands of the meticulous historian. Historical truth, rather, is to be discovered in a moment of insight into the data, which presupposes precisely the personal perspective of the historian. However, since historians may not agree on the value of each interpretive key, it is always helpful when scholars are transparent about their own.

While I insist that this subjective dimension is integral to the historian's work, it is simultaneously true that the historian must work in the most rigorous and honest manner possible. This is the objective dimension. In gathering data and trying to identify "what really happened," all of the critical methods of exegesis should be applied with care, according to the peculiarities of each documentary source. This work is always painstaking and difficult, but the temptation to sidestep or truncate this phase of research must be avoided at all costs if the work is to have any value.

2. A Subjective Perspective: Christian

To do history from a Christian vantage point has unavoidable implications. It means above all recognizing that history is

always in some manner a nexus point of nature and grace. The lengthy story of salvation recorded in Sacred Scripture shows, if anything, that history is the stage for the in-breaking of the Universal into the particular. And, as was made shockingly and definitively manifest in the Incarnation of the Son of God, the Particular also now has universal implications. This means that the Christian historian, while exhausting the rigors of the critical methods to arrive at some hypothesis, can and must sometimes ask questions like, "Is this consistent with God?" and "Does God work this way?"

3. Historical-Theology and the Stigmatization

I can show concretely some implications that the historical-theological approach as I understand it has for the topic of this book by using as a point of departure an issue raised by an active scholar on the subject.

Kees van Dooren has expressed dissatisfaction with what he thinks are equivocal treatments by certain historians. The issue, he says, is that these scholars insist that the stigmata of Francis can be demonstrated to be historical "fact," whereas their divine origin cannot be proved.[19] He quotes, for example, Jacques Dalarun who has written that "it is for the historian to ascertain that an earthquake took place here at a certain time on a certain day" but not to "explain why earthquakes happen."[20] Statements like these, says van Dooren, are simply "an attempt to escape the delicacy of the problem."[21] If we can say that Francis had wounds on his body but not that they were of divine origin, the scholar wants to know why they should be called "stigmata."

My answer to this question would bring us back to the relationship between the objective and subjective dimensions of historical analysis.

According to the demands of objective study, I suggest that the historian—any historian—must in the case at hand proceed

in the following manner. First, he or she must use the scientific means at his or her disposal (systematic, unbiased, and rigorously reasoned methods) to determine as much as possible which documentary sources are available and in what ways they are reliable for knowledge of the event that is past and is no longer able to be known through direct experience. Then, the scholar makes (nothing more than) a more or less probable hypothesis as to "what really happened."

To do so in our case means that the historian must ask and answer these questions: (1) Did Francis have wounds in his hands and feet and side? (2) If so, is there anyone who claims that Francis thought that he had experienced them as of divine origin? (3) If yes, do we have good reason to believe either that the witness was mistaken that Francis claimed this as his experience or that the witness or Francis fabricated the story?

Then, if the answers to the aforesaid questions are affirmative, affirmative, and negative respectively, it remains for the Christian historian to try to answer the question of whether this experience, which has been provisionally but reasonably attributed to Francis, is consistent with divine activity. If so, he or she can attempt to offer an interpretation of what that divine action meant in the life of Francis, in particular, and perhaps what it means for Christian life in general.

III. The Stigmata Debate

Controversy over the reality of Francis's stigmata is not new but is in fact traceable all the way back to the thirteenth century.[22]

At the very beginning, of course, it was as if Francis's stigmata were too new and shocking to be freely talked about. But this did not last long. Perhaps, as I will have occasion to consider later, the detraction that would come was often mere rejoinder. For, after the initial hesitancy over the miraculous wounds subsided, caution was replaced with bravado, and the stigmata

became a rallying cry of the group that he founded, seen, as they were, as a mark of approval for Francis and for them.[23] Disputes over their authenticity followed almost necessarily.

Later, the stigmata were sometimes thought to be an irresponsible or even blasphemous attribution, especially in the era of the Reformation.

After the Age of Enlightenment had made its mark, efforts began to focus on finding better, natural explanations for their origin, if there really were wounds in the first place. Of course, proponents of the supernatural wounds did not allow this without a fight. The height of this debate was at the end of the nineteenth and the beginning of the twentieth century.[24] It took place largely in Italian and German scholarly journals, with the German school bearing the more critical character.[25] It is not necessary here to retrace this lengthy and sometimes tedious debate—I will bring up its participants in Part Two only when recent historians have made themselves heirs of their positions. I note only that even when the debate was textually based (not always the case by any means), the unspoken presupposition behind the critical arguments against the stigmata was that the philosophical category of the miraculous is inadmissible.

The debate waned for decades but has resurfaced in recent ones, enjoying advances but not resolution.

The unsettled state of the historical question has likewise prevented solid spiritual studies from being accomplished. Of course this is true, for the spiritual treatment can never precede the historical. Too often, spiritual studies have been based on truisms and superficial elements. Sometimes they have been too hasty in equating the experience of Francis with that of other stigmatics, never founding that presumption on solid analysis of the data. But most frequently, the problem has been in exegetical method, misunderstanding the documentary dossier of Francis by naïvely assuming that one need only line up the various

accounts and harmonize them in order to arrive at an historical reconstruction on which to base the spiritual reading; the dossier of Francis is just not that simple.

Happily, we are in a better position than ever to avoid these pitfalls. A couple of converging factors have brought this about. First, we are in the fortunate position today of inheriting the so-called Franciscan Question in a rather stable form, as I have already explained. After more than a century of rigorous philological and exegetical study of the documentary dossier of Francis of Assisi, we are now in a position to confidently propose hypotheses about the early narratives, their sources, and their relationships with one another; in some cases, the dossier is of such integrity that, if we proceed carefully, we can propose hypotheses about the historical facts behind the narratives in a way that might even satisfy even historians of the old positivist school.

The second converging factor is the constructive direction of spiritual-theological methodology in certain sectors, where greater value is being given to what we can call the historical particular.[26] In other words, the singular and unrepeatable experience of Francis is recognized as important, which not only helps to avoid hasty conflations with others' but, more importantly, makes possible the identification of the unique work of God in this one man's life.

This is to say that we are not simply interested in Francis insofar as he too is an example of that supernatural phenomenon known as stigmatization, a category familiar to us today. Rather, we should first be interested in what it meant concretely in the life of Francis of Assisi, an individual who lived in a particular place at a particular time 800 years ago before there even was that phenomenon at all.

What did Francis think when he first looked down and saw on his hands, feet, and side these marks? How did it fit

in his own conception of his own vocation? What did it mean to the man who had set out to "follow the Lord's footsteps" and "live according to the form of the Holy Gospel" so many years before? This is what is interesting. This is what should precede any effort to systematize any spiritual categories generally applicable to every Christian life. Francis of Assisi was a man whose life was consciously and radically rooted in the objective doctrines of Christianity, but he experienced their effects in his life in subjective, irrepeatable ways, because every life is the life of an irrepeatable subject. And if the subject in question is an exemplary Christian—in this case among the most exemplary of Christians ever—then the particulars of his or her experiences are interesting and important for the rest of us, which is why some are beginning to speak of the "'lived theology' of the saints."[27]

IV. Structure and Plan of This Book

In Part One, I will introduce the earliest written materials about Francis's stigmata. There I will try to give initial indications on the importance and value of each early source, distinguishing primary sources from those that build on or deviate from them.

Part Two of the book will seek to determine what finally can be known of the historical event of Francis's stigmatization through a detailed analysis of the recent scholarly discussions about the early sources presented in the first part. This part of the book is the longer and more tedious stretch, but it seems to me to be necessary if we are ever going to move forward with the debate. As I evaluate each of four scholarly positions, I will inch forward little by little towards an understanding of the state of the question. By the end, I will be able to summarize the results in a cohesive fashion and even offer a provisory reconstruction of the event.

In the final part of my book, I want to try something

difficult but important, namely to see what can be guessed of Francis's personal experience of the stigmata. The reason why this is so difficult—even foolhardy—is because Francis never writes explicitly about the stigmata at all, and the biographical sources say he was very secretive about them. What, then, could we know of his experience? The answer to this depends first on being able to determine in Parts One and Two something certain about his experience based on first-hand information given to personal confidants. The rest we will have to surmise. This we can try to do in two ways. First, we have to establish reliable understandings of his personal spirituality and vision, and this is made possible through recent advances in the study of his writings. If we can do that, we will have a chance of guessing how an extraordinary phenomenon such as this one would fit in the larger picture of this man's spiritual self-understanding. Second, we must see how the La Verna event fits in the real life situation in which Francis finds himself. That is, what was this real person going through in his real life when this event occurred? What was the real-life experience that contextualized the mystical phenomenon? In this way the individual in all his uniqueness will come alive, the caricatures of a lawn-statue saint will be done away with, and the real holiness of this most important of figures can shine through.

---

1 Francis, son of Peter of Bernardone, born and died in Assisi (24 June [?] 1182–4 October 1226), founder of the Order of Friars Minor. For basic biographical details see Roberto Rusconi, *Francesco d'Assisi, santo (Francesco di Pietro di Bernardone)*, in *Dizionario biografico degli Italiani*, vol. 49, a cura di Alberto Maria Ghisalberti (Roma: Istituto della Enciclopedia Italiana, 1997), 664-678; and Roberto Rusconi, *Francis of Assisi in the Sources and Writings*, translated from the Italian by Nancy Celaschi, OSF (St. Bonaventure, NY: Franciscan Institute, 2008). An excellent new attempt at the very difficult biography is: André Vauchez, *François d'Assise. Entre histoire et mémorie* (Paris: Librairie Arthème Fayard, 2009); Italian translation: *Francesco d'Assisi. Tra storia e memoria*, edizione italiana a cura di Grado Giovanni Merlo (Torino: Giulio Einaudi Editore, 2010). The Assisian is traditionally understood to be the first person to have borne on his body "stig-

mata," wounds of supernatural origin patterned after the manner of the crucifixion marks of Jesus Christ.

2 Cf. Fernando Uribe, *Introduzione alle fonti agiografiche di san Francesco e santa Chiara d'Assisi (secc. XIII-XIV)*, traduzione dell'edizione spagnola rivista ed ampliata, Saggi 7 (S. Maria degli Angeli-Assisi: Edizioni Porziuncola, 2002), 3-34.

3 The manuscript Sabatier discovered—currently catalogued as MS 1743 at the Mazarin in Paris—had the date of MCCXXVIII. This 1228 would have meant our 1227 since it was under the Pisan calendar. Therefore, this work would have been written after the death of Francis but before the canonization, and therefore before *1 Celano* (the true first biography of Francis, commissioned by the Holy See). Later, however, better manuscripts would be found showing that the first "X" was a copyist error in place of another "C." The year should be 1318.

4 The critical edition is: Thomas de Celano, *Vita prima S. Francisci* [=*1 Celano*], in *AnalFranc* X, 3-115; now also in: *Fontes*, 275-424; English translation: *The Life of Saint Francis by Thomas of Celano*, in *FA:ED* I, 180-308.

5 Thomas de Celano, *Vita secunda S. Francisci* [=*2 Celano*], in *AnalFranc* X, 127-268; now also in *Fontes*, 443-639; English translation: *The Remembrance of the Desire of a Soul (The Second Life of Saint Francis) by Thomas of Celano*, in *FA:ED* II, 239-393. As the editors of the English-language volume reflect in their choice of title for the work, the standard title, *Vita secunda*, may need to be reconsidered. The incipit may be better, and reads: *"Memoriale in desiderio animae" de gestis et verbis sanctissimi patris nostri Francisci*. An introduction to the work is found at F. Uribe, *Introduzione alle fonti*, 88-116. A recent proposal for a new critical edition is in: Felice Accrocca, "Le due redazioni del *Memoriale nel desiderio dell'anima* di Tommaso da Celano," *FrateFr* 72 (2006): 153-186.

6 The critical edition is in Lorenzo Di Fonzo, "L'Anonimo Perugino tra le Fonti Francescane del Sec. XIII. Rapporti Letterari e Testo Critico," *MiscFranc* 72 (1972): 117-483, at 435-465; now also in *Fontes*, 1311-1351; English translation: *The Beginning or Founding of the Order and the Deeds of Those Lesser Brothers Who Were the First Companions of Blessed Francis in Religion (The Anonymous of Perugia) by John of Perugia*, in *FA:ED* II, 34-58.

7 For the text see: Théophile Desbonnets, "Legenda trium sociorum. Edition critique," *ArchFrancHist* 67 (1974): 38-144, text at 89-144; now also in *Fontes*, 1373-1445; English translation: *The Legend of the Three Companions*, in *FA:ED* II, 66-110. On the place that *Three Companions* held in the late nineteenth and twentieth-century historiographical debate, and for a general introduction to the work, see F. Uribe, *Introduzione alle fonti*, 15-20 and 195-228, with particular attention on the relationship between the Greccio letter and the legend at 196-201.

8 Cited and examined at length in Part One.

9 Thomas de Celano, *Tractatus de miraculis B. Francisci* [=*3 Celano*], in *AnalFranc* X, 269-330; now also in *Fontes*, 643-754; English translation: *The Treatise on the Miracles of Saint Francis by Thomas of Celano*, in *FA:ED* I, 399-468. Essential introduction to the work is found at F. Uribe, *Introduzione*, 116-125. Though for simplicity's sake I am not treating this work here, it does add important bio-

graphical information. For example, this work is our early source for information on Lady Jacoba da Settesoli.

10 *Florilegium* is a technical term for a compilation or anthology of texts. *Florilegia* of all sorts were frequently made in the Middle Ages, whether as collections of theological positions of Patristic authors, collections of *exempla* used for preaching purposes, etc. Here "*Florilegium*" will be capitalized and refer to a specific collection of stories made in 1246. It is not to be confused with the fourteenth-century work known as the *Fioretti*, or *Little Flowers of Saint Francis*.

11 " . . . de amoeno prato quosdam flores, arbitro nostro, pulchriores excerpimus" (*Three Companions* 1:9).

12 The literary form of a *legenda* was characterized by being more or less chronological and including the three elements of *conversio*, *conversatio*, and *miracula* (conversion, converted manner of life, miracles).

13 Later, we will have the occasion to use a similar such compilation, one normally called Manuscript "Little."

14 *"Compilatio Assisiensis" dagli scritti di fra Leone e Compagni su s. Francesco d'Assisi. Dal Ms. 1046 di Perugia*, II edizione integrale riveduta e corretta con versione italiana a fronte e varianti, a cura di Marino Bigaroni, Pubblicazioni della Biblioteca Francescana, Chiesa Nuova 2 (S. Maria degli Angeli—Assisi: Edizioni Porziuncola, 1992). English translation: *The Assisi Compilation*, in *FA:ED* II, 118-230. For preliminary indications see: F. Uribe, *Introduzione*, 24-28; 273-307.

15 This work, which may contain many of the episodes original to the *Florilegium*, is also a *florilegium*.

16 Hence the modern appellation, "The Assisi Compilation."

17 In 1311, Ubertino of Casale writes that he has before his eyes a book and scrolls (*rotuli*) written by Leo and kept in the friars' closet (*armario fratrum*) in Assisi. Cf. F. Uribe, *Introduzione*, 285-286, which cites the *Declaratio* of Ubertino from Franz Ehrle, *Zur Vorgeschichte des Concils von Vienne*, in *Archiv für Litteratur und Kirchengeschichte des Mittelalters* 3 (Berlin: Weidmannsche Buchhandlung, 1887), 162-206, at 168.

18 In my understanding of how history is to be done I am deeply influenced by Henri I. Marrou, *The Meaning of History*, translated by Robert J. Olsen (Montreal: Palm, 1966).

19 Kees van Dooren, "The Stigmatization of St. Francis, Fact or Fiction?," in *Verum, pulchrum et bonum. Miscellanea di studi offerti a Servus Gieben in occasione del suo 80° compleanno*, a cura di Y. Teklemariam (Roma: Istituto Storico dei Cappuccini, 2006), 155-183, at 178-180.

20 Jacques Dalarun, *The Misadventure of Francis of Assisi: Towards a Historical Use of the Franciscan Legends*, translated by Edward Hagman, O.F.M. Cap. (St. Bonaventure, NY: Franciscan Institute, 2002), 130.

21 K. van Dooren, "Fact or Fiction?," 179.

22 The essential introduction to medieval doubts about Francis's stigmata and the papal responses remains the magisterial work: André Vauchez, "The Stigmata of St. Francis and Its Medieval Detractors," translated by Edward Hagman, O.F.M. Cap., *GreyfrRev* 13 (1999): 61-89.

23 An excellent and fuller treatment of this is in: Giovanni Miccoli, "Francis and La Verna," *GreyfrRev* 19:1 (2005): 1-65.
24 An extremely useful and much needed study, which traces the entirety of the debate in detail, has recently been completed: Liviana Bortolussi, "Le stigmate di San Francesco nel dibattiti del '900," Dissertatio ad Lauream (Pontificia Universitas Antonianum, 2010). Apart from chronicling the story of the debate, Bortolussi especially focuses on highlighting the ideological perspectives that fueled it.
25 Since these studies will bear the longer lasting influence, I note the most important contributions: Karl August Von Hase, *Franz von Assisi: Ein Heiligenbild* (Leipzig: Breitkopf und Härtel, 1856), 143-202; Karl Hampe, "Die Wundmale des hl. Franz von Assisi," *Historische Zeitschrift* 96 (1906): 385-402; Michael Bihl, "Die Stigmata des hl. Franz von Assisi," *Historisches Jahrbuch der Görres-Gesellschaft* 28 (1907): 529-550; Josef Merkt, *Die Wundmale des Heiligen Franziskus von Assisi*, Beiträge zur Kulturgeschichte des Mittelalters und der Renaissance, Herausgegeben von Walter Goetz, Heft 5 (Leipzig: B. G. Teubner, 1910); Michael Bihl, "De stigmatibus s. Francisci Assisiensis (Occasione recentis cuiusdam libri)," in *ArchFrancHist* 3 (1910): 393-432; Karl Hampe, "Die frühesten Stigmatisationen und der hl. Franz von Assisi, in Internationale Wochenschrift für Wissenschaft, Kunst und Technik," 4 (1910): 1485-1494; Karl Hampe, "Altes und Neues über die Stigmatisation des hl. Franz von Assisi," in *Archiv für Kulturgeschichte* 8 (1910): 257-290. Apart from Bortolussi, an earlier, less complete, summary of the discussion was Octavian Schmucki, *The Stigmata of St. Francis of Assisi*, translated by C. F. Connors (St. Bonaventure, NY: The Franciscan Institute, 1991), Chap. 1.
26 See especially: Giovanni Moioli, "Teologia spirituale," in *Dizionario teologico interdisciplinare*, vol. 1 (Torino: Marietti, 1977): 36-66; Giovanni Moioli, *L'esperienza spirituale. Lezioni introduttive*, a cura di Claudio Stercal del Centro Giovanni Moioli, Contemplatio 6 (Milano: Glossa, 1992, rist. 2006); Giovanni Moioli, "Teologia spirituale," in *Nuovo dizionario di spiritualità*, a cura di Stefano De Fiores e Tullo Goffi, 7ª edizione (Milano: Edizioni San Paolo, 1999), 1597-1609.
27 E.g., John Paul II, *Novo millenio ineunte* (2001), no. 27.

PART ONE: THE EARLIEST WRITINGS ABOUT THE STIGMATA

Chapter 1: *THE LETTER OF ELIAS*

In Part One, I will devote several short chapters to providing basic introductions to the written documentary sources most relevant to the discussion. Addressing for now only what is essential for introductory purposes, I will recapitulate this material at the end of Part Two, adding additional nuance based on what is learned through dialogue with recent historiography.

For each source, I will supply full citations of the pertinent texts, which is necessary since detailed reference will be made to them frequently. The citations will be in English, but with the best critical edition facing, since only on (our best approximation of) the original can a discussion like this one be founded.

In the enormous dossier of early documentary Francis literature, there are numerous texts that speak of the saint and his stigmata, but of these I will concentrate only on certain ones.

First, I consider three texts (or portions thereof) that can be considered the three original or primary texts at the basis of our potential historical knowledge of the phenomenon: (1) *The Encyclical Letter on the Passing of St. Francis*, by Brother Elias; (2) *The Life of St. Francis*, by Thomas of Celano; and (3) the autograph gloss made by Brother Leo on the autograph blessing of Francis for the same brother.

Second, I will draw attention to three other texts, which do not speak explicitly of the stigmata of Francis but do nevertheless figure in the discussion to such a degree that it is necessary to introduce and cite them as well. They are sections or episodes taken from: (1) the canonization Bull of Francis, *Mira circa nos*, by Gregory IX; (2) the early fourteenth-century manuscript

known today as *The Assisi Compilation*; and (3) the similar but later compilation commonly called *Manuscript Little*.

Finally, I will briefly survey the other major early sources that speak of the stigmata for the sake of giving a complete picture.[1]

I. INTRODUCTION TO *THE LETTER OF ELIAS*

Before I cite in full the portion of the text relevant to my study and explain its significance, I will briefly introduce the source in its basic elements and then devote a necessary excursus to the question of its authenticity.

The letter in question, called by its modern editors *Epistola encyclica de transitu S. Francisci*,[2] is understood to have been written by Brother Elias Bombarone (often called "of Cortona" or "of Assisi"), who was acting as Vicar General of the Order at the time of Francis's death (having been appointed to that position by Francis himself in 1221).[3] He signs his name at the beginning (*Letter of Elias* 1/1) and at the end (10/33).

At issue is a letter that appears to be a kind of encyclical announcement of the death of the saintly founder and so is seemingly written on or after October 4, 1226, though scholars speculate that parts of it appear to be the result of a longer period of anticipatory drafting, especially because of frequent and subtle biblical allusions.

As it comes down to us, the letter is addressed to the Provincial Minister of the friars in France, but it is presumed that copies were sent to all the provinces, as would have been customary. And, in fact, external testimony says as much, in the form of the notice given by early Franciscan chronicler Jordan of Giano, who says that Elias "addressed a letter of consolation to the brothers throughout the Order" (*Jord. Giano Chronicle* 50).[4]

As for content, the letter begins with the personal lament of Elias for the death of Francis and an invitation to the friars to mourn also (*Letter of Elias* 1/1-2/6). The author describes what a

light Francis was for the world (3/7-11) and says that this, along with the fact that at death Francis forgave the brothers their faults, gives reason to temper mourning with rejoicing (4/12-14). He then makes his announcement that assures the letter a central place in this study, namely that Francis "appeared crucified, bearing on his body five wounds that are truly the stigmata of Christ," and goes on to describe those wounds (5/17-5/19). After describing the glorious state of Francis's body at death (6/20-22), Elias encourages the brothers to praise God and hold fast Francis's memory, praying too for a share in his grace (7/23-24). Those last words, followed by an "Amen," close what can be considered the first of two parts of the letter and have also encouraged scholars in thinking that this was the original ending to the letter. The second part of the letter shifts to a more sober style, announcing plainly the precise day and hour of Francis's *transitus* (8/25), and repeats the exhortations to mourn and yet rejoice (8/26-9/31). Elias closes with the suffrages required of the friars, a final "Amen," and his signature (10/32-33).

II. Excursus: On the Letter's Authenticity

The authenticity of this encyclical letter must be addressed, especially since it was called into serious question some years ago,[5] creating a doubt that was in some manner canonized by the editors of an important translation volume of the Francis sources.[6] There are external and internal problems with the letter. The tremendous external difficulty is the lack of even a single manuscript copy of the encyclical. It seems to pop up out of nowhere when German friar Wilhelm Spoelberch publishes it in 1620.[7] Though he refers to a letter at the Minors' house in Valenciennes that would purportedly be the original one sent by Elias to France,[8] that manuscript is now gone. One would presume that a circular letter like this one would have left more traces.

Felice Accrocca points out a number of internal problems

with the text as well. For example: (1) the text seems to show evidence of editorial seams (as noted above), which lessens its integrity as an original composition;[9] (2) the suffrages to be offered by the brothers seem anachronistic, more representative of the 1260 Constitutions of Narbonne;[10] (3) the portrait of Francis also seems anachronistic, the identification between him and Christ being more typical of later texts;[11] and (4) where some would point to literary borrowings of *The Letter of Elias* in *1 Celano*,[12] the discrepancies in their descriptions of the stigmata make it seem that the parallel passages are just awkward summaries of *1 Celano* by the later forger.[13]

On the basis of these external and internal indications, Accrocca concludes that it is likely that the letter is a forgery. He suggests that such might have been motivated by the need to respond to the Protestant objections to the (by then) pervasive idea of Francis as "alter Christus."

However, one thing is sure: whether or not we have the authentic letter today, one such certainly existed, a fact we know from the notice of Brother Jordan that I mentioned earlier. I will show why I believe that the substantial, though perhaps not total, concordance of the modern critical edition of the text with the one described by Jordan can be shown to be very plausible. I will briefly respond to the objections in the order I presented them above.

First, it is hard to doubt that the text has been manipulated by someone, probably Spoelberch, and perhaps others too (who knows what path the MS transmission might have taken, of which there is no remaining trace?). After all, Accrocca proves that Spoelberch had no pretensions about touching up texts and reordering material in his editions. Nevertheless, along the lines of what Giovanni Miccoli has said, a discovery that the editor combined two letters, or even adjusted some of the language according to the tastes of the age, is not yet the discovery of a

forgery but only of a more or less corrupted text that must be approached with due care.[14]

As for the suffrage prescriptions, the practice is not so strange or forward-looking since the Friars Preachers' Constitutions of 1228 have exactly the same ones (with a discrepancy in the number of Paters, which most think is a copyist's error anyway, since it is so disproportionate to what the clerics are asked; "five" should be "five hundred").[15] That no prescriptions instituted by Francis (or anyone else) were already in place only suggests that Elias composed those prescriptions in consultation with someone outside the order, which in fact accords well with the more recent, nuanced hypothesis of Accrocca.[16]

The third objection, concerning the anachronism of Francis's conformity to Christ, in some manner begs the question of Part Two of this book and so will have to be re-evaluated later. For the moment I will comment only briefly. Miccoli downplays the idea that *The Letter of Elias* presents Francis as radically conformed to Christ since the text merely says that *tąle signum* before Francis was only in Christ.[17] And while he is correct that the presentation is still far removed from the stronger language later developed by Bonaventure, for example, Accrocca is right to point out the possible biblical allusions that would be parallels between Christ and Francis; however, and this is also something I will have to prove later in a better context, I do not think that *The Letter of Elias* places any more emphasis on such a parallel than does *1 Celano*, written, it is true, after the canonization yet before any real opportunity for hagiographical or polemical development. For the present, I offer just one quotation to give some sense of comparison between the two sources: "In fact, there appeared in him the form of the cross and passion of the spotless lamb who washed away the sins of the world. It seemed he had just been taken down from the cross, his hands and feet pierced by nails and his right side wounded by a lance" (*1 Celano*

112:9). This seems more of a development of the announcement of *The Letter of Elias* than vice-versa. I do not see any reason to suggest that statements like those in *The Letter of Elias* could not have been written so early. Quite the opposite, a forgery written after a work such as Bartholomew of Pisa's *De conformitate*, as follows from the hypothesis, would probably be stronger.[18]

I come now to the last objection listed above, the discrepancy in the descriptions of the stigmata. Accrocca explains that this suggests that *The Letter of Elias* was merely an awkward summary of *1 Celano*. Yet the force of what will become the "canonized" version of the story (not just the written one but the iconographic one too, as Chiara Frugoni's research shows)[19] is simply too great to allow a forger from the seventeenth century to prescind not only from the description of the wounds, but also from the circumstances of their reception (La Verna, the Seraph, etc.), which are not even alluded to in *The Letter of Elias*. Instead, it would be much easier to account for such a bare presentation in a primary source that was immediately making the announcement while still in the stupor of the unheard-of discovery.[20]

A final support for the authenticity of *The Letter of Elias* as we know it is that Julian of Speyer apparently knew that text.[21] Julian wrote in the years immediately following the writing of the first and official legend of Francis written by Thomas of Celano (*1 Celano*), and he very seldom does other than represent Thomas's material in a different style. So it is striking when he shows evidence of knowing not just Thomas but apparently also one of Thomas's written sources, *The Letter of Elias*, choosing at times the language of the latter, which had been modified by Thomas. This comes out clearly in Accrocca's 2003 reassessment of his study,[22] some observations of which I in part recreate here. For Julian, the miracle is from all ages unheard-of, which is much closer to Elias's version, where "such a sign" (namely the "news of a miracle") is unheard-of. Whereas,

for Thomas what is unheard-of is the "great joy". Here are the texts:

Et his dictis, annuntio vobis gaudium magnum et **miraculi novitatem. A saeculo non est auditum** tale signum . . . (*Letter of Elias* 5/15-16).	Sed temperabat moestitiam **gaudium inauditum**, et miraculi novitas eorum mentes in stuporem nimium convertebat (1 *Celano* 112:6).	. . . donec in se ipso tandem vidit gloriosissimum illud miraculum: **miraculum**, inquam, omnibus, ut arbitror, **retroactis saeculis inauditum** (*Julian Speyer Vita* 61:6).

Then, too, in Elias and Julian the verb used for the way blood exited the side wound is *evaporare*, whereas for Thomas it is *emittere*.

Latus vero eius lanceatum apparuit et saepe **sanguinem evaporavit** (*Letter of Elias* 5/19).	Dextrum quoque latus quasi lancea transfixum, cicatrice obducta, erat, quoad saepe **sanguinem emittebat** . . . (*1 Celano* 95:4).	In latere vero dextro cicatrice obductum vulnus apparuit, quod et sacrum **sanguinem** saepius **evaporans** . . . (*Julian Speyer Vita* 62:4).

Taken together, the above considerations defend the substantial authenticity of the text as we have it, "substantial" because we know the methods of Spoelberch, and we do not have a manuscript tradition that would allow us to examine variant readings. So, the substance is authentic, but possibly not all of the individual words or phrases. Indeed, we know that the text has problems of integrity, since, as Lempp had already shown, it seems that there are two letters here combined. Also,

a comparison of the text with the description given by Jordan of Giano[23] gives the impression that elements once present are now missing (e.g., the descriptions of miracles worked by Francis and the call for a chapter of election).[24]

So, even though certain reservations remain, we can at least conclude the following: though we may want to be careful in founding entire arguments on any single word in the text, or on the whole as a single letter written in a single moment for a single audience, it nevertheless remains to be seen whether the use of the text as a primary source for historical knowledge of Francis's stigmata will be affected by such difficulties, especially since the relevant portion of the letter comes from the first part of the text as we have it, which seems for its part to be integral.

III. THE TEXT

[5/15] Et his dictis, annuntio vobis gaudium magnum et miraculi novitatem. [5/16] A saeculo non est auditum tale signum, praeterquam in Filio Dei, qui est Christus Dominus. [5/17] Non diu ante mortem frater et pater noster apparuit crucifixus, quinque plagas, quae vere sunt stigmata Christi, portans in corpore suo. [5/18] Nam manus eius et pedes quasi puncturas clavorum habuerunt, ex utraque parte confixas, reservantes cicatrices et clavorum nigredinem ostendentes. [5/19] Latus vero eius lanceatum apparuit et saepe sanguinem evaporavit.

[6/20] Dum adhuc vivebat spiritus eius in corpore, non erat in eo adspectus, sed despectus vultus eius et nullum membrum in eo

[5/15] And, having said these things, I announce to you a great joy and the news of a miracle. [5/16] Such a sign has never been heard of except in the Son of God, who is Christ the Lord. [5/17] Not long before death, our brother and father appeared crucified, bearing on his body five wounds, which are truly the stigmata of Christ. [5/18] For his hands and feet had, as it were, the openings of nails, pierced on both sides, revealing scars and showing the blackness of nails. [5/19] His side truly appeared opened by a lance and frequently emitted blood.

[6/20] As long as his spirit lived in the body, there was no beauty in him for his appearance was that of a man despised, and no part of

remansit absque nimia passione. [6/21] Ex contractione nervorum membra eius rigida erant, sicut solent esse hominis mortui, sed post mortem eius, pulcherrimus adspectus est, miro candore rutilans, laetificans videntes. [6/22] Et membra quae prius rigida erant, facta sunt mollia nimis, sese vertentia huc atque illuc secundum positionem suam tamquam pueri delicati.

his body was without great suffering. [6/21] By reason of the contraction of his sinews, his limbs were stiff, much like those of a dead man. But after his death his appearance was one of great beauty, gleaming with a dazzling whiteness, giving joy to all onlookers. [6/22] His limbs, which had been rigid, became marvelously soft and pliable, so that they would be turned this way and that, like those of a young child.

IV. SIGNIFICANCE

The first known text ever to mention the stigmata of Francis bears the following features. The text (1) is an announcement of something not otherwise considered to be common knowledge in the Order; (2) refers to a miracle; (3) dates the miracle to "not long before Francis's death"; (4) says that the miracle is how Francis appeared crucified, since he bore five wounds; (5) considers those wounds to be truly (*vere*) the wounds of Christ; (6) describes the wounds in hands and feet as having quasi nail holes (front and back) and the blackness of nails; and (7) describes the side wound as appearing to have been pierced by a lance and often bleeding. Next, the following lacunae will be noted in the passage: (1) there is no precise date of the appearance of the wounds; (2) there are no external circumstances, such as location or what Francis was doing at the time the wounds appeared; and (3) there is no mention of witnesses.

I have also cited lines 6/20-6/21, which follow the stigmata passage and speak of the glorious state of Francis's body after death, because it will become important in one of the later discussions in Chapter 11.

1 I cannot consider any of Francis's own writings to be primary sources in this first, historiographical part of the discussion, since he never mentions the stigmata. However, based on the findings of Parts One and Two, I will suggest in Part Three that we have well-founded reasons for seeing in certain of his writings not only ancillary indications about Francis's experience of the stigmata but key insights into the heart of it.

2 For initial indications see: F. Uribe, *Introduzione alle fonti*, 367-377. Among important contributions since 2002 I note: Felice Accrocca, "La lettera (o le lettere) di frate Elia sul transito di san Francesco," *FrateFr* 69 (2003): 503-520, to which I will return. For the text, which I cite below, the edition is: *Epistola encyclica de transitu S. Francisci a Fr. Helia tunc Ordinis Vicario Generali ad omnes provincias Ordinis missa* [=*Letter of Elias*], in *AnalFranc* X, 525-528 and *Fontes*, 253-255; English translation: *A Letter on the Passing of Saint Francis Attributed to Elias of Assisi*, in *FA:ED* II, 489-491. (I have modified it in several places). When I cite *The Letter of Elias* I will give both the divisions that appear in *AnalFranc* and the line numbers adopted by *Fontes*, since in this case the latter does not retain also the former, which is by now standard.

3 For more on Elias's person one may again begin with the preliminary indications and bibliography in F. Uribe, *Introduzione alle fonti*, 367-369. The discussion on Elias in recent years has been dominated by Giulia Barone, "Brother Elias Revisited," translated by Giles Bello, *GreyfrRev* 13, Supplement (1999): 1-18; and Giulia Barone, *Da frate Elia agli Spirituali* (Milano: Edizioni Biblioteca Francescana, 1999).

4 *The Chronicle of Brother Jordan of Giano*, in *XIIIth Century Chronicles* [=*Jord. Giano Chronicle*], translated by Placid Hermann O.F.M., introduction and notes by Marie-Therese Laureilhe (Chicago: Franciscan Herald Press, 1961), 1-78. Critical edition: *Chronica Fratris Jordani*, editit, notis et commentario illustravit H. Boehmer, Collection d'études et de documents sur l'histoire religieuse et littéraire du Moyen-âge 6 (Paris: Librairie Fishbacher, 1908).

5 Felice Accrocca, "Is the 'Encyclical Letter of Brother Elias on the Transitus of St. Francis' Apocryphal?," translated by Robert Stewart, O.F.M., *GreyfrRev* 13, supplement (1999): 18-64. Accrocca's was the first and much needed full length study on the subject, but some of the unresolved problems were already pointed out in Regis Armstrong, "'Mira circa nos,' Gregory IX's View of Saint Francis of Assisi," *Laurentianum* 25 (1984): 385-414.

6 *FA:ED* II, 485-488. The American volumes are arranged in a hypothetical chronological order, and instead of finding its way into the beginning of vol. 1, *The Letter of Elias* is placed after Thomas of Celano's *Treatise on Miracles* in vol. 2 and vaguely dated "after 1253" (the year of Elias's death). More accurately, between *The Letter of Elias* and the *Treatise* is in fact placed another work, *An Umbrian Choir Legend*, but after recent studies the dating for that source is disputed, such that it too should likely be placed much earlier. The new study is Jacques Dalarun, *Vers une résolution de la question franciscaine. La* Légende ombrienne *de Thomas de Celano* (Paris: Fayard, 2007).

7 *Speculum vitae b. Francisci et sociorum eius*, Pars II, Opera & studio f. Guilielmi Spoelberch (Antverpia: Ex Officina Gerdus Wolfschatii, 1620). For more on Spoelberch's work one may see Jérôme Goyens, "Les éditions du 'Speculum vitae B. Francisci' parue en 1620 et 1623," *ArchFrancHist* 20 (1927): 116-131.
8 *Speculum vitae*, II, 102, n. 2; cited in F. Accrocca, "Encyclical," 21.
9 F. Accrocca, "Encyclical," 41-43, where it is noted that this had already been pointed out by Eduard Lempp, *Frère élie de Cortona. Etude biographique*, Collection d'études et de documents sur l'histoire religieuse et littéraire du Moyen-âge 3 (Paris: Librairie Fishbacher, 1901), 72, n. 1.
10 F. Accrocca, "Encyclical," 56-58.
11 F. Accrocca, "Encyclical," 45-48.
12 Francis's first legend, finished in 1229, which I will introduce later.
13 F. Accrocca, "Encyclical," 52.
14 Giovanni Miccoli, "Considerazioni sulle stimmate," in *Il fatto delle stimmate di S. Francesco*, Atti della tavola rotonda tenuta alla Porziuncola di Assisi il 17 settembre 1996 (Assisi: Edizioni Porziuncola, 1997), 13-39, at 16 (Miccoli's article is now found also in *Franciscana* 1 [1999]: 101-121).
15 "A festo sancti Dyonisii usque ad adventum pro anniversario fratrum clericus psalterium, sacerdos tres missas, laici D 'Pater noster' dicant. Idem faciat quilibet fratrum pro defuncto fratre sui conventus. Idem fiat per totum ordinem pro magistro ordinis et a comprovincialibus pro priore provinciali defuncto. Idem etiam fiat pro visitatore a domibus, quas visitare debet, si in visitatione moriatur. Idem etiam fiat pro diffinitoribus generalis capituli, sive prioribus provincialibus, sive aliis fratribus et eorum sociis, si eos in via mori contigerit, quod fit pro magistro ordinis mortuo. Item in unaquaque provincia pro fratre illius provincie defuncto quilibet sacerdos celebret unam missam, et quilibet conventus unam in communi, et unusquisque aliorum vij psalmos . . ." (*Die Constitutionen des Prediger-Ordens vom Jahre 1228, in Archiv für Litteratur- und Kirchengeschichte des Mittelalters* I, ed. Heinrich Denifle [Berlin: Weidmannsche Buchhandlung, 1885], 221, no. 22). I thank Conrad L. Harkins, O.F.M., for pointing this out to me.
16 F. Accrocca, "La lettera (o le lettere)," 516-519.
17 G. Miccoli, "Considerazioni," 19, n. 13.
18 Bartholomaeo de Pisa, *De conformitate vitae Beati Francisci ad vitam Domini Iesu*, in *AnalFranc* IV-V, edita a Patribus Collegii s. Bonaventurae (Quaracchi, 1912).
19 I will discuss her work in Chapter 8.
20 Cf. G. Miccoli, "Considerazioni," 18.
21 German Friar Minor who wrote a vita of Francis for the friars in Paris, largely based on *1 Celano*, probably between 1232-1235. Iulianus de Spira, *Vita s. Francisci,* in *AnalFranc* X, 333-371; now also in *Fontes*, 1025-1095; *The Life of Saint Francis by Julian of Speyer*, in *FA:ED* I, 368-420.
22 F. Accrocca, "La lettera (o le lettere)," 515-516.
23 "After the death of Blessed Francis, Brother Elias, the vicar of Blessed Francis, addressed a letter of consolation to the brothers throughout the Order who were so dismayed over the death of so great a father. In the letter he announced to each

and all that on the part of Blessed Francis he blessed them and absolved them from every fault. Furthermore, he made known to them the stigmata and the other miracles the Most High God had deigned to perform through Blessed Francis after his death, and he commanded the ministers of the Order to come together for the election of a Minister General" (*Jord. Giano Chronicle* 50).

24 Meanwhile, it is also plausible, as some have noted, that Jordan has (so many years after the fact) conflated various missives in his memory.

Chapter 2: THE CANONIZATION BULL

I. Introduction to The Canonization Bull

Chronologically, the next relevant documentary source is the Bull of canonization, *Mira circa nos*,[1] which does not mention the stigmata, at least not explicitly.

Francis was solemnly canonized on July 16, 1228 at Assisi by Pope Gregory IX,[2] who also authored the official canonization Bull, promulgated three days later from Perugia.[3] Perhaps the scope of the document—the official proclamation of the sanctity of Francis—explains its style, which is rich in biblical figures and allegories but sparse in biographical details, as I will have occasion to discuss (Chapter 10).

Scholars generally think this source is relevant for the stigmata discussion, but for two opposing reasons. For some, the relevance of the document is precisely the egregious omission of all mention of the stigmata. The omission would be confirmatory evidence that, at least at the time of canonization, Gregory had serious doubts about the reality of this new miracle announced by Elias and so remained silent about it. Others, however, now say that there may in fact be an implicit allusion to the stigmata in the document. I will discuss these two perspectives later, but for now I will cite the passage that some suspect may make reference to the stigmata.

II. The Text

Et in terram visionis accedens, super unum sibi montium demonstratum, videlicet excellentiam	And approaching the land of vision on one of the mountains shown to him (namely the

fidei, carnem suam quasi filiam unigenitam, quae ipsum interdum deceperat, cum Jephte Domino in holocaustum obtulit, igne supposito charitatis, illam fame, siti, frigore, ac nuditate, vigiliis multis, & jejuniis macerando; qua cum vitiis, & concupiscentiis crucifixa, dicere poterat cum Apostolo: Vivo ego, jam non ego, vivit autem in me Christus: quoniam jam non sibi vixerat, sed Christo potius, quo pro peccatis nostris mortuus est, & resurrexit propter justificationem nostram, ut nullatenus peccato ulterius serviamus.

excellence of faith), he offered in holocaust to the Lord his flesh—which previously had deceived him—as a kind of only-begotten daughter (like Jepthah did), laying it on the fire of love, and mortifying it by hunger, thirst, cold and nakedness, many vigils, and fasting. When he had crucified it with its vices and concupiscence, he was able to say with the Apostle: I live, now no longer I, but Christ lives in me. Truly he no longer lived for himself, but rather for Christ, who for our sins died and rose for our justification so that we might no longer serve sin in any way.

III. SIGNIFICANCE

This portion of the Bull speaks of Francis offering his flesh to the Lord as a holocaust on a mountain; he makes this offering by mortifying his flesh in many ways and is said to "crucify it." May one wonder if there is a connection between the "mountain" of *Mira circa nos* and the mountain of La Verna, which Thomas of Celano later mentions as the place of stigmatization? Should the allusion to crucifixion be taken literally? If so, is Gregory remembering the stigmatization of Francis as something that resulted from human asceticism (therefore tempering Elias's use of the word "miracle"), or is he instead merely veiling it in these terms for some other reason? I will return to these questions later.

---

1 The edition, cited below, is: *Mira circa nos*, in *Bullarium franciscanum romanorum pontificum* [=*BullFranc*]. *Constitutiones, epistolas, ac diplomata continens tribus ordinibus minorum, clarissarum, et poenitentium a Seraphico Patriarcha Sancto*

Francisco institutis concessa, studio et labore fr. Joannis Hyacinthi Sbaraleae, Tomus I (ab Honorio III ad Innocentium IV) (Roma: Typis Sacrae Congregationis de Propaganda Fide, 1759), 42-44; English translation: *Mira circa nos of Gregory IX*, in *FA:ED* I, 565-569. For preliminary introduction to the source and further bibliography, see: F. Uribe, *Introduzione alle fonti*, 378-384.

2 Gregory had worked closely with the fledgling Order in his previous capacity as Cardinal Protector until he was elected Supreme Pontiff in 1227, the year after Francis died.

3 There are, nevertheless, copies of the Bull already sent beyond Italy as early as July 9.

Chapter 3. **THOMAS OF CELANO, THE LIFE OF ST. FRANCIS**

I. Introduction to *1 Celano*[1]

The first *legenda* of Francis was commissioned by Pope Gregory IX and written by Friar Thomas of Celano, who probably joined the Order in 1215 amid a group of "literate men and nobles" (*1 Celano* 57:1), which means that in some capacity he knew Francis personally. Thomas participated in the second missionary attempt of the friars in Germany,[2] where he seems to have remained (serving also as Custodian for a time) until returning to Italy at least by the time of the canonization, if not as early as the death of Francis.[3]

It was probably around the time of the canonization that the pope asked Thomas to begin working on the *vita*, which he seems to have finished quickly since we have notice in one codex that Gregory approved it just over seven months later, on February 25, 1229. At the latest, Thomas finished writing before May 25, 1230, since the *translatio* of Francis's body was celebrated on that day but is not mentioned in the legend.

Thomas's *incipit* refers to the work as the *Vita beati Francisci*, but since Thomas was later called upon to write other hagiographical works on the same saint, the legend has long been called the *Vita prima* or *First Celano* to distinguish it from the others. In recent years scholars have begun to lament this since it might encourage viewing the legend only in view of what comes later (especially in terms of alterations of the story), obscuring therefore not only the intrinsic value of the legend but also the hagiographic originality and genius of it.[4]

How Thomas came to be nominated to write the legend is unknown, but he undoubtedly proves himself worthy of the task, demonstrating excellent command not only of the Latin language but also of the "language" of the genre of hagiographic literature. Thomas understands well how to assist in the promulgation of the cult of the new saint by situating Francis among the preexisting models of sanctity, showing that Francis is everything that someone would expect a saint to be. At the same time, Thomas's genius (and intention) is seen in his ability to push the boundaries of the genre, allowing also, when possible, very concrete elements of the personality, humanity, and historical particulars of the saint to shine through.[5] This last aspect contributes much to the current consensus that *1 Celano* is fundamental for coming to reliable historical knowledge of Francis.

It is difficult to know what precise sources Thomas has at his disposal when he writes the *vita*. He says that he will report not only things that he himself heard from the mouth of Francis but also things he has learned from trustworthy witnesses (cf. *1 Celano*, prol., 1:1), but it would seem that the vast majority of his information is from the latter. Nor do we know if those witnesses gave their testimony to Thomas in oral or written form. Philological evidence supporting the view that Thomas used *The Letter of Elias* is hard to deny. Traces of Francis's own writings are also discernible at times. Presumably there was written documentation from the canonization process that Thomas would have been given. And, of course, the Bull of Canonization would have been available for reference. Beyond this we do not know about his written sources.[6] I will return to the question of Thomas's witnesses later.

Thomas divides his work into three books, as announced in the Prologue (*1 Celano*, prol., 3:1-5). Book I (our 1-87) treats Francis's life more or less chronologically up to the Christmas at Greccio of 1223. Book II (88-118) is about the last two years of

Francis's life, with an emphasis on Francis's stigmata, illnesses, and death. The final *opusculum* (119-150) concerns what occurs after Francis is entombed at the Church of St. George in Assisi, especially the canonization and (as promised in the prologue) a collection of post-mortem miracles (introduced with its own *incipit*) (127-150).

As for the treatment of the stigmata of Francis, Thomas will have to fill in the gaps left by Elias, who had announced the stigmata but without saying anything about the circumstances surrounding their origin. Here follows a list of Thomas's interventions on the subject.

Thomas does not mention the stigmata explicitly in Book I, but he may do so implicitly when Francis, very early in his conversion process, is said to have "changed in mind but not in body [*immutatus . . . sed mente non corpore*]" (*1 Celano* 6:1).[7]

With the beginning of Book II comes the first explicit mention of the stigmata, in a chapter that acts as a prolegomenon to what follows (*1 Celano* 88-90). The last lines of that section announce that Francis was truly "marked with the marks of the passion and the cross on five parts of his body" (90:7), that this should be considered "a great sacrament" (90:8a; cf. Eph 5:32), and that the hidden meaning of it was revealed in part to a certain person by Francis himself (90:8c).

Above all, there are two major stigmata narratives (cited below), which are likewise found in Book II.

The first describes the event in which the stigmata first appear on Francis's body, an event situated in the larger narrative context of a retreat from secular crowds, a time of secret solitude in a quiet place (cf. 91:1), namely the hermitage at La Verna (94:1). It is a retreat during which Francis shows a certain dissatisfaction, a desire to turn to God to find out how he might not leave unfulfilled the divine plan he believes he had begun carrying out some time earlier (cf. 91:5; 92:7). That prayer of Francis

is mysteriously answered when he randomly opens the book on the altar three times to passages that predict the passion of Jesus, which shows Francis that the fulfillment of his own life's mission will be through trials, tribulations, and struggles (93:1-4).

With this larger narrative context for the first account, the actual stigmata-event description (which seems to have something of a narrative autonomy from what precedes it) is as follows. At La Verna, Francis has a vision of a man who is seraph-like: as a man, the figure has hands and feet affixed to a cross, but as a seraph he has six wings (94:1). Afterwards, while Francis is trying to understand the vision's meaning, nail marks begin to appear on his body just like (*quemadmodum*) the ones he had seen on the crucified man-seraph above him (94:7). Thereupon follows Thomas's first detailed description of the five wounds (95:1-4), closing with the identification of the two witnesses to the side wound while Francis was still living: Elias and Rufino (95:5-8). An excursus on Francis's solicitude to conceal the wounds not only from strangers but also from those close to him ends the narrative (95:9-96:1-2).

The second major stigmata narrative in *1 Celano* (still in Book II) is situated after the death of Francis.[8] First, Thomas tells how the grief of the friars and of the Assisian people is suddenly tempered when they discover the new miracle (*miraculi novitas*): Francis had wounds in his hands, feet, and side that made him seem like one just taken down from the cross (112:6-9). Then follows the second description of the stigmata (113:1), which is briefer than that of 95:1-4. This description is also related to that of *The Letter of Elias*, though it seems to modify it. Next, Thomas goes on to describe how the people become spontaneously devoted to these wounds since they experience them as a sacramental reminder of Christ (113:3; 114:2). Only a dull-witted person (*hebes*), he says, would not know what all of this means: Francis is a saint (113:8).

There are a few other minor references to the stigmata before the end of Thomas's work.[9] Both Book II and Book III end by invoking the intercessory power of the wounds (cf. 118:6; 151:2).

II. The Text

94:1 Faciente ipso moram in eremitorio, quod a loco in quo positum est Alverna nominatur, duobus annis antequam animam redderet caelo, vidit in visione Dei virum unum, quasi Seraphim sex alas habentem, stantem supra se, manibus extensis ac pedibus coniunctis, cruci affixum. 2 Duae alae supra caput elevabantur, duae ad volandum extendebantur, duae denique totum velabant corpus. 3 Cumque ista videret beatus servus Altissimi, admiratione permaxima replebatur, sed quid sibi vellet haec visio advertere nesciebat. 4 Gaudebat quoque plurimum et vehementius laetabatur in benigno et gratioso respectu, quo a Seraphim conspici se videbat, cuius pulchritudo inaestimabilis erat nimis, sed omnino ipsum crucis affixio et passionis illius acerbitas deterrebat. 5 Sicque surrexit, ut ita dicatur, tristis et laetus, et gaudium atque moeror suas in ipso alternabant vices. 6 Cogitabat sollicitus, quid posset haec visio designare, et ad capiendum ex ea intelligentiae sensum anxiabatur plurimum spiritus eius.

94:1 While he was staying in a hermitage called La Verna after the place where it is located, two years prior to the time that he returned his soul to heaven, he saw standing over him in the vision of God a man like a seraph having six wings, hands extended and feet joined, affixed to a cross. 2 Two of his wings were raised up over his head, two were stretched out for flight, and two covered his whole body. 3 When the blessed servant of the most High saw these things, he was filled with the greatest awe, but could not decide what this vision meant for him. 4 Moreover, he greatly rejoiced and was much delighted by the kind and gracious look that he saw the Seraph giving him. The Seraph's beauty was beyond comprehension, but the fact that the Seraph was fixed to the cross and the bitter suffering of that passion thoroughly frightened him. 5 Consequently, he got up both sad and happy as joy and sorrow took their turns in his heart. 6 Concerned, he kept thinking about what this vision could mean. His spirit

was deeply anxious to grasp a sensible meaning of it.

[7] Cumque liquido ex ea intellectu aliquid non perciperet et multum eius cordi visionis huius novitas insideret, coeperunt in manibus eius et pedibus apparere signa clavorum, quemadmodum paulo ante virum supra se viderat crucifixum.

[7] While he was unable to perceive anything clearly understandable from the vision, and its strangeness was very much pressing upon his heart, the marks of the nails began to appear on his hands and feet, just as he had seen them a little while earlier on the crucified man hovering over him.

[95:1] Manus et pedes eius in ipso medio clavis confixae videbantur, clavorum capitibus in interiore parte manuum et superiore pedum apparentibus, et eorum acuminibus exsistentibus ex adverso. [2] Erant enim signa illa rotunda interius in manibus, exterius autem oblonga, et caruncula quaedam apparebat quasi summitas clavorum retorta et repercussa, quae carnem reliquam excedebat. [3] Sic et in pedibus impressa erant signa clavorum et a carne reliqua elevata. [4] Dextrum quoque latus quasi lancea transfixum, cicatrice obducta, erat, quod saepe sanguinem emittebat, ita ut tunica eius cum femoralibus multoties respergeretur sanguine sacro.

[95:1] His hands and feet seemed to be pierced through the middle by nails, with the heads of the nails appearing on the inner part of his hands and on the upper part of his feet, and their points protruding on opposite sides. [2] Those marks on the inside of his hands were round, but oblong on the outside; and a small piece of flesh was visible like the top of nails, bent over and flattened, protruding from the rest of the flesh. [3] On his feet, the marks of nails were stamped in the same way and raised above the surrounding flesh. [4] His right side was marked with an oblong scar, as if pierced with a lance, and this often dripped blood, so that his tunic and undergarments were frequently stained with his sacred blood.

~

[112:6] Sed temperabat moestitiam gaudium inauditum, et miraculi

[112:6] But incredible joy lightened their grief and the newness of

novitas eorum mentes in stuporem nimium convertebat. [7] Versus est luctus in canticum, et ploratio in iubilationem. [8] Numquam enim audierant, nec legerant in scripturis quod oculis monstrabatur, quod et persuaderi vix potuisset eis, si non tam evidenti testimonio probaretur.

[9] Resultabat revera in eo forma crucis et passionis Agni immaculati, qui lavit crimina mundi, dum quasi recenter e cruce depositus videretur, manus et pedes clavis confixos habens et dextrum latus quasi lancea vulneratum.

[10] Intuebantur namque carnem illius, quae nigra fuerat prius, candore nimio renitentem, et ex sui pulchritudine beatae resurrectionis praemia pollicentem. [11] Cernebant denique vultum eius quasi vultum Angeli, quasi viveret non sicut mortuus esset, et caetera membra eius conversa in teneritudinem et habilitatem innocentiae puerilis. [12] Non sunt contracti nervi eius, ut mortuorum solent, non indurata cutis, non rigida effecta sunt membra, sed huc atque illuc vertentia se, veluti ponebantur.

[113:1] Cumque tam mira pulchritudine cunctis cernentibus resplenderet, et caro eius candidior esset

the miracle turned their minds to amazement! [7] Mourning turned into song, weeping to jubilation. [8] For they had never heard or read in Scripture about what their eyes could see: they could not have been persuaded to believe it if it were not demonstrated by such clear evidence.

[9] While it seemed as if he had just been taken down from the cross—with hands and feet having the piercings of nails and the right side as if wounded by a lance—there truly showed forth in him the form of the cross and the passion of the spotless Lamb who washed away the sins of the world.

[10] They looked at his skin that was black before but now shining white in its beauty, promising the rewards of the blessed resurrection. [11] They saw his face like the face of an angel, as if he were not dead, but alive. All his limbs had become as soft and moveable as in childhood innocence. [12] His muscles were not taut, as they usually are in the dead, his skin was not hard, his limbs were not rigid but could be easily moved back and forth.

[113:1] And while all saw him shining with such remarkable beauty, and his flesh became even whiter,

effecta, cernere mirabile erat in medio manuum et pedum ipsius non clavorum quidem puncturas sed ipsos clavos ex eius carne compositos, ferri retenta nigredine, ac dextrum latus sanguine rubricatum. [2] Non incutiebant horrorem mentibus intuentium signa martyrii, sed decorem multum conferebant et gratiam sicut in pavimento albo nigri lapilli solent.

it was marvelous to discern in the middle of his hands and feet indeed not the piercings of nails but nails themselves—composed of his flesh, retaining the black color of iron—and the right side reddened with blood. [2] These signs of martyrdom did not provoke horror in the minds of the onlookers, but conferred great beauty and grace, like little black stones in a white pavement.

[3] Accurrebant fratres et filii, et collacrimantes deosculabantur manus et pedes pii patris eos derelinquentis, necnon et dextrum latus, in cuius plaga illius memoria celebris agebatur, qui ex eo loco sanguinem et aquam pariter fundens, mundum reconciliavit Patri.

[3] His brothers and sons hurried to him and, weeping together, kissed the hands and feet of their dear father who had left them, and even the right side, the wound of which made them remember the One who poured out blood and water from His own side and reconciled the world to the Father.

[4] Maximum donum sibi exhiberi credebat quivis de populo, si admittebatur non solum ad deosculandum, sed etiam ad videndum sacra stigmata Iesu Christi, quae sanctus Franciscus portabat in corpore suo.

[4] People considered it a great gift to be allowed to kiss or even to see the sacred marks of Jesus Christ which Saint Francis bore in his body.

III. SIGNIFICANCE

Thomas of Celano's work brings many new pieces of information not known from *The Letter of Elias* (or *Mira circa nos*): (1) the date is changed, or at least made more specific, though still remaining vague: the event occurs two years before Francis's death during the time he was at the hermitage; (2) the place is named La Verna (94:1); (3) witnesses are mentioned: some part

of the mysterious thing was made known to a certain unnamed person by Francis (90:8), and Elias and Rufino experienced the side wound while Francis was still alive (95:6); plus, the second narrative informs us that after Francis's death the "whole city of Assisi" becomes a witness to the wounds (112:3), and all begin to venerate them (113:3-4); (4) the reader is told the remote circumstances of the event: a time of retreat from worldly crowds (91:1) in which Francis is experiencing a dissatisfaction in bringing to completion God's plan (91:5; 92:7), and during which he understands that his prayer will be answered through trials and suffering (93:1-4); (5) the proximate circumstances are also made known: the appearance of the wounds is in some manner related to a mystical experience, the apparition of a mysterious man-seraph (94:1-4); Francis is trying to understand this apparition when the wounds appear on his body (94:6-7); and (6) more details (apparently modifications) of what the wounds looked like are given (95:1-4; 113:1).

---

1 For a general introduction to the life and work of the hagiographer, Thomas of Celano, see F. Uribe, *Introduzione alle fonti*, 55-62, while for preliminary remarks and further bibliography on *1 Celano* one should see ibid., 62-85. Among contributions since published I note: Felice Accrocca, "*La Vita beati Francisci di Tommaso da Celano*. Un'opera elevata e complessa," in FrateFr 70 (2004): 485-505; and Raimondo Michetti, *Francesco d'Assisi e il paradosso della minoritas. La Vita beati Francisci di Tommaso da Celano*, Nuovi Studi Storici 66 (Roma: Istituto Storico Italiano per il Medio Evo, 2004). I cited the text in the General Introduction.

2 Jordan of Giano is our source and dates the mission to 1221 (*Jord. Giano Chronicle* 4; 19), but it might actually have been 1219 since the letter of Pope Honorius III (*Cum dilecti filii*), which the friars apparently took with them on that second attempt, is dated to the earlier year (cf. *FA:ED* I, 558).

3 Some have wondered if the use of the first person in the apposite passage is merely quoted verbatim by Thomas from his source or indicates instead his own experience of being at the death of Francis and viewing the stigmata (cf. *3 Celano* 5:6-7).

4 Cf. F. Accrocca, "*La Vita beati Francisci*," 485, n. 2; R. Michetti, *Il paradosso*, 37-48.

5 Among the many who have drawn attention to this in recent years I note J. Dalarun, *Misadventure*. We have come a long way from Nino Tamassia, most of whose work was dedicated to showing how the Francis of Thomas of Celano was nothing more than a literary tapestry woven out of hagiographical commonplaces. Cf. Nino Tamassia, *Saint Francis of Assisi and His Legend*, translated by Lonsdale Ragg, (London: T. Fisher Unwin, 1910).

6 Dalarun proposes that the three books of *1 Celano* correspond in rough manner to three sources, such that the writings of Francis (with the *Testament* as a loose outline) correspond to Book I, *The Letter of Elias* to Book II, and *Mira circa nos* together with the miracles collected for the Process to Book III. The three books would be thus associated each with a particular source-person: Francis, Elias, and Gregory, respectively (J. Dalarun, *Misadventure*, 104-108, 118, 124). Dalarun's treatment of witnesses will come up again later.

7 In a later work, Thomas will use a similar phrase that clearly intends to reference the stigmata. Whence, after Francis has a transforming encounter with a leper, but before he hears the crucifix speak to him at San Damiano, he is thus described: "With his heart already completely changed—soon his body was also to be changed [*Mutatus perfecte iam corde, in brevi mutandus et corpore*]" (*2 Celano* 10:1). Then, after the encounter with the speaking crucifix, Thomas says, "From that very hour his soul melted as the Beloved spoke to him. A little while afterward, his heart's love showed in the wounds of his body [*Patuit paulo post amor cordis per vulnera corporis*]" (*2 Celano* 11:5).

8 Before this is the minor mention in *1 Celano* 98:6, which explains the multiplication of Francis's illnesses in this way: "But he had not yet filled up in his flesh what is lacking in the sufferings of Christ [cf. Col 1:24], even though he bore the marks on his body [cf. Gal 6:17]. So God multiplied his mercy on him, and he contracted a serious disease of the eyes."

9 *1 Celano* 115:8; 117:8; 118:6; 119:3; 151:2.

Chapter 4: *THE "RUBRICS" OF LEO*[1]

I. Introduction to *The "Rubrics" of Leo*

Remarkably, one of the sources for historical knowledge of the stigmata is an autograph testimony (meaning we have the original) of Brother Leo, special companion to Francis in the latter years of the founder's life.[2] I am speaking of a gloss that Leo carefully makes on another autograph, one penned by Francis himself, today preserved in Assisi at the Basilica of St. Francis.

In a sense, the tiny goatskin parchment (currently only 10 cm by 13.5 cm) actually hosts three different autograph writings, two of Francis and one of Leo.[3] On the flesh side of the *Chartula* (Latin for "little parchment") of Francis is *The Praises of God* (Fig. 1), which constitute a seventeen-line prayer of praise written by Francis. On the hair side (Fig. 2) is a blessing written by Francis for Brother Leo based on the blessing of Aaron (Num 6:24-27). On the same side, under the blessing, Francis has drawn a picture of a Tau-shaped cross, the base of which seems to rest in a man's mouth. The man's head lies horizontally and may be intended to be depicted as underground, such that the view would be the cross-section of a mountain. Interpretations of the drawing abound. The most common is that the Tau represents the cross of Christ on Mount Calvary, the grace from which flowed down to the dead, saving Adam, who according to some traditions was buried in that very spot.[4] Somewhat intertwined with the Tau are words placed on two lines: under the right side of the transom are (from left to right): *dominus bene*, while lower (and straddling the vertical bar after the "e" in Leo's name) are (from left to right) *f. leo te dicat*. Apparently

it is meant to read, in a more common word order: *Dominus te benedicat, frater Leo*, though more creative interpretations have been given.[5]

Also on the hair side, in three places, is Leo's red-ink gloss (*The Rubrics of Leo*) in handwriting smaller and finer than Francis's. Above *The Blessing for Br. Leo* is a seventy-two word explanation of the circumstances that occasioned the writing of *The Praises of God.* Therein is found the relevance for this study, since the *laudes* were written "after the vision and message of the Seraph and the impression of Christ's stigmata on his body." As one scholar writes, "Placing his own declaration there, Leo changed the nature of the parchment from a private sign of affection on the part of Francis into a public testimony to the veracity of the apparition and the manifestation of the stigmata."[6] Underneath the blessing is Leo's attestation that Francis, with his own hand, had written that blessing for Leo. Beneath the drawing is his attestation that the "*thau cum capite*" was also drawn by Francis's own hand.

Fig. 1: Parchment of Francis, Flesh Side (*Centro di documentazione francescana della Basilica e Sacro Convento di San Francesco in Assisi*)

Fig. 2: Parchment of Francis, Hair Side (*Centro di documentazione francescana della Basilica e Sacro Convento di San Francesco in Assisi*)

If Leo's gloss dates Francis's double autograph to the days in between the feasts of the Assumption of Mary and Michaelmas two years before Francis's death (*Rubrics of Leo* 1-4), it does nothing to indicate its own date of composition. For the moment, the introductory indications regarding its dating are as follows. The strict *terminus a quo* has to be the canonization on July 16, 1228, since Francis is already called *beatus* (*Rubrics of Leo* 1).[7] On the other end of the spectrum, Leo's death is known to be November 13, 1271, which leaves several decades in between. There have been many hypotheses for arriving at a securer date between these two. Some would propose a date that would correspond to other similar events: for example, maybe Leo glossed the parchment when he also glossed the "Breviary of Francis" and consigned it to the Monastery of St. Clare around 1257 or 1258.[8] Others have suggested that we must push the date back in order to account for how Leo was able to give details about the circumstances of the stigmata event not otherwise found together in a single source until Bonaventure's writing in the 1260's.[9] Still others argue from paleographic evidence: Leo's well-preserved rubrics compared with Francis's poorly-preserved writing show that the former must have been done very late, probably closer to the date of Leo's death.[10] Today, the majority favor a post-1263 dating. I will return to this important question in Chapter 10.

II. THE TEXT

1 Beatus Franciscus duobus annis ante mortem suam fecit quadra 2 gesimam in loco Alverne ad honorem beate Virginis matris dei et beati 3 Michaelis archangeli a festo Assumptionis sancte Marie Virginis usque ad festum sancti 4 Michaelis septembris. Et facta est

1 Two years before his death Saint Francis made a 2 Lent at La Verna, in honor of the blessed virgin Mother of God and of Saint 3 Michael the archangel, from the feast of the Assumption of the holy Virgin Mary to the September feast of holy

super eum manus domini. Post visionem et allocuti [5] onem Seraphym et impressionem stigmatum Christi in corpore suo fecit has laudes ex alio [6] latere cartule scriptas, et manu sua scripsit, gratias agens Deo de beneficio sibi [7] collato.

[4] Michael. And the hand of the Lord was on him. After the vision and [5] message* of the Seraph and the impression of Christ's stigmata on his body, he made these praises written on the other [6] side of this note and wrote them with his own hand, giving thanks to God for the favor [7] granted him.

[8] Beatus Franciscus scripsit manu sua istam benedictionem mihi fratri Leoni.

[8] Saint Francis wrote this blessing for me, Brother Leo,† with his own hand.

[9] Simili modo fecit istud signum thau cum capite manu sua.

[9] Similarly, he made with his own hand this Tau sign with a head.

III. SIGNIFICANCE

This source, if compared to *The Letter of Elias* and *1 Celano*, would seem to add the following details: (1) the date is like the one given in *1 Celano*, but still more specific: not merely two years before Francis's death, but during the "Lent" that lasts from the feast of the Assumption to the feast of St. Michael (v. 3); (2) the seraph apparently not only appeared to Francis but also spoke to him (vv. 4-5); (3) Francis gave thanks for the favor granted him by writing *The Praises of God*; and (4) perhaps Leo is including himself as a witness, in the sense that he is apparently informed by Francis as to the literary intention of *The Praises of God*, which is said to be directly related to the stigmata.

Meanwhile, *The Rubrics of Leo* would omit the following aspects recounted in the other versions: (1) there is no description of the stigmata; (2) the seraph is neither described, called a man, nor said to be crucified; (3) none of the remote circumstances are given.

1 For this study, I have adopted the title *The Rubrics of Br. Leo* in order to have a convenient way to refer to the autograph gloss that Leo placed on the autograph *Chartula* of Francis, which I will describe presently. There are actually other autograph glosses of Leo, but they do not pertain directly to this study.
2 For Leo's biographical details see Enrico Menestò, "Leone e i compagni di Assisi," in *I compagni di Francesco e la prima generazione minoritica*, Atti del XIX Convegno Internazionale, Assisi, 17-19 ottobre 1991 (Spoleto: Centro Italiano di Studi sull'Alto Medioevo, 1992), 33-58.
3 The most authoritative study of the autograph writings of Francis and Leo is Attilio Bartoli Langeli, *Gli autografi di frate Francesco e di frate Leone*, Corpus Christianorum Autographa Medii Aeui V (Turnout: Brepols, 2002). This study contains further bibliographic indications and is the source for the paleographic details that here follow. Bartoli Langeli's edition of the text of *The Rubrics of Leo*, which I cite below, is found at 31-32. An English translation is in *FA:ED* I, 108, but I have re-translated it in several places. I am using the divisions of Bartoli Langeli, which are simply diplomatic divisions following the lines as they appear on the parchment itself. See now also *Scripta*, 116 for the same text but with minor editorial variations.
4 On this idea: Duane Lapsanski, "The Autographs on the 'Chartula' of St. Francis of Assisi," *ArchFrancHist* 67 (1974): 18-37, at 36-37. For other theories and plentiful bibliography, see: Octavian Schmucki, "The Passion of Christ in the Life of St. Francis of Assisi: A Comparative Study of the Sources in the Light of Devotion to the Passion Practiced in His Time," translated by Ignatius McCormick, O.F.M. Cap., *GreyfrRev* 4, Supplement (1990): 18-20. A recent and original theory is in Michael Cusato, "Of Snakes and Angels: The Mystical Experience behind the Stigmatization Narrative of 1 Celano," in *The Stigmata of Francis of Assisi: New Studies, New Perspectives* (St. Bonaventure, NY: Franciscan Institute Publications, 2006), 29-74, esp. 56-74.
5 See, for example: A. Bartoli Langeli, *Gli autografi*, 40-41. But with this should be compared Giovanni Pozzi, "Lo stile di san Francesco," Italia medioevale e umanistica 41 (2000): 7-72, at 57-58.
6 C. Frugoni, *L'invenzione*, 76.
7 Raoul Manselli, "Un giorno alla Verna: San Francesco e frate Leone," in *Francesco e i suoi compagni*, Bibliotheca Seraphico-Capuccina 46 (Roma: Istituto Storico Dei Cappuccini, 1995; originally, 1983).
8 C. Frugoni, *L'invenzione*, 76.
9 Cf. Josef Merkt, *Die Wundmale des Heiligen Franziskus von Assisi*, Beiträge zur Kulturgeschichte des Mittelalters und der Renaissance, Herausgegeben von Walter Goetz, Heft 5 (Leipzig: B. G. Teubner, 1910), 44-47.
10 M. Cusato, "Of Snakes and Angels," 45-46.
* *Allocutio* is normally translated as "conversation," "message," or "speech." I, however, am torn between this and the secondary and related meaning, "consolation" or "consoling word." In the biographical dossier of Francis the word is used both ways. When it is used next to *visio* it seems simply to refer to speech (e.g.

Legend of the Three Companions 15:7, regarding the speaking crucifix), and so I leave it that way here. Still, one document uses it precisely to speak of consolations "of saints and angels" kept secret, immediately following the discussion of the stigmata (*A Life of St. Francis by an Anonymous Monk of a German Monastery*, XXVII:82). The consolation that the seraph brings, according to *Assisi Compilation* 118 (*consolatio*, however), becomes integral to the overall argument of this book.

† Among the modifications I have made to this translation, I have added the appositive "Brother Leo," which was probably left out by typographical error.

Chapter 5: *THE ASSISI COMPILATION*

I. Introduction to *The Assisi Compilation*

The fourteenth-century manuscript we call the *Compilatio Assisiensis*, which is a kind of *miscellanea* of episodes[1] about Francis, apparently copied and compiled at Assisi by an anonymous friar for personal use, may be considered in some of its parts a potential primary source for events related to the stigmata of Francis, because it seems to contain an episode from the *Florilegium* concerning Francis's La Verna retreat of 1224.

Introductory comments about *The Assisi Compilation* should include the fact that caution is always in order when making use of it. For though it contains episodes that all can agree are pristine and more primitive than the same episodes found in *2 Celano*, it also contains episodes that have been interpolated at some later date, often probably well after Bonaventure's writing of the *Major Legend*. In fact, the actual compilation was put together and then used in the ambit of the Spiritual Franciscans, and its interventions and interpolations are sometimes of a polemical nature.[2] A more dramatic example of this is the episode in the current *Assisi Compilation* 17, where the ministers and Elias scatter in confusion after the theophanic irruption of the Lord who announces that he wants the *Rule* observed *"ad litteram, ad litteram, ad litteram, et sine glossa, et sine glossa, et sine glossa"* and that those who refuse should leave the Order (*Assisi Compilation* 17:12, 14).[3] Thus, while the compilation is of consummate importance, the historian must go forward attentively.

The episode relevant to this book is *Assisi Compilation* 118.

Even though the passage does not mention the stigmata, it does concern a Lent that Francis made on La Verna and a seraph that appeared to him there, which obviously gives reason to think that this is a version of the story that Thomas of Celano had told. The anonymous fourteenth-century editor of the *Speculum perfectionis* thought for his part that the two episodes were related, whence he speaks of the temptations and sufferings Francis experienced during that Lent (showing literal correspondence with numerous phrases of *Assisi Compilation* 118), saying that this was "at the time he received on his body the stigmata of the Lord on the holy mountain of La Verna" (*Mirror of Perfection* 99:6).[4] But it could be, as some argue, that both episodes indeed speak of the same La Verna event but should not be so nonchalantly harmonized as the compiler of *Mirror of Perfection* has done, because the authors of the *Florilegium* were intentionally trying to separate the stigmata from the La Verna event, since they were two events falsely joined together in *1 Celano.*

If *Assisi Compilation* 118 did originally belong to the *Florilegium*, unassailable proof will not be found in *2 Celano*, for the episode *per se* is not there. But I suspect that Thomas did in fact have that story, at least in some form, among his source materials in 1246-1247, since *2 Celano* 197 treats for the first time the special devotion of Francis to the angels, particularly to St. Michael, and seems not only to borrow the concept from the story but also some of the language.[5]

Even if the episode in *Assisi Compilation* 118 was not sent in with the *Florilegium* in 1246, it had certainly been written down and consigned to the right people by 1260, when the recently elected Minister General, Brother Bonaventure of Bagnoregio, set to compiling "one good legend" out of all the existing ones, as the General Chapter of 1257 had requested.[6] *Major Legend* VIII:10:6-13 tells the same story of Francis on La Verna receiving a divine sign in the form of birds that come and fly around

his cell and how this was a premonition of the seraph vision.[7] There is no way to know with certainty what the episode looked like when Bonaventure received it and what modifications he made, but in essence, all the crucial elements from *The Assisi Compilation* version appear there.[8]

I suppose it is logically possible that the version appearing in *The Assisi Compilation* is an embellishment of the one from the *Major Legend* (i.e., originates with Bonaventure and not the *Florilegium*), but I find it very improbable. Everything we know of the origin of *The Assisi Compilation* and the similar compilations of the early fourteenth century indicates that the intention of the compilers was to supply materials not available in Bonaventure's version. If it is ever to be argued that any of the very few episodes that appear in both do not originate in the *Florilegium* but in *Major Legend*, it will have to be on the basis of something that *The Assisi Compilation* adds, and it will probably be of a polemical nature, considering the tendencies of the Spiritual camp. Since I do not see anything like this in *Assisi Compilation* 118, I will operate as if our episode is faithfully transmitted from the *Florilegium*.[9]

I think that even though Thomas hypothetically had the episode in his *Florilegium* packet, it is understandable that he did not incorporate it wholesale into his new work, if only because of the method by which he chose to deal with his new sources. Book I of *2 Celano* reworks much of the material of *1 Celano*'s Book I on the basis of certain new materials apparently received along with the *Florilegium*, like some form of *Three Companions*, a source that primarily contributes information about the earlier part of the Francis story, especially his conversion. But Thomas does not re-write Book II of *1 Celano*, which treated just the last two years of Francis's life (including the stigmata). Instead, he makes his new Book II a kind of *speculum*, opting for a more thematic rather than chronological approach. And, here again, I

propose that he chose this approach because he probably felt governed by the types of new materials he was told to incorporate, for we remember that the *Florilegium* was not a chronological legend but a somewhat random smattering of "flowers."[10] In other words, Thomas's materials apparently were new, chronological episodes about the earlier parts of Francis's life and a hodgepodge of non-chronological later episodes that were recalled by companions of the saint; and these correspond to his new Book I and Book II respectively. So Thomas does not seem to have been given a new body of material that would have necessitated a rewriting of his former Book II.[11] It seems to me, therefore, that Thomas did not find a place to insert the narrative of *Assisi Compilation* 118 wholesale, nor a place (if he even saw such a need, which is also doubtful) where he could re-present the stigmatization narrative of *1 Celano*, reworked in light of this new version of the story.

II. THE TEXT

[118.1] Quodam tempore ivit beatus Franciscus ad heremitorium montis Alverne; [2] et quia valde remotus est locus ille, tantum placuit ei quod voluit ibi facere quadragesimam ad honorem sancti Michaelis. [3] Iverat autem illuc ante festum Assumptionis gloriose virginis Marie, et numeravit dies a festo sancte Marie usque ad festum [sancti] Michaelis, quod essent quadraginta dies, [4] et ait: "Ad honorem Dei et beate Virginis Marie, matris eius, et beati Michaelis, angelorum principis et animarum, volo hic facere quadragesimam."

[118:1] Once, blessed Francis went to the hermitage of Mount La Verna, [2] and, because that place is very remote, he liked it very much and he wanted to make a Lent in honor of Saint Michael. [3] He went there before the feast of the Assumption of the glorious Virgin Mary, and he counted the days from the feast of Saint Mary to the feast of Saint Michael, which are forty days, [4] and he said: "I want to make a Lent here, in honor of God, the Blessed Virgin Mary, His mother, and blessed Michael, the prince of the angels and souls."

[5] Et factum est, dum introisset in cellam ad manendum in ea continue, rogavit Dominum in prima nocte, ut sibi ostenderet in aliquo quod cognoscere posset utrum esset voluntas sua quod maneret ibi. [6] Nam beatus Franciscus semper sollicitus fuit, cum staret in aliquo loco continue ad orationem vel cum iret per mundum predicando, cognoscere voluntatem Domini, secundum quam sibi magis placere posset; [7] quia quandoque timebat ne, sub specie remotius manendi in oratione, corpus vellet quiescere recusando laborem eundi per mundum ad predicandum, pro quo Christus de celo in hunc mundum descendit; [8] immo, qui sibi dilecti a Domino videbantur, hos faciebat rogare Dominum ut ostenderet illis suam voluntatem, utrum deberet ire per mundum predicando, an aliquando maneret in aliquo remoto loco ad orationem.

[5] And it happened as he entered his cell where he was to stay constantly, he asked the Lord on the first night to show him in some way how he might know if it were His will for him to remain there. [6] For, when he stayed continually in some place to pray, or when he went through the world preaching, blessed Francis was always solicitous to know the will of the Lord, about how he could please him better. [7] Because he was sometimes afraid that, under the pretext of remaining in prayer in a remote place, the body wanted to rest, refusing the labor of going through the world preaching, for which Christ came down from heaven into this world. [8] Indeed he would have those he considered beloved by the Lord ask the Lord to show them His will, whether he should go through the world preaching or stay for a while in a remote place to pray.

[9] Et summo mane in aurora, cum staret in oratione de diversis generibus aves venerunt super cellam ubi manebat, non coadunate simul, sed prius veniebat una et cantabat, dulcem faciendo versum suum, et postea recedebat; [10] et alia veniebat et cantabat et recedebat; et sic omnes fecerunt. [11] Et plurimum de hoc admiratus est beatus Franciscus et habuit inde

[9] In early morning at dawn, while he stood in prayer, birds of various kinds came over the cell where he was staying. They did not come altogether, but first one would come and sing, making its sweet verse, and then go away, [10] and another one come and sing and go away; and all did likewise. [11] And Blessed Francis marveled greatly at this and

maximam consolationem; sed cepit meditari quid hoc esset. [12] Et dictum fuit ei a Domino in spiritu: "Hoc signum est quod Dominus bene faciet tibi in cella ista et multas dabit consolationes."

received great consolation from it. But he began to meditate on what this might be. [12] And the Lord told him in spirit: "This is a sign that the Lord will do good for you in this cell and give you many consolations."

[13] Quod ita verum fuit; nam inter alias multas consolationes occultas et manifestas, quas sibi contulit Dominus, ostensa est sibi a Domino visio Seraphyn, de qua multam habuit consolationem in anima sua inter se et Dominum toto tempore vite sue. [14] Et factum est, dum socius eius portaret ei comestionem ipso die, narravit ei omnia que sibi acciderant.

[13] It was truly so. For, among the other many consolations, hidden and manifest, which the Lord granted him, there was shown to him by the Lord a vision of a Seraph, from which, for the whole time of his life, he had great consolation in his soul between himself and the Lord. [14] And it happened that while his companion brought him food that day, he told him everything that happened to him.

[15] Et licet habuerit multas consolationes in cella illa, multas [tamen] tribulationes fecerunt sibi de nocte demones, sicut idem socio suo narravit. [16] Unde quadam vice dixit: "Si scirent fratres quot tribulationes faciunt michi demones, nullus esset illorum quin pietatem magnam et compassionem de me haberet." [17] Et ideo sicut multotiens dixit sociis suis, non poterat de se satisfacere fratribus et ostendere illis.

[15] And, although he had many consolations in that cell, demons also gave him many trials at night, as he himself told his companion. [16] That is why he once said: "If the brothers knew how many trials the demons cause me, there would not be one of them who would not have great piety and compassion for me." [17] As a result, as he often said to his companions, he was unable by himself to satisfy the brothers or sometimes to show them the friendliness that the brothers desired.

III. SIGNIFICANCE

The significance of this episode is found in its deviation from the other versions of the story, particularly because the source materials composed in 1244-1246 are considered sometimes to be corrections of the official version of the story that was not always correct in all of its details.

I would summarize the differences between *Assisi Compilation* 118 and the previously mentioned stories in the following way: (1) there are no stigmata; (2) central to the story is a special sign in the form of birds; (3) the seraph is not said to speak, as in *The Rubrics of Leo*.

But, to repeat, it nevertheless seems to be the same La Verna episode, made evident by the following similarities: (1) the specifics of the location of La Verna and the timing of the Lent are the same as *The Rubrics of Leo*, except for the mention of "two years before"; (2) as in *1 Celano*, Francis is struggling to discern what God wants from him (though the details of that are divergent); (3) Francis receives a kind of celestial communication, though it is not said to be from the seraph but rather from the Lord; (4) Francis tells everything to his companion, which seems similar to *1 Celano* 90:8.

---

1 More specifically, it is a *miscellanea* found at ff. 94-127 of the current Cod. 1046 of the Perugia Biblioteca Augusta, and it is especially by means of the other materials therein that we are able to date the whole codex to around 1311.

2 Cf. F. Uribe, *Introduzione alle fonti*, 292.

3 The other version of the story is free from this dramatic theophany, but not from odd undertones, whence Elias claims to have lost the draft Francis has made of the *Rule* (cf. *Major Legend* 4:11:7-8).

4 The text of this other compilation, which was probably made in 1318, just a few years after *The Assisi Compilation*, is *Le Speculum perfectionis ou Mémoires de frère Léon sur la seconde partie de la vie de Saint François d'Assise*, tom. 1, préparé par Paul Sabatier (Manchester: The University Press, 1928); now also in *Fontes*, 1849-2053; English translation: *A Mirror of the Perfection of the* Status *of a Lesser Brother (The Sabatier Edition)*, in *FA:ED* III, 253-372. A new critical edition,

which I am not using, has been announced: Anonimo della Porziuncola, *Speculum perfectionis status fratris Minoris*, a cura di Daniele Solvi, Edizione Nazionale dei Testi Mediolatini 12 (Firenze: SISMEL, 2006).

5

. . . voluit ibi facere quadragesimam **ad honorem sancti Michaelis**. Iverat autem illuc ante **festum Assumptionis** gloriose virginis Marie, et numeravit dies a festo sancte Marie usque ad **festum** [sancti] Michaelis, quod essent **quadraginta dies**, et ait: "Ad honorem Dei et beate Virginis Marie, matris eius, et beati Michaelis, angelorum principis et **animarum** . . . (*Assisi Compilation* 118:1-4).	. . . Michaelem, eo quod **animarum** repraesentandarum haberet officium, saepe dicebat excellentius honorandum. Nam **ad honorem sancti Michaelis**, inter **festum Assumptionis** et **festum** eius, **quadragenam dierum** devotissime ieiunabat . . . (*2 Celano* 197:5-7).

6 Cf. F. Uribe, *Introduzione alle fonti*, 240. The text of the legend will be found at: Bonaventura de Balneoregio, *Legenda maior S. Francisci*, in *AnalFranc* X, 555-652; now also in *Fontes*, 777-961; English translation: *The Major Legend of Saint Francis by Bonaventure of Bagnoregio*, in *FA:ED* II, 525-683.

7 Bonaventure takes the cue from the birds in his source story and combines therein another episode (cf. *2 Celano* 168).

8

Assisi Compilation 118	*Major Legend* VIII:10
Francis goes to La Verna to make the Lent of St. Michael (vv. 1-4)	Francis goes to La Verna for the Lent of St. Michael (v. 6a)
He prays to know if it is God's will that he remain there or if he should go out preaching (vv. 5-8)	—
Birds come and go to his cell as a sign, which gives him a great consolation (vv. 9-11)	Birds fly around his cell as if rejoicing at his arrival and enticing him to stay (v. 6b)
The Lord tells him that it is a sign that the Lord will do good for him there [i.e., if he stays] and give many consolations (v. 12)	He tells his companion that this is a sign that God's will is that they stay (v. 7)
The Lord's word would come true since he would have a vision of a seraph that would give him consolation for his whole life, which he told his companion about (vv. 13-14)	The birds seem to have been a premonition of when he was "lifted up on the wings of contemplation" and exalted with a vision of a seraph (v. 13)
But there were also trials from demons (vv. 15-17)	—

9 The episode has parallels in the other similar compilations: *MS Upsala* 53, *MS Little* 159, but offer no significant variants.
10 Admittedly, there are many episodes in Book II unaccounted for in terms of sources, and so we can only push this argument so far.
11 It is well to recall also, with Accrocca, that it does not seem that Thomas's task was to replace *1 Celano* but to write a work complementary to it. After all, there is no indication that *1 Celano* was ever replaced by *2 Celano* as the official legend, but it retained that honor until 1263 when *Major Legend* was promulgated (cf. F. Accrocca, *La* Vita beati Francisci, 485, n. 2). In this light, Thomas must have been satisfied with anything in *1 Celano* not explicitly modified by what he wrote in *2 Celano*, which includes his narrative of the stigmatization event.

Chapter 6: *MANUSCRIPT "LITTLE"*

I. Introduction to *Manuscript "Little"*

A manuscript currently catalogued at the Oxford Bodleian Library as Cod. lat. theol. d 23, which is often called *MS Little* after the scholar who drew attention to it, contains at ff. 104^r-141^v, among other things, a collection of episodes not unlike *The Assisi Compilation.*[1] The compilation of *MS Little,* therefore, is also in some manner related to the *Florilegium.* In fact, of all the similar fourteenth- and fifteenth-century compilations, this manuscript alone is able to offer early versions of a certain number of the unaccounted-for episodes in *2 Celano.*[2] The episode that pertains to my study is one of these, *MS Little* 154 (f. 121), "How St. Francis wrote those things he was meditating upon in his heart."

This episode is pertinent because it describes the day on La Verna when a companion of Francis (who we know is Leo because of *Rubrics of Leo* 8) desires and receives from Francis a little parchment with the saint's own writing on it. Therefore, if this story is in any way traceable to Leo (or to his collaborators Rufino and Angelo, for that matter) then this episode would be another primary source that would help to clarify the events of those early autumn days at the hermitage.

Though *2 Celano* 49 is an example of one of the times that Thomas chooses to copy quite closely from his source,[3] it still seems that the fifteenth-century compilation has, for the most part, preserved the original story better. One can see, for example, how Thomas has taken a statement from the end of the episode ("And the friar marveled greatly and rejoiced, especially

because, without having asked his question, the holy father, by the will of God, satisfied his desire"), developed it, and moved it towards the beginning in order to emphasize that the point of the story is the prophetic gift of Francis (cf. *2 Celano* 49:3), which is the theme of all the episodes in this section of *2 Celano* (27-54). Also, *2 Celano* 49:6 makes sure to add that the friar's temptation (which was the reason he wanted the writing from Francis) disappeared immediately, something not mentioned in *MS Little*, which makes the latter the more probable *lectio difficilior*.

I will also have occasion to show later that *MS Little* 154 is closely related to *The Rubrics of Leo*, whereas *2 Celano* 49 is less so, a fact that makes us conclude not only that the episode is of Leonine origin, but also that *MS Little* preserves it better.

II. THE TEXT[4]

1 Socius beati Francisci cum maneret cum ipso in monte Alverne, quando stetit ibi in carcere, desiderabat habere aliquem [sic] recreabile scriptum manu sua de verbis Domini, maxime quia erat tunc tribulatus maligna et gravi temptatione non carnis sed spiritus.	1 While a companion of Saint Francis was staying with him on Mount La Verna—when he stayed there in a cell—he desired to have something encouraging of the words of the Lord written with his [Francis's] own hand, because he [the companion] was then greatly troubled by a grave and wicked temptation, not of the flesh but of the spirit.
2 Et dixit ad eum quadam die b. Franciscus: Da michi cartam et atramentum, quoniam volo scribere quedam verba Domini et ejus laudes, quas meditatus sum in corde meo. Ille vero dedit ei. 3 Ivit b. Franciscus et scripsit illa verba et illas laudes Domini, et in fine scripsit suam benedictionem	2 And one day Saint Francis said to him: "Give me paper and ink, because I want to write some words of the Lord and his praises that I have meditated upon in my heart." He did give them to him. 3 Saint Francis went and wrote those words and those praises, and at the end wrote his

illi, dicens ad eum: [4] Accipe hanc cartam et custodias regulam† [sic] diligenter usque ad diem mortis tue. [5] Et plurimum admiratus et letatus est frater ille, maxime quia sine rogamine et dicto suo satisfecit sanctus pater de voluntate Domini desiderio suo.

blessing for him, saying to him: [4] "Take this paper and guard the Rule [sic] carefully until the day of your death."‡ [5] And the friar marveled greatly and rejoiced, especially because, without having asked his question, the holy father, by the will of God, satisfied his desire.

[6] Nam post mortem beati Francisci plura miracula et magna Dominus operatus est per illam litteram in illis quibus [sic] signati fuerunt in magnis infirmitatibus suis cum illa carta.

[6] And after the death of Saint Francis, the Lord worked through that letter many great miracles for those with great infirmities who were signed with that parchment.

III. Significance

Similar to the last source, the significance of this one is that it seems to tell the story of La Verna that the previous sources also told but with divergent data. Above all, there is no mention of either the stigmata or an apparition of a seraph. Likewise, the motivation that Leo had indicated in *The Rubrics of Leo* for Francis's writing here seems to be changed, or at least there is no mention of writing in thanksgiving for the benefit received (stigmata and seraph vision).

One could easily ask after examining the last three sources, all hypothetically but credibly traceable to Leo: are these sources the result of a creative memory of the events, growing over time and according to the needs at the time of writing? Or is there some explanation that would allow for a reasonable harmonization of the sources? These are the types of questions that will have to be addressed in Part Two.

---

1 From this point forward I will mean by "MS Little" only the part of the codex that concerns this discussion, namely the folios just cited. The manuscript was brought to the attention of the scholarly world by Andrew George Little,

"Description of a Franciscan Manuscript, formerly in the Phillipps Library, now in the possession of A. G. Little," in *Collectanea Franciscana*, vol. 1, British Society of Franciscan Studies 5, ediderunt A. G. Little, M. R. James, H. M. Bannister (Aberdonia: Typis Academicis, 1914), 9-113. Though Little does transcribe many episodes, the manuscript has not had a full printing, much less a critical edition. Some indications about this are found in Felice Accrocca, "Un'inedita e incompleta trascrizione del *Ms. Little* ad opera di Paul Sabatier," *ArchFrancHist* 90 (1997): 587-590. Based on Sabatier's personal transcriptions of no. 134-140 and 147-198, Accrocca has recently printed no. 170–183 in Felice Accrocca, "I *Miracoli del Beato Francesco*, ovvero la forza narrative di Tommaso," *FrateFr* 73 (2007): 557-590, at 583-590. Of these, Little had not printed 172-174. For an overview of the compilation and its place in the philological and historiographical Francis debate, begin with: F. Uribe, *Introduzione alle fonti*, 320-330. The relationship of *MS Little* to *The Assisi Compilation* and the other similar compilations is complex. One basic element to keep in mind is that *MS Little* is significantly later, probably dateable to the second quarter of the fifteenth century.

2 *MS Little* 153b = *2 Celano* 50; *MS Little* 154 = *2 Celano* 49; *MS Little* 155 = *2 Celano* 214-215; *MS Little* 187 = *2 Celano* 51; *MS Little* 194 = *2 Celano* 39; *MS Little* 195 = *2 Celano* 110; *MS Little* 197 = *2 Celano* 111. Taken from John R. H. Moorman, *The Sources for the Life of S. Francis of Assisi* (Manchester: Manchester University Press, 1940, reprint 1966), 95, 107.

3 Cf. J. Moorman, *The Sources*, 115.

4 I cite the text as reported in A. G. Little, *Description of a Franciscan Manuscript*, 80. The internal divisions and English translation are mine.

† I note that *regulam* may be a copyist interpolation. Moorman omits it (without explanation) when he cites the text. Moorman does not mention that he has seen the manuscript, so I presume that Little has transcribed it correctly but that Moorman takes it to be a later contamination. His would be a reasonable conclusion since the word does not appear in the versions of Thomas of Celano and Bonaventure (which I return to), and since such an interpolation would be consistent with the ambit in which these compilations were made and copied, namely that of the Spirituals, who valued highly the idea of Leo as guardian of the true memory of the intention of Francis for the Rule.

‡ If *regulam* is indeed an interpolation, then this sentence would better read: "Take this paper and guard it carefully until the day of your death."

Chapter 7: **THE OTHER EARLY SOURCES**

There are many other early texts that speak of the stigmata of Francis, and some of them will find auxiliary places in the discussions of Part Two; however, there are no other sources to be considered foundational or primary (at least not specifically for the La Verna event at the origin of the phenomenon) but only ones that in one way or another depend on those outlined above.

For the sake of completeness, and also because it will help to highlight what is peculiar to the sources introduced above, I will here briefly mention a few of the more important secondary texts and say something about their significance. The latest work I will mention is Bonaventure's, since, generally speaking, his work can be considered the chronological cut-off point for possible new historical facts about Francis, though there are oral traditions of various levels of integrity that are passed on beyond his time, and many of the witnesses to pre-Bonaventurian material come (as we have already seen) from texts compiled after his death.

I. *The Life of St. Francis* by Julian of Speyer

The *vita* written by Julian of Speyer, already mentioned in conjunction with the authenticity of *The Letter of Elias*, is interesting in its minor deviations from *1 Celano*, which generally seems to be the former's only source.[1] For example, Francis does not see a *vir quasi seraph* (seraph-like man), but simply *unum quasi seraph* (one like a seraph) (cf. *Julian Speyer Vita* 61:1), which is vaguer, and perhaps more like *The Rubrics of Leo* and *The Assisi Compilation*. Also, the time that elapses between the appearance of the seraph and the appearance of the wounds is emphasized, Julian

adding that Francis was considering "for a long time [*diutius*]" (*Julian Speyer Vita* 61:5) what the vision had meant before the wounds began to appear. Finally, Julian alters the description of the wounds by saying that there appeared in Francis's hands and feet something like "prints of nails [*fixurae clavorum*]" (*Julian Speyer Vita* 62:1), whereas Thomas had said that there were the "heads of nails" (*1 Celano* 95:1), and again that there were "indeed *not* the holes of nails" (*1 Celano* 113:1). Julian is either moving back towards what Elias had written or perhaps simply opting for a biblical allusion to Thomas the Apostle who will not believe unless he sees in the hands of Jesus the prints of the nails ("Unless I see in his hands the print of the nails [*fixuram clavorum*] . . ." John 20:25b).

II. THE *ANONYMOUS OF PERUGIA*

An intriguing and authoritative source that we normally call the *Anonymous of Perugia*,[2] probably written in 1240-1241, speaks only briefly of the stigmata, which is no surprise since only the first and the last of the twelve chapters concentrate on Francis alone, while those sandwiched in between tell more the story of the early fraternity as it grows into an officially sanctioned Order. Since the passage is brief I can cite it in full:

46:5 Volens autem Dominus ostendere dilectionem quam habebat in eum, posuit in membris eius et latere eius Stigmata dilectissimi Filii sui. 6 Et quoniam desiderabat famulus Dei Franciscus venire in domum suam et locum habitationis gloriae suae, vocavit eum Dominus ad se, et sic.

46:5 And the Lord, desiring to show how much love he had for him, placed in his members and in his side the Stigmata of his most beloved Son. 6 And since the servant of God Francis desired to come into his house and the dwelling place of his glory, the Lord called him to himself, and thus he gloriously passed to the Lord.

Of note here would be the clear understanding that the Stigmata

were of divine origin, placed on the body of Francis by God the Father out of love.

III. THE REMEMBRANCE (2 CELANO)

As I have already mentioned, Thomas does not treat again the La Verna event when he writes *2 Celano*. He does, however, devote a section of Book II to the hiding of the stigmata (*2 Celano* 135-139). The choice for this theme is significant, giving evidence of what we also know from external data, that there was need already by this time to defend the veracity of Francis's wounds, done in this case by emphasizing anew the secrecy that had been described in the first legend. Sometimes there is an edge to the portrayal: in response to a companion who sees the stigmata on his feet and asks what they are, Francis replies: "Mind your own business" (135:6)! A new name is added to the witnesses of the wounds: Brother Pacifico once tricked Francis into letting his wounds be seen (*2 Celano* 137). More detail is added to the story of how Elias saw the side wound (*2 Celano* 138).

Furthermore, the development in Thomas's understanding of the stigmata is evident even in these few pages. He is more explicit about certain things that were only implicit or present seminally in *1 Celano*. For example, through the stigmata, the lover of Christ (Francis) has been transformed by love of Christ into Christ's image ("Christi amor in eamdem imaginem transformarat amantem," *2 Celano* 135:2). Words like *imago* and *transformare* that will one day have great success are already present here.

IV. THE TREATISE ON MIRACLES (3 CELANO)

The second of this work's fourteen chapters (*3 Celano* 2-13)[3] is dedicated to "the miracle of the stigmata and the manner in which the seraph appeared to him." The following are the characteristic features of the section.

Emphasis is placed on the newness and the singularity of this miracle: no one should look for a model for this, nor should one seek rational explanation, since it is truly miraculous (2:3).

Thomas now sees foreshadowings of this event in Francis's earlier life (saying that the mystery of the cross had shone around him for a long time; cf. 2:4-8), thus taking up and developing a theme he had briefly announced in *2 Celano* 10-11, where interior preparation for the exterior wounds had begun when Francis heard the crucifix speak to him at San Damiano.

3 Celano 4 retells the story of the La Verna event with some minor changes and some developments. A change, probably of little significance, is that the appearance of a *vir quasi Seraph cruci affixus* (cf. *1 Celano* 94:1) is abbreviated to *seraph in crucem positum*. A development is that the connection between the seraph appearance and the appearance of the wounds is made stronger in two ways. First, more clearly than in *1 Celano*, the text explains that the meaning of the incomprehensible vision is made evident in the appearance of the wounds: "But understanding came from discovery: while he was searching outside himself, the meaning was shown to him in his very self" (*3 Celano* 4:7). Second, Thomas now adds the word *statim* (4:8) to emphasize how soon the wounds began to appear (though still after the vision is over).

Furthermore, an addition to the description of the wounds is made: after Francis's death, someone sees that the wounds that were really the nails themselves could be moved around, such that, if pushed on one side, the other immediately showed the effect (5:4).

Similar to *Anonymous of Perugia*, special emphasis is placed on the divine origin of the wounds since they were "marvelously fashioned by divine power from his own flesh [*ex eius carne virtute divina mirifice fabrefactos*]" (*3 Celano* 5:4).[4]

There are also curious passages in the first person plural,

which I briefly mentioned earlier in connection with the theory that Thomas was present at the death of Francis. For example:

> We who say these things have seen these things; we have touched with our hands what we are writing by hand. With tears in our eyes, we have sketched what we profess with our lips, and what we once swore, while touching sacred things, we declare for all time. Many brothers besides us saw it while the saint was alive; at his death, more than fifty of them with countless lay people venerated it (*3 Celano* 5:6-7).

Frugoni has noted the similarity of this passage to the testimony of Brother Bonitius, who was ordered at the Chapter of Genoa to "tell the brothers the truth about the stigmata of the saint, because many in the world were doubting this matter," and who "replied with tears: 'These sinful eyes have seen them; and these sinful hands touched them'" (*Coming to England*, XIII).[5]

The chapter ends with four lengthy post-mortem miracle stories, each of which centers around the resolution of doubts about the stigmata (*3 Celano* 6-13).

V. *THE MAJOR LEGEND* BY BONAVENTURE

The stigmata of Francis are very important to Bonaventure's theological vision of the life of Francis. Taking his cue from Thomas of Celano, who saw foreshadowings of the stigmata in Francis's encounters with the cross, Bonaventure sees six such encounters (*Major Legend* I:3; I:5; II:1; III: 5; IV:9; IV:10), which culminate in the most important, seventh one. This culminating one is paradigmatic because it is a kind of seal printed by God on the body of Francis to confirm the saint's mission and his place in history (cf. Prol., 2:3-4; IV:11:10; XIII:9:5).

All of Chapter XIII is dedicated to the stigmata of Francis. The following are its salient features.

Major Legend XIII:1-3 retells the La Verna story following *1 Celano* in broad strokes, but with some modifications that should be considered hagiographical and theological developments.

Francis no longer opens the Gospel book three times by himself but has an unnamed companion do it for him (XIII:2:2). And the result is slightly different: Francis understands that as he has imitated Christ in his life (*"sicut Christum fuerat imitatus in actibus vitae"*) he now must be conformed to him in his passion ("sic conformis ei esse deberet in afflictionibus et doloribus passionis," XIII:2:3). With this phrase Bonaventure introduces a theme that will become standard in subsequent literature: *imitatio* that leads to *conformitas.* Bonaventure is the first to add a date for the La Verna event, which is probably not a real but a symbolic date based on the liturgical coincidence noticed in hindsight:[6] "around the feast of the Exaltation of the Cross" (XIII:3:2).

The modifications to the seraph apparition and appearance of the stigmata are curious and have been well analyzed by Frugoni.[7] The man-seraph, which was a vague entity, is now much more Christ-like. Bonaventure makes it a gradual revelation: when the celestial being is descending from heaven, it is a Seraph with six wings (*Major Legend* XIII:3:2), but when it finally arrives at Francis it is now apparent that between the wings is a crucified man (XIII:3:3); and when the crucified man looks graciously at Francis he is explicitly called "Christ under the appearance of a seraph" (XIII:3:6). Next, bringing to completion the seminal idea of *3 Celano*, the time between the seraph apparition and the manifestation of the wounds is removed: it is while the vision is still disappearing that the wounds appear (*"disparens igitur visio . . . impressit effigiem,"* XIII:3:9); actually, to be more precise, the wounds do not merely appear anymore, but are *impressed.* And *visio* is the subject of *impressit*, so the seraph is the agent.

Immediately after this, Bonaventure offers the name of a witness not previously associated with the stigmata event, namely Brother Illuminato (*Major Legend* XIII:4:3). It is not clear from the account—in which Illuminato inspires Francis

to share his secret—if Illuminato is present on La Verna during the days of the stigmatization or if instead his account concerns something that happens later. Either way, Illuminato convinces Francis to speak about the vision, although some things Francis will never say, namely certain things told to him during the vision (XIII:4:8). This passage would be the only source other than *The Rubrics of Leo* that indicates the vision spoke.

The legend closes with ten chapters of miracles. The first of those chapters is devoted exclusively to the power of the stigmata. Bonaventure introduces a series of stigmata-related miracles by asserting that the certainty of the miracle of the stigmata is not in doubt because Pope Gregory IX himself testified that he had doubted but then believed after Francis appeared to him in a dream (*Major Legend, Miracles* I:2). The miracles that follow in the text are taken from *3 Celano* (*Major Legend, Miracles* I:3-6).

VI. THE LEGEND OF THE THREE COMPANIONS

The source I introduced earlier in connection with the Greccio letter, *Three Companions*, is a very important early work, understood now to be a written source for *2 Celano*, but probably in an earlier form than we have it today.[8] Almost all agree that the last two chapters are a post *Major Legend* addition, which means that the stigmata passage in Chap. XVII (there are eighteen in total) is probably not very useful as original source material. The first verse echoes the emphasis on the efficient causality of God, as in *Anonymous of Perugia*, *3 Celano*, and many passages of *Major Legend*, but adds to the divine motive (love for Francis) the desire to show the world Francis's love and his constant meditation on the Passion.

69:1 Cuius dilectionis fervorem et iugem passionis Christi memoriam	69:1 While he was still alive in the flesh, the Lord adorned him

quam gerebat in corde volens ipse Dominus ostendere toti mundo, singularis privilegii mirabili praerogativa ipsum adhuc viventem in carne mirabiliter decoravit.

with a wonderful prerogative of a unique privilege, wishing to show the whole world the fervor of love and the incessant memory of the Passion of Christ that he carried in his heart.

The next verses also betray the influence of the Bonaventurian text. *Three Companions* 69:2 speaks of the "seraphic ardor of [Francis's] desires," which has a parallel in *Major Legend* XIII:3:3. Then there is the repetition of that specific date of "around the feast of the Exaltation of the Holy Cross" (*Three Companions* 69:3a). And Bonaventure's influence is seen again when it is said that the very beautiful crucified man had features that were clearly those of the Lord Jesus (*"effigiemque Domini Iesu clarissime praetendentis,"* 69:3b).

---

1 I say this with caution, of course, since I have already argued that *Julian Speyer Vita* knows *The Letter of Elias*. Frankly, more study is owed to this work, which has often been neglected because it is so much a mere re-writing of *1 Celano*. Cf. Emanuela Prinzivalli, "A Saint to Be Read: Francis of Assisi in the Hagiographic Sources," translated by Edward Hagman, O.F.M. Cap., *GreyfrRev* 15:3 (2001): 253-298, at 265-266.

2 Some argue that the incipit would serve better as a title; certainly it is more descriptive of the content: *De inceptione vel fundamento Ordinis et actibus illorum fratrum Minorum qui fuerunt primi in religione et socii B. Francisci*. For introductory indications: F. Uribe, *Introduzione alle fonti*, 173-193. I cited the edition and translation in the General Introduction. Today, it seems that the author of the work can be traced to a John of Perugia, companion of Brother Giles, who says that he is writing the work as one who was companion to the first companions of the saint (*Anonymous of Perugia* 2), and who is mentioned as a witness in the Greccio letter I spoke of earlier in connection with the *Florilegium* (*Three Companions* 1:4).

3 This collection of miracles is written by Thomas of Celano—once again, at the request of the Order (cf. *3 Celano* 198:7)—after *2 Celano* and before *Major Legend*. It complements and perhaps completes *2 Celano* not unlike the way the miracles of Book III in *1 Celano* relate to the whole of that work, although stylistically and conceptually this collection is more advanced than the previous one. Text already cited.

4 Along these lines I should mention the content of a minor liturgical work that has been attributed to Thomas of Celano by modern scholars since Michael Bihl, "De S. Francisci Legenda ad usum chori auctore Fr. Thoma Celanensi iuxta

novum codicem Senensem," *ArchFrancHist* 26 (1933): 343-389. (A small group of Italian scholars, however, are working on reopening the question of attribution.) The *Legenda ad usum chori*—according to its prologue meant to be read in the Office for Saint Francis—briefly describes the La Verna event, but adds a striking expression indicating that the seraph is the agent and impresses the stigmata on Francis: " . . . vidit Seraphim crucifixum, qui crucifixionis suae signa sic in eo expresse evidenter impressit" (*4 Celano* 11:1). This clear phrase has made some want to post-date the work. I do not know if the language is sufficient for arriving at that conclusion, but I would say that, with the current knowledge of the manuscript tradition, it is very difficult to know if the integral work should be dated all the way back to 1230 as is customarily said, and our passage is one of those that would be in doubt. The best manuscript we have, Cod. 338 of the Sacro Convento, probably dates to the mid or late 1240's but only contains nos. 1-8, roughly the first half of the critical edition. And most other manuscripts known to the editors of *AnalFranc* lack all or some of the later paragraphs (cf. *AnalFranc* X, xxi-xxiv). For the text: Thomas de Celano, *Legenda ad usum chori* [=*4Celano*], in *AnalFranc* X, 118-126; 720-721; now also in: *Fontes*, 427-439; English translation: *The Legend for Use in the Choir by Thomas of Celano*, in *FA:ED* I, 319-326.

5 Critical edition: *Tractatus fr. Thomae vulgo dicti de Eccleston de adventu Fratrum Minorum in Angliam* [=*Coming to England*], edidit notis et commentario illustravit Andrew G. Little, Collection d'études et de documents sur l'histoire religieuse et littéraire du Moyen-âge 7 (Paris: Librairie Fishbacher, 1909); English translation: *The Chronicle of Brother Thomas of Eccleston, The Coming of the Friars Minor to England*, in *XIIIth Century Chronicles*, translated from the Latin by Placid Hermann O.F.M., Franciscan Herald Press, Chicago, 1961, 79-191; Cf. C. Frugoni, *L'invenzione*, 67.

6 Cf. Jacques Dalarun, "The Great Secret of Francis," in *The Stigmata of Francis of Assisi: New Studies, New Perspectives* (St. Bonaventure, New York: Franciscan Institute Publications 2006), 9-26, at 21.

7 C. Frugoni, *L'invenzione*, esp. 174-180.

8 The version of the work as we have it today, with a fairly strong manuscript tradition, seems to owe its existence to a second push within the Order to enrich the written sources available. This one begins in 1276 at the Chapter held at Padua, which made a request for written materials not unlike the request that had once been made in 1244 at Genoa, and which is easily contrasted to the decree of 1266 to purge all sources other than the official one.

PART TWO: HYPOTHESIZING WHAT REALLY HAPPENED

Chapter 8: **FIRST CRITICAL THEORY: APPARITION OF THE SERAPH, INVENTION OF THE STIGMATA**

In this second part of my study, I will determine the state of the historical question of Francis of Assisi's stigmata by reviewing and evaluating the recent historiography of the same, which, as I have explained, is a *de facto* continuation of a nineteenth- and early twentieth-century debate. I have chosen what seem to me to be the four most important recent treatments of the subject and have devoted a chapter to each. In each chapter, I will present the position in question and then offer an evaluation of it. In a fifth chapter, I will try to summarize the results of my analysis in a cohesive manner in an effort to understand the current state of the question as well as propose a hypothetical reconstruction of the historical event at issue.

I. First Critical Theory

With the publication of *Francesco e l'invenzione delle stimmate* (1993), the Italian medievalist Chiara Frugoni reopened the nineteenth-century debate over the nature and historicity of the stigmata allegedly borne by Francis of Assisi.[1]

Frugoni's large tome is multi-layered, inter-disciplinary, and extensive. The bulk of the scholar's book, summarized in a rough way, shows how the notion of Francis's stigmata develops over time well beyond its original conception.[2] I may say here in anticipation of an evaluation of her work, this is probably the strength of the book, but it is not what I am concerned with.

Instead, I plan to analyze only one small part of Frugoni's larger project, namely her understanding not so much of the

development of the stigmata's treatments in the decades after Francis's death, but of the historical reality at their origin. Since her work is extensive, and this reading is found in disjoined pieces throughout the chapters, I will try to present a simple and summary form of the main of her argument. Before explaining her argument in detail, I will briefly summarize the end result.

Frugoni's reading of the written documentary sources of the stigmata is understood best by starting with her conclusion: there are from the beginning two versions of the story, the one of Elias and the one of certain companions of Francis (the latter being the true one). An apparent third version, the one of Thomas of Celano (*1 Celano*), is rather a kind of irenic attempt to employ both versions. As for a version of Francis himself, there is of course no direct commentary on what really happened at La Verna or regarding any stigmata, but clues are found in his *The Praises of God* showing that the version of the companions reflects Francis's true experience.

From this point of view, the story told in *1 Celano* contains not one organic story but two woven together. Thomas tells how Francis is in the hermitage at La Verna two years before his death, has a vision of a man-seraph affixed to a cross, and afterwards bears flesh-nails in his hands and feet and a scar in his side, red with blood. But neither Elias nor the companions in question tell this same story; certain aspects are found in one, certain in the other.

1. The Version of Brother Elias[3]

The "version of Elias" is that found in the passage of *The Letter of Elias* I cited in Part One, Chapter 1. Elias makes an incredibly audacious claim in his letter, says Frugoni: at his death Francis appeared divine—like Christ, that is—because he was found bearing on his body five wounds that were truly the wounds of Christ (*quae vere sunt stigmata Christi*). Yes, Francis *apparuit crucifixus* (*Letter of Elias* 5/17). And lest Elias leave any

room for doubt in his literary intention, he makes it clear that Francis bore the same wound that distinguished Christ's crucifixion from others', and which became also the verification of his divinity, namely the side wound. Francis's side wound also appeared to have been opened by a lance, and it bled (*Letter of Elias* 5/19).

It is no exaggeration, explains Frugoni, when Elias says that what he is announcing is unheard of (cf. *Letter of Elias* 5/15). While miraculous stigmata may later become known phenomena, they are not so at the time of Francis's death. The news of this miracle (*miraculi novitatem*) invokes the full sense of such a phrase in that it is also a novelty of a miracle, one with a specific newness (*Letter of Elias* 5/16).

2. The Version of Leo and the Companions[4]

There appears to be, however, a contradictory version of the story, argues Frugoni, clues of which are found in various places, above all *The Rubrics of Leo* and *Assisi Compilation* 118.

The salient characteristics of this version are that there is a vision of and message from a seraph, while no miraculous wounds appear on the body of Francis.[5]

The Rubrics of Leo speak of Francis bearing stigmata, borrowing language from *Gal* 6:17. But Frugoni says that this usage is different from Elias's. Paul's reference to *stigmata* (the word used in the Vulgate) is not, she argues, to outward scars (like those Paul himself bore from being scourged for his witness to Christ) but to the invisible mark of baptism.[6] Frugoni sees Leo using the phrase *"impressionem stigmatum Christi in corpore suo"* to refer to the invisible, spiritual favor (*beneficium*) bestowed on Francis during the experience with the seraph.[7]

The episode reported in *Assisi Compilation* 118 goes hand-in-hand with the one in Leo's rubrics, according to Frugoni, further witnessing to an alternative "companions' version." It too tells a story of Francis on La Verna making a Lent from the

Assumption to the feast of Saint Michael and culminates with the vision of a seraph, which apparently constitutes a *beneficium* promised Francis by the Lord.[8] So, once again, there is a seraph, but no stigmata.

Frugoni thinks there are other traces of a seraph-separated-from-stigmata tradition in the early documentation, including one example—apparently also traceable to Leo—related in *The Coming of the Friars Minor to England* of Thomas of Eccleston:

> . . . Brother Leo, the companion of St. Francis, told Brother Peter, the minister of England, that the apparition of the Seraph came to St. Francis while he was rapt up in contemplation and more clearly even than was written in his life; and that many things were revealed to him at that time that he did not communicate to any living person. But he did tell Brother Rufinus, his companion, that when he saw the angel from afar, he was greatly afraid, and that the angel had treated him harshly; and he told him that his Order would continue to the end of the world, that no one of evil will would remain long in the Order, that no one who hated the Order would live long, and that no one who truly loved the Order would come to a bad end. But Saint Francis commanded Brother Rufinus to wash and anoint with oil the stone on which the angel had stood; this he did. These things Brother Warin of Sedenfeld wrote down from the lips of Brother Leo (*Coming to England* XIII).

Here again there is (1) an apparition of a seraph; (2) a communication by the seraph to Francis; and (3) no mention of the stigmata.

3. *1 Celano*, the Compromise Version[9]

Thomas of Celano has to reconcile the two versions of the story, one of which he certainly has in the form of a written source (*Letter of Elias*), the other he probably knows only through the oral testimony of companions of Francis, such as Leo.

Many aspects of the companions' version are found in Thomas's story. From them he takes the specifics of time and place (*1 Celano* 94:1), and the involvement of a seraph (*1 Celano*

94:1-4)—both of which are missing in Elias's account.

But a comparison of *1 Celano* and *The Letter of Elias* shows that Thomas also knew that source and draws data from it.[10] One example of the influence of Elias's letter on Thomas's stigmata narrative is the emphasis on the side wound (*1 Celano* 95:4-8; 112:9; 113:1, 3), completely absent in the companion version. Another example is how, in addition to the earlier narrative of the stigmata appearing after the seraph disappears (*1 Celano* 94:7-95:4), there is also in *1 Celano* the later scene where the stigmata are discovered at Francis's death (*1 Celano* 112-113).

This last example brings up an important find of Frugoni, namely that the two separate moments in which Thomas speaks of the stigmata (*1 Celano* 94-96 and 112-113) seem to correspond roughly to his two sources, though with the necessary modifications needed to create a coherent narrative and reconcile the two versions. The first one corresponds to the seraph account of the companions, the second to the stigmata-discovered-at-death account of Elias.

Thomas, Frugoni would say, is obviously struggling to make a coherent story out of the sources given him, and so he uses each one to complete the other. He must employ Elias's tale, but it is not useable as is: Thomas needs to be able to put such an unprecedented *miraculi novitatem* in context and give its circumstances of occurrence. Meanwhile, the hagiographer also remembers how the companions told him of a pinnacle event of Francis's life, one from which he enjoyed great benefit and consolation for his entire life, the vision and message of a seraph; this second story he uses to explain the first in *1 Celano* 94-96 (in fact beginning at 91, as will be shown).

The following would be some ways that the seraph account in Thomas of Celano bears elements from both "versions" without being completely consistent with either: (1) while there is no seraph in *Letter of Elias*, there is one in the companion version

and *1 Celano*, but here he is not a normal seraph but a man-seraph, and he is cruciform, thus adapted to the needs of Thomas's episode; (2) the seraph that speaks in the companion sources is mute in Thomas's version, and thus Francis is left confused about the meaning of the vision, which the hagiographer can then resolve by the account of the appearance on Francis's body of wounds like the ones he had seen earlier on the crucified man (cf. *1 Celano* 94:6-7); (3) there is no description of the stigmata in *The Rubrics of Leo* (since they were intended spiritually) nor any stigmata at all in *Assisi Compilation* 118, while in *The Letter of Elias* and *1 Celano* there are descriptions of the wounds and a clear borrowing from the former in the latter (cf. *Letter of Elias* 5/18-19; *1 Celano* 95:1-4).

4. *1 Celano*, the "Spiritual" (Not Physical) Version

Though in some ways Elias's version wins out (there is a description of the stigmata and the seraph is mute), Thomas is obviously resistant to it: a close inspection of his work, argues Frugoni, shows that he "spiritualizes" not only the stigmata but Francis's whole experience in order to make the narrative more consistent with the companions' version.

An example of this spiritualizing tendency, the author suggests, would be Thomas's change in the description of the wounds on Francis's body. As stated, Thomas seems to have the text of Elias in front of him while writing and borrows language from it, even as far as the description of the stigmata. But at one point he makes a decisive shift. Whereas Elias had spoken of "something like the holes of nails" in Francis's hands and feet,[11] Thomas insists that in Francis's hands and feet were *not* the holes of nails, but the nails themselves, composed from his flesh.[12] Frugoni wants to say that this goes along with the spiritualizing trend of Thomas's narrative because it shows that the stigmata are not physically imposed on Francis from without (for example, by the seraph), but come from within.

The intention of Thomas to interiorize and spiritualize the experience of Francis can be demonstrated further, according to Frugoni, after first showing that the wider context of the seraph episode is meant to be a mirror of Christ on Mount Olivet. The scene preceding the apparition of the seraph, which spans *1 Celano* 91-93, shows Francis in solitude (apparently already on La Verna) struggling to know something of the will of God, and he opens the Gospel book three times in order to discover it. Each time the book falls open to the Passion or, more precisely, to a passage that predicts the suffering that Christ is *about* to endure.[13] This has to be a reference to the Garden of Gethsemane on the Mount of Olives because that is the only Passion prediction narrative that could be considered at the same time a "passage of the Passion of our Lord."[14] Another piece of evidence that Thomas desires to associate this experience with Mount Olivet, though I do not recall that Frugoni explicitly notes this, is a textual allusion, where just before the first opening of the book Francis "rises from prayer" as Jesus had done in the Garden.[15]

And so, Frugoni proposes, if Francis's experience on La Verna is like the Passion, but specifically the aspect of the Passion that was Christ's *mental* anguish on the mount, then the interior (and not physical) suffering he endures is the salient characteristic of the narrative. And just as Christ's mental anguish manifested itself physically in the sweat of blood (Luke 22:44), so did Francis's manifest itself in flesh-nails that were produced from his own body. This is the idea Thomas wanted to communicate, according to Frugoni.

For the scholar, Mount Olivet also gives the key to understanding how Thomas wants the seraph to figure in his spiritual-not-physical narrative, if one considers the episode (present only in some biblical manuscript traditions) of the angel coming to minister to Christ during his interior trial ("And an angel from heaven appeared to comfort him," Luke 22:43). In this way,

when the seraph appears to Francis during his own time of interior struggle and on his own mount, it is more like an angel coming to comfort him than it is like Christ coming to inflict wounds on him,[16] as later hagiographers and iconographers will depict.

Finally, according to Frugoni, Thomas's narrative insists on the spiritual-not-physical presentation—vague and dream-like—of Francis's apparition.[17] The being that appears to Francis is quite a mystery and seemingly indeterminate. He is first called "a man" (*virum unum*) but immediately qualified as "almost like a seraph [*quasi Seraphim*]" (*1 Celano* 94:1). Soon, though, he is referred to simply as a "seraph," but one affixed to a cross and suffering (94:4). Then, after the vision is gone and Francis is considering its meaning, the being is now called not a seraph or a man-like-a-seraph, but simply, a "crucified man" (*"virum . . . crucifixum,"* 94:7). It seems that Thomas does not intend to present the celestial being as concrete and/or physical, and this lends to the idea that the experience of Francis is meant to be understood also as interior and spiritual.

5. What Really Happened?

So, in the end, what does Frugoni think is the reality of the event that inspired these documents? Her position can again be explained in relation to the different "versions" of the story, after being clarified by the context of the last years of Francis's life.

The context of his last years is widely known: Francis had great interior and exterior sufferings. The precise nature of the interior ones is still debated, but it seems fair to say that the governance of the Order became increasingly difficult for him, and that he did not always feel himself to be in agreement with all of the other friars in the direction of the Order. His physical sufferings were manifold, including a very painful eye disease that left him increasingly deprived of his vision.[18] Really, writes Frugoni, "towards the end of his life Francis was one big wound."[19] The versions of Elias and the companions, suggests Frugoni, should

therefore be taken as efforts to understand, accept, and explain this reality of the revered founding father reduced to such a state.

Elias, for his part, would be trying in his own way to understand and to offer some explanation to the Order he is at the moment charged with guiding. He then receives an illumination when he hears Leo say how this broken and beaten Francis reminds him of someone who has just been taken down from the cross; Salimbene de Adam many years later reports having heard Leo say just such a thing.[20] So, Elias is not creating *ex nihilo*, but he certainly gets carried away when he describes the wounds as "truly the wounds of Christ" (*Letter of Elias* 5/17). Francis was, after all, "one big wound," as Frugoni says, and maybe there were wounds on his hands and feet too. If so, "it is possible that the heads of the nails of flesh described by Thomas of Celano were in fact leprous excrescences."[21] Of course, it goes without saying that it would be politically expedient for the acting Vicar of the Order, who also later would be charged with raising money to build the grandiose basilica in honor of the founder, to be able to say that the same founder was a new, unprecedented image of Christ himself. In the end, the invention of the miraculous stigmata should be attributed to Elias.[22]

The effort of Leo and the companions is more to understand and contextualize the *mental* anguish Francis suffered during those last years (and particularly during that Lent on La Verna), and it seems Francis helped them to do so by telling them of an illumination he received during a mystical experience or dream related to a seraph. Somehow on La Verna Francis was able to overcome his depression, and he dressed up this moment of resolution in the image of a seraph, and he shared this with his most intimate companions, like Leo, who told the story and eventually recorded it in documentary form in places like *The Rubrics of Leo* and the source that is now found in *Assisi Compilation* 118.[23]

This is Chiara Frugoni's account of how the story of Francis of Assisi's stigmata came to be invented.

II. EVALUATION OF THE FIRST CRITICAL THEORY

Considering that the next two hypotheses also give valuable commentary on Frugoni's position, I limit myself here to a single point of evaluation, concerning a weakness in her reading of Thomas of Celano.

I am dissatisfied with the thesis of Frugoni that Elias proposes a reading that is rejected from the beginning by many central figures like Gregory IX, the special companions, and the first and official hagiographer, Thomas of Celano. I read all of these differently than does she, but for the moment I will concentrate only on Thomas.

Frugoni sees Thomas minimizing a possible identification of Francis with Christ[24] by distancing himself from the exaggerations of Elias, but I think the sheer force of the larger hagiographic Thomasian narrative suggests the opposite intention. I will (1) show this on a macro level, insofar as the larger relationship of Book I (*1 Celano* 1-87) to Book II (88-118) argues against the theory; then (2) show on a micro level that each of the two stigmata passages (94-96 and 112-113) individually argues against it as well; and (3) make some conclusions about the reading of Thomas.

1. Showing a New Identification with Christ

The transition from Book I to Book II of *1 Celano* demonstrates Thomas's intention to read Francis as, at once, rooted in the traditional type of sainthood and, at the same time, going beyond it in a new way, being connected with his likeness unto Christ in his stigmata.

In Book I of his work, Thomas demonstrates, according to the normal exigencies of hagiographic literature (sometimes even with literal borrowings), that his saint is like the saints

who have come before.[25] For example, even Francis's life of sin was like other saints-to-be since "with his crowded procession of misfits he used to strut about impressively and in high spirits, making his way through the streets of Babylon" just as St. Augustine had.[26] And Francis's first inklings towards re-thinking his life, where he begins to notice that earthly things are not fully satisfying, are reminiscent of St. Benedict's own similar thoughts.[27] Or, after Francis's permanent turn away from his family business to a life of penitence, he has a significant encounter with a leper, which reminds every medieval reader or listener of a similar encounter had by St. Martin of Tours.[28] Not much later in the narrative, there is a shift in Francis's life from an eremitical form of living to a more apostolic one, when Francis goes into a church and hears the commissioning of the Apostles proclaimed from the Gospel, which strongly resembles an episode from the life of St. Antony.[29] And there is even a physical description of Francis—and we remember that Thomas himself had seen the founder with his own eyes—that borrows words from the description of St. Bernard of Clairvaux.[30] Finally, a fine argument has been made that, more than anything else, Thomas's account of the conversion of Francis is based on that of St. Paul.[31]

But, after insisting one last time on this reading at the beginning of Book II,[32] the narrative immediately initiates a significant shift in tone and message, in which Thomas declares—and then repeats again and again—the altogether *newness* (perhaps an allusion to *Letter of Elias* 5/15) of the current saint,[33] specifically as compared with previous saints: no, Francis is not a mere repetition of previous saints, but instead "his glorious life clarifies the perfection of earlier saints by a brighter light (*1 Celano* 90:6a).[34] Next to prior saints, insists the hagiographer, this saint is brighter, more perfect, and simply *different*. He then goes on to explain (by means of his first mention of the stigmata, and

before even having told the story of it) in what precisely this specific *novitas* is to be found:[35]

> [T]he passion of Jesus Christ and his cross prove this and manifest it fully. Truly the venerable father was marked in five parts of his body with the sign of the passion and the cross as if he had hung on the cross with the Son of God (*1 Celano* 90:6b-7).[36]

This is how Book II begins, clearly set apart from the first, intentionally setting a new tone and working toward a different end, and centering it all on the stigmata.[37]

2. The First Stigmata Account in Narrative Context

With this type of shift from Book I to Book II having taken place, the successive references to Christ-like parallels in Francis take on special significance and seem to distance Francis from previous saints, aligning him in a peculiar way with Christ.

The narrative of the first stigmata pericope builds in the following way. We find Francis going up Mount La Verna, as Christ had gone up the Mount of Transfiguration, taking with him his special companions.[38] And considering that the Christian tradition has so often understood the Transfiguration event to have been a preparation for the Passion, it is no surprise that La Verna suddenly becomes in the next scene another Gethsemane, as Frugoni points out. Francis, seeking the will of the Father, decides to prostrate himself in prayer to ask that he be enlightened when he rises and opens the book of the Gospels. He is then described by Thomas as rising just as does Jesus from prayer in the Garden. And in the very same line, Thomas makes an allusion to the speech of Azariah, who prays that he and the other two young men in the fiery furnace be accepted as a sacrificial offering, obviously understood by Thomas as a foreshadowing of Christ's own self-offering.[39]

These are strong parallels, especially in the context created, yet they do not finish without culminating in the most vivid parallel of them all, but in this case one that is without a *topos* in

the then-standard hagiographical literature that a writer would be expected to reference: after a vision of a crucified man-seraph, four flesh-nails appear on Francis's hands and feet, and a bleeding, oblong scar appears on his right side (*1 Celano* 94-95:4). And we have to notice that all five wounds are certainly physical in Thomas's presentation.

So the first stigmata pericope confirms the methodology I identified Thomas as having used in the transition from Book I to Book II, where the hagiographer does something unusual by emphasizing the break of Francis from normal models to emphasize instead his greater, even physical, identification with Christ, demonstrating it above all by the stigmata.

3. The Second Stigmata Account in Narrative Context

The episode of the viewing of Francis's dead body is another specific and relevant example of how Thomas intentionally juxtaposes Francis's traditional sanctity with this new form of sanctity in order to emphasize Francis's uniqueness, a uniqueness in a novel identification with Christ.

When Thomas relates Francis's actual moment of death he wants the reader to know that it resembles that of the first martyr, St. Stephen: "And then that most holy soul was released from the flesh, and as it was absorbed into the abyss of light, his body *fell asleep in the Lord*."[40] The same Stephanic imagery is reinforced a few scenes later at the description of the dead body of Francis. Thus, while the people gather around to see him they see that *his face* is like *the face of an angel*, just as Stephen's face had been before the council of those who sat in judgment of him.[41]

And why Stephen? Stephen is a model for Francis because Stephen was the first to be like Christ. The author of Luke-Acts clearly intends to parallel the two.[42] We see that (1) both Stephen and Christ forgive their executioners; (2) both are killed for the same reason, namely threatening to destroy the Temple; (3) only Stephen and Christ in all early Christian literature use

the epithet "Son of Man" in reference to the Christ; and (4) they have the same last words.[43] For this reason, Stephen was also a model in ancient and medieval hagiography, and not just for Francis.

But once again—and here is the point—having set this scene and having understood all of Thomas's literary allusions and his concern to set Francis in a context familiar to the medieval reader and hearer, we experience the same hagiographer suddenly shaking us out of the *topos*, introducing once again the "new miracle" (*1 Celano* 112:6); for, even while Francis is shining with wonderful beauty for all the onlookers,[44] it is marvelous in that same moment for the people to discern on his body four nails, formed from his own flesh, and a side wound reddened with blood (*1 Celano* 113:1).[45]

Francis is like Christ just as Stephen was, but Thomas wants to say that there is something new and unique about Francis's way of being Christ-like. Francis's body becomes "sacramental," in the broad sense of the term, because it becomes a reminder to the people of their Savior (cf. *1 Celano* 113:3; 114:2). But this sacramental nature of Francis's stigmata is first of all concrete and physical, which is why Thomas can say that the people consider it such a great gift to *kiss* or even merely *see* those wounds.[46]

I reach the same conclusion as in the last section: Thomas has created a new context into which he inserts old *topoi*, thereby intending to offer a proven saint who also means something new, and the newness is intimately connected to the physical, Christ-like wounds that have appeared on Francis's body.

4. Conclusions about Thomas's Presentation

There are two questions to ask of Thomas at the conclusion of this evaluation. First, how does he want the reader to view the stigmata of Francis? Second, from where would he like the reader to believe the stigmata originate?

In light of the preceding demonstration, I think that in answer to the first question it must be said that, made of Francis's flesh or not, the wounds are certainly presented by Thomas as a concrete, specific, and material (that is, physical) identification of Francis's body with the body of Christ.

My answer to the second question is that, while it is true that Thomas does not say that the seraph produced the flesh-nails, he equally refrains from saying that Francis produced them himself in any manner, for example by auto-suggestion. Meanwhile, the mere proximity—even if causality itself is not taken for granted—of the appearance of the wounds to a theophanic event like a seraph appearance certainly creates the implication that what follows is in the category of the miraculous (via the seraph or otherwise) and is therefore something worked from outside of Francis. Thomas explicitly uses the word miracle (*1 Celano* 112:6), which by medieval theological definition always and everywhere means something worked from beyond the natural realm. Certainly, if Thomas desires to distance himself from the so-called version of Elias he has to be clearer about it.

This is my preliminary response to the first critical theory. In the next two presentations and evaluations other necessary clarifications will come to light as well.

---

1 C. Frugoni, *L'invenzione*, cited earlier. Her position may also be found in summary form in the popular biography: Chiara Frugoni, *Francis of Assisi: A Life*, translated by John Bowden (New York: Continuum, 1995), 119-147; and in an academic paper given in the United States: Chiara Frugoni, "Saint Francis, A Saint in Progress," in *Saints: Studies in Hagiography*, edited by Sandro Sticca (Binghamton: Medieval and Renaissance Texts and Studies, 1996), 161-190. The initial responses to the author's theories were: André Vauchez, "Autour de la stigmatisation de saint François: une histoire de textes et d'images," *Revue Mabillon* 66 (1994): 270-274 (now also in *Francesco d'Assisi e gli Ordini mendicanti*, Saggi 10 [S. Maria degli Angeli—Assisi Edizioni Porziuncola, 2005], 73-79); Pietro Zerbi, "'L'ultimo sigillo' (Par. XI, 107). Tendenze della recente storiografia italiana sul tema delle stigmate di s. Francesco," *Rivista di storia della chiesa in Italia*

48 (1994): 7-42; Roberto Rusconi, "Attraversando Francesco," *Cristianesimo nella storia* 16 (1995): 599-625; Servus Gieben, "Chiara Frugoni, *Francesco e l'invenzione delle stimmate*" (Recensione), *CollFranc* 65 (1995): 279-281; Stanislao da Campagnola, "'L'invenzione delle stimmate di Francesco. Una storia per ipotesi da Frate Elia a san Bonaventura," *Commentari d'arte* I/2 (1995): 21-34; Anna d'Alessandro, "Chiara Frugoni, *Vita di un uomo: Francesco d'Assisi*" (Recensione), *Antonianum* LXXI (1996): 581-586; Anna d'Alessandro, "Il Medioevo tra storia e santità. Sulle tracce dell'uomo Francesco" (*Chronica*: 10 maggio 1996 presentazione del libro: Chiara Frugoni, *Vita di un uomo: Francesco d'Assisi*, riportando integralmente il testo dell'intervento di Fortunato Iozzelli, 610-619), *Antonianum* LXXI (1996): 604-619; Giovanni Miccoli, "Considerazioni sulle stimmate," in *Il fatto delle stimmate di S. Francesco*, Atti della tavola rotonda tenuta alla Porziuncola di Assisi il 17 settembre 1996 (Assisi: Edizioni Porziuncola, 1997): 13-39; Stanislao da Campagnola, "Il 'fatto' delle stimmate nelle fonti documentarie," in ibid., 41-48. A more recent evaluation worthy of mention makes up the first part of K. van Dooren, *Fact or Fiction?*, 155-183, already cited.

2 In this vein the title of Frugoni's work is apparently a provocative word play. Primarily, I am sure, the title indicates a work that will show the unfolding "discovery" of the stigmata that the Order makes over time; and this is the etymological meaning of *invenzione*, from the Latin *invenire*. Still, modern parlance knows *invention* to mean less the happening upon something that is in fact there for the finding, and more the creation of something not previously there at all. I will use the word in its colloquial sense.

3 What follows refers especially to C. Frugoni, *L'invenzione*, 51-71.

4 Cf. C. Frugoni, *L'invenzione*, 72-87.

5 The first to hypothesize that the seraph and stigmata were not originally part of the same story was K. Hampe, "Die Wundmale," 385-402. Recently, another German scholar has reached a similar conclusion, but not necessarily by the same means, as he reports in a brief article: Paul Bösch, "Opinationes de stigmatibus Francisci. Annotationes ad quaestionem disputatam," *CollFranc* 76 (2006): 561-565, at 561-562. This article is in response to critiques of his full length book, *Franz von Assisi—neuer Christus. Die Geschichte einer Verklärung* (Düsseldorf: Patmos Verlag, 2005). His own reasons for reaching the same conclusions as Hampe and Frugoni are found at 204-216. Thanks to Paulus Maria Tautz, C.F.R. for helping me with this German text.

6 C. Frugoni, *L'invenzione*, 58.

7 Cf. C. Frugoni, *Francis of Assisi*, 143.

8 "Hoc signum est quod Dominus bene faciat tibi in cella ista et multas dabit consolationes" (*Assisi Compilation* 118:2).

9 Cf. C. Frugoni, *L'invenzione*, 52; 56-59; 148; 153-157; 165-166.

10 This chart will show the dependence:

1 Celano	*Letters of Elias*
[107:6] . . . **nullum in eo remanserat membrum absque nimio passionis** dolore.	[6/20] . . . **nullum membrum in eo remansit absque nimia passione.**
[109:10] Fratribus meis tam absentibus quam praesentibus offensas **omnes** et **culpas remitto**, et eos, sicut possum, absolvo; quibus tu haec denuntians, ex parte mea omnibus **benedices**.	[4/14] Iucundamini, quia antequam tolleretur a nobis tamquam alter Iacob omnes filios suos **benedixit** et **omnibus remisit culpas**, quae in eum factae fuissent vel cogitatae ab aliquo nostrum.
[112:5] Verumtamen filii lamentabantur **tanto patre** orbati, et pium cordis affectum **lacrimis** et suspiriis ostendebant.	[8/26b] viam demus **lacrimis, tanti patris** solatio destituti.
[112:6] Sed temperabat moestitiam **gaudium inauditum**, et **miraculi novitas** eorum mentes in stuporem nimium convertebat.	[5/15] . . . annuntio vobis **gaudium magnum** et **miraculi novitatem**. [16] A saeculo **non est auditum** tale signum . . .
[112:10] Intuebantur namque carnem illius, quae nigra fuerat prius, **candore** nimio renitentem, et ex sui pulchritudine beatae resurrectionis praemia pollicentem. [11] Cernebant denique vultum eius quasi vultum Angeli, quasi viveret, non sicut mortuus esset, et caetera **membra** eius conversa in teneritudinem et habilitatem innocentiae **puerilis**. [12] Non sunt **contracti nervi eius**, ut mortuorum solent, non indurata cutis, non **rigida** effecta sunt **membra**, sed huc atque illuc vertentia se, veluti ponebantur.	[6/21] Ex **contractione nervorum membra** eius rigida erant, sicut solent esse hominis mortui, sed post mortem eius, pulcherrimus adspectus est, miro **candore** rutilans, laetificans videntes. [6/22] Et **membra** qua prius **rigida** erant, facta sunt mollia nimis, sese vertentia huc atque illuc secundum positionem suam tamquam **pueri** delicati.

11 "Nam manus eius et pedes quasi puncturas clavorum habuerunt" (5/18).

12 "Erat in medio manuum et pedum ipsius non clavorum quidem puncturas sed ipsos clavos ex eius carne compositos" (113:1).

13 " . . . cum aperuisset librum occurrit sibi primo passio Domini nostri Iesu Christi, et id solum quod tribulationem eum passurum denuntiabat" (*1 Celano* 93:2).

14 I am not sure that Frugoni explains it this way, but I believe myself to be clarifying her position.

15 "Surgens quoque ab oratione" (*1 Celano* 93:1); "Et cum surrexisset ab oratione" (*Luc* 22:45).
16 Cf. C. Frugoni, *L'invenzione*, 82.
17 Though much of Frugoni's presentation of this point works as a comparison with later narratives (like *3 Celano* and *Major Legend*), I repeat that I am trying to pinpoint what in her proposal indicates what was historically there at the event itself, and I think her point stands firm (and is ultimately stronger, since it is less dependent on rhetorical value) without framing the discussion in those terms.
18 Cf. Octavian Schmucki, "Le malattie di Francesco durante gli ultimi anni della sua vita, in Francesco d'Assisi e francescanesimo dal 1216 al 1226," Atti del IV Convegno Internazionale della S.I.S.F., Assisi, 15-17 ottobre 1976 (Rimini: Maggioli Editore, 1977), 315-362; and Ottaviano Schmucki, "Infermità, malattia, malato, salute, assistenza ai malati," in *Dizionario francescano*, col. 827-872; 2413-2417.
19 C. Frugoni, *L'invenzione*, 59.
20 "Nam, sicut dixit michi frater Leo, socius suus, qui presens fuit quando ad sepeliendum lavabatur in morte, videbatur recte sicut unus crucifixus de cruce depositus" (Salimbene de Adam da Parma, *Cronica*, due volumi, testo latino a cura di Giuseppe Scalia, traduzione di Berardo Rossi, prefazione di Luigi Malerba [Parma: Monte Università Parma Editore, 2007], vol. 1, 542 [Scalia edition, 282]). Cf. C. Frugoni, *L'invenzione*, 69-70; 93. I believe that the first to suggest this theory was actually N. Tamassia, *Francis and His Legend*, 112-113.
21 C. Frugoni, *Francis of Assisi*, 141.
22 Frugoni's argument, as I have said, is scattered here and there throughout the book, but on this she is unequivocal: " . . . sono propensa ad addebitare a Elias, sollecito compagno nel vegliare le ultime malattie e presente alla fine del santo, la decisione di tramutare in miracolo il compianto dei frati sul corpo morto e martoriato di Francesco, le piaghe finalmente visibili in stimmate, e di divulgare il prodigio con la massima risonanza possibile. [. . . .] Per Elia, il riconoscere nelle piaghe di Francesco morto le stimmate fu il modo di placare il ricordo del fondatore scoraggiato e incupito, si ricomporre i patimenti fisici di Francesco, trasformandoli nel privilegio accordato da Dio in modo unico e irripetibile" (C. Frugoni, *L'invenzione*, 82-83).
23 "Da una parte—sarà la mia tesi—Francesco sul monte della Verna ebbe nel buio di una lunga crisi la gioia di un'illuminazione e vestì l'esperienza ineffabile dell'immagine del Serafino, facendone parte a Leone e ai pochissimi compagni che lo avevano seguito. Dall'altra ci sono i frati che assistevano all'incalzante deperire fisico del loro compagno, che vedevano la sua tristezza accentuarsi" (C. Frugoni, *L'invenzione*, 82).
24 Cf. C. Frugoni, *L'invenzione*, 156-157: "Likewise, the biographer does not at all identify Francis with Christ; he limits himself to a comparison . . ."; and, in the episode of La Verna "there is not any temptation to suggest an *alter Christus* and the stigmata are a stage, not the culmination of the imitation of the Savior." Frugoni is right, of course, that the language of *alter Christus* arrives much later and that it indicates the full state of hagiographical development. But I will show

that Thomas clearly does identify Francis with Christ in a novel and forceful way that does not temper Elias's presentation at all.

25 Of great help in identifying these *topoi* are the notes of the Quaracchi fathers in *AnalFranc* X.

26 *1 Celano* 2:5; cf. *Confessiones* II:3:8 (*PL* 32; *CCSL* 27).

27 *1 Celano* 3:4; cf. Gregorius Magnus, *Vita S. Benedicti* (*Liber secundus Dialogorum*), prol. (*PL* 66, col. 126). Cf. *FA:ED* I, 185, n. b.

28 *1 Celano* 17:4; cf. Sulpicius Severus, *Vita sancti Martini*, 18:3 (*PL* 20, col. 170).

29 *1 Celano* 22; cf. *Vita Antonii*, 2 (*PG* 26, col. 841-842, with the translation of Evagrius Ponticus).

30

. . . **Statura mediocris** parvitati **vicinior**, caput mediocre ac rotundum [. . . .] **barba** nigra, pilis non plene **respersa** . . . crura **subtilia**, parvuli pedes, **tenuis cutis**, **caro paucissima**, aspera vestis, somnus brevissimus, manus largissima (*1 Celano* 83:8-10).	**Statura mediocritatis** honestae, longitudini tamen **vicinior** apparebat [. . . .] **Barba** subrufa, circa finem vitae eius **respersa** canis . . . Corpus omne **tenuissimum** et **sine carnibus** erat, ipsa quoque **subtilissima cutis** . . . (*Vita Bernardi*, 3:1:1 [*PL* 185, col. 303]).

31 Cf. Felice Accrocca, *"Alter apostolus." Per una rilettura della* Vita beati Francisci, in *La leggenda di un santo di nome Francesco. Tommaso da Celano e la* Vita beati Francisci, Istituto teologico San Bernardino–Verona Settimana di studi francescani, 31 agosto—6 settembre 1997 (Milano: Edizioni Biblioteca Francescana, 1999), 143-260, esp. at 198-209.

32 He begins the book by reminding the reader of what should be clear by this point in the narrative: twenty years before death, Francis "embraced Christ completely following the life and footsteps of the Apostles" (*1 Celano* 88:3). That is to say, the new saint excelled on the normal path of sanctity, which is one of imitation of the other great followers of Christ who have come before.

33 "Quoniam in **novissimo** tempore **novus** evangelista, quasi unus ex paradisi fluminibus, in toto terrarum orbe 'fluenta Evangelii' pia irrigatione diffudit et viam Filii Dei atque doctrinam veritatis opere praedicavit. Facta est proinde in eo et per eum orbis terrarum insperata exsultatio et sancta **novitas**: antiquae religionis germen inveteratos diu et veteres multum subito **innovavit**. Datus est spiritus **novus** in cordibus electorum et in medio eorum effusa est unctio salutaris, cum velut unum de luminaribus caeli, Christi servus et sanctus **novo** ritu, **novisque** signis desuper radiavit. **Renovata** sunt per eum antiqua miracula, dum in deserto mundi huius, ordine **novo** sed antiquo more, plantata est vitis fructifera, proferens flores suavitatis in odorem virtutum sanctarum, ubique sacrae religionis palmites extendendo" (*1 Celano* 89:4-7). For newness as a Leitmotif in *1 Celano* I suggest William J. Short, "Francis, the 'New' Saint in the Tradition of Christian Hagiography," in *Francis of Assisi: History, Hagiography, and Hermeneutics in the Early Documents*, edited by Jay M. Hammond (Hyde Park, NY: New City Press, 2004),

153-163. For a list of the uses of *novus* and related words: George Mailleux, *Thesaurus Celanensis. Concordance, Index, Listes de fréquence, Tables comparatives*, Corpus des Sources Franciscaines I (Louvain-la-Neuve: Publications du CETEDOC, Université Catholique de Louvain, 1974), esp. at 400.

34 "Et quidem gloriosa vita ipsius priorum sanctorum perfectionem illustrat lumine clariore."

35 Cf. R. Michetti, *Il paradosso*, 236-237.

36 "[P]robat hoc passio Iesu Christi et eius crux plenissime manifestat. Revera in quinque partibus corporis passionis et crucis signaculo pater venerabilis et signatus ac si in cruce cum Dei Filio pependisset."

37 Cf. R. Michetti, *Il Paradosso*, 233: "Il secondo opuscolo della *Vita beati Francisci* non si presenta come la mera prosecuzione del primo, ma assume i caratteri peculiari di un prodotto autonomo . . . Si tratta di una soluzione assolutamente originale e del tutto inusuale all'interno del genere agiografico. Se è vero che la maggior parte delle leggende agiografiche tende a conferire una particolare rilevanza al momento della morte del santo . . . difficilmente si avverte la necessità di isolare in un apposito e circoscritto spazio temporale e letterario, come avviene nell'opera in esame, l'ultimo periodo della sua esistenza."

38 "**Assumpsit** proinde **secum** socios valde paucos . . ." (*1 Celano* 91:3); cf. ". . . et **adsumit** Petrum et Iacobum et Iohannem **secum**" (Marc 14:33).

39 " . . . **in spiritu humilitatis animoque contrito** . . ." (*1 Celano* 93); ". . . sed **in anima contrita et spiritu humilitatis** suscipiamur" (Dan 3:39).

40 "Sanctissima illa anima carne soluta est, qua in abysso claritatis absorpta, corpus **obdormivit** in Domino" (*1 Celano* 110:4); cf. "Et cum hoc dixisset **obdormivit**" (Act 7:60).

41 "Cernebant denique *vultum eius quasi vultum Angeli*, quasi viveret, non sicut mortuus esset" (*1 Celano* 112:11); cf. ". . . et intuentes eum omnes qui sedebant in concilio viderunt *faciem eius tamquam faciem angeli*" (Act 6:15).

42 Cf. Thomas Heffernan, *Sacred Biography: Saints and their Biographers in the Middle Ages* (New York: Oxford University Press, 1988), 116-117.

43 "Pater in manus tuas commendo **spiritum meum**" (Luc 23:46); cf. "Domine Iesu suscipe **spiritum meum**" (Act 7:59).

44 As other saints had before, as I will show later.

45 Which had not been seen in other saints before him. "Cumque tam mira pulchritudine cunctis cernentibus resplenderet, et caro eius candidior esset effecta, cernere mirabile erat in medio manuum et pedum ipsius non clavorum quidem puncturas sed ipsos clavos ex eius carne compositos, ferri retenta nigredine, ac dextrum latus sanguine rubricatum" (*1 Celano* 113:1). This single Latin sentence is a clear example of how Thomas chooses to juxtapose these two elements, holding them tightly against one another. It is an effort to introduce, perhaps with some hesitation, the utter newness of Francis, but in a way that is still rooted in the necessary demands of the genre and public expectation.

46 "Maximum donum sibi exhiberi credebat quivis de populo, si admittebatur non solum ad deosculandum, sed etiam ad videndum sacra stigmata Iesu Christi, quae sanctus Franciscus portabat in corpore suo" (*1 Celano* 113:4).

Chapter 9: **SECOND CRITICAL THEORY: FACT OF THE STIGMATA, UNCERTAINTY OF THEIR ORIGIN**

I. Second Critical Theory

The paper Giovanni Miccoli presented in September of 1996 is brief, but is one of the more acute treatments of the questions raised by Chiara Frugoni's book, which he engages directly. The roundtable discussion in which Miccoli participated had gathered to ask the question on everyone's mind after Frugoni's erudite volume: is it still possible to speak of the stigmata of Francis as an historical event, a "fact," or are they instead something invented by some of his early disciples?[1] By way of summary, Miccoli answers that, speaking as an historian, one must say that what contemporaries decided to call the "stigmata" of Francis are indeed an historical fact, in the sense that all the early witnesses testify to have known them. The scholar bases this assertion on the substantial agreement in the primary sources.

1. Rubrics of Leo: Witness to a Non-Stigmata Seraph Tradition?[2]

Miccoli sees *The Rubrics of Leo* as a primary source not only in that it is an autonomous testimony (regardless of its dating), but also in that it is written by someone who was with Francis during the days in question.

The most noteworthy feature of the source is that it situates the stigmata in the context of a mystical experience (that of the seraph), even if it still presents them as distinct. For Leo says

that Francis's *Praises of God* are an action of thanksgiving for a two-fold favor (*beneficium*), namely the "vision and conversation with the Seraph" and the "imprint of the stigmata" on his body. Miccoli emphasizes the point: it is a single *beneficium* with a double manifestation; that is, there are two distinct aspects of a single event, distinct but not disjoined since both are fruits of the same *beneficium*.

This point speaks directly to Frugoni's hypothesis that Leo is the chief proponent of the seraph-without-stigmata tradition. Because in this reading *The Rubrics of Leo* do not present two separate stories—distinct, yes, but separate, no. Rather, Leo presents two stages or aspects of the *single* story that begins with the "hand of God" over Francis on La Verna and ends with him giving thanks by writing the *laudes* that Leo holds in his hand as he writes.

It remains for Miccoli to answer Frugoni's suggestion that, even though Leo does use the word *stigmata*, he means it only in a metaphorical way, and he raises two arguments against it. First, nothing in the text itself supports her interpretation. Rather, Leo speaks of the *impressio* of the stigmata, thus using a word that normally indicates something quite physical, for example the stamping of a coin or even a physical assault. Second, if the note is written, as all assume, after *The Letter of Elias*, it would be virtually impossible to explain Leo's so casual use of this word *stigmata* if he does not agree to Elias's use of it; further explanation would be needed.

And in the light of this reading of *The Rubrics of Leo*, Frugoni's interpretation of the statement of Leo to Salimbene of Parma (which would have originally been uttered in the presence of Elias and inspired the invention of the stigmata) also weakens considerably.

2. A Non-Stigmata Seraph Tradition?[3]

Miccoli also addresses the theory of traces in the early

documentary sources of an alternative non-stigmata version of the seraph story, and he concludes that the evidence is insignificant.

While it is true that the stigmata are not mentioned in some accounts, silence is not necessarily evidence that the author denies the fact; instead, perhaps it is taken for granted. The story in *MS Little* 154 / *2 Celano* 49, for example, speaks of La Verna and *The Praises of God* without mentioning *either* the seraph *or* the stigmata, and yet the source of the account, Leo, the owner of the parchment, insists that they are all part of the same story. So perhaps that episode simply has a different scope.

Similarly, the story told in *Assisi Compilation* 118 seems to have as its aim the communication of a specific point that may not include the stigmata but has nothing in it that would deny the well-known La Verna event. The scope of the story concerns how Francis received consolations on La Verna, including in the form of the Seraph's appearance.

As for Thomas of Eccleston's account of the alleged oral witness of Leo concerning aspects of the seraph's appearance left out of the legend, again the same point must be made: the scope of the story simply seems to be other than the stigmata. Certainly by the time of the writing of *Coming to England*, the stigmata are taken for granted by a chronicler of the Order. If the non-mention was suspicious in any way, something would be said about it. At any rate, this episode lacks some credibility since it appears to suffer from developmental embellishment (which is to be expected in a later chronicle reporting oral testimony several times removed); in this case one is tipped off by those secret words that the seraph had entrusted to the founder in assurance of the destiny of the Order, which lacks verisimilitude.

3. *1 Celano* as a Primary Source[4]

Thomas of Celano's *legenda* should also be considered a primary source insofar as it not only uses *The Letter of Elias*

but apparently conveys for the first time information gained from direct oral testimony. So, when Thomas links the seraph to the stigmata, while keeping them still distinct, he is obviously having recourse to the oral testimony of Leo, testimony which will later be recorded in red ink by the hand of the very same witness. And when Thomas modifies the description of the stigmata, he could only be repeating what he has learned from witnesses. The precision and the realism of the description, which also demands very much since it diverges from the one offered by Elias, evokes the feeling of sworn testimony, or a kind of "verbal process."[5]

4. Basic Harmony of the Primary Sources on the "Fact"

The preceding analyses of the sources leads Miccoli to conclude that on the question of the stigmata the primary sources do not admit of substantial or effective diversity of witness.

Thomas, then, would not substantially deviate from Elias. The first announcement of the stigmata, which does not have all of the later facts, would be explained in terms of a leader caught up in the emotion of the moment as he announces the great revelation and so fails to clarify the particulars, which he probably did not go to the trouble of getting properly informed about at that time. The official hagiographer must fill in the gaps, and, with the other witnesses, he acquires some clarifications that deviate somewhat from Elias's account but do not negate its substance. One thing is sure: the new witnesses apparently have such a tranquil certainty about the new details that they do not perceive any difficulty in offering clarifications of the message that came from the then-highest authority in the Order.

Nor would Thomas be contradicting the probably later testimony of *The Rubrics of Leo*. When Thomas takes the same position on the time and place as *The Rubrics of Leo* but does not also mention any communication from the seraph, it is simply

testimony to the fact that when Thomas is writing there are still uncertainties about some of the details of the mysterious events of La Verna, which is understandable considering Francis's reluctance to speak of them.

So, Miccoli concludes, the primary sources agree in substance because each presents the same datum: the body of Francis was consistently seen by its viewers as bearing the stigmata of Christ. This is a simple conclusion forced upon the historian by the concordant sources; it remains the fundamental objection to the thesis of Frugoni.[6]

5. Uncertainty about the "Fact" of the Cause[7]

Speaking as an historian then, Miccoli insists on the "fact" of the appearance of the "stigmata" on Francis's body, but he goes on to say that the same historical certitude is absent when it comes to positing the *cause* of the fact.

In other words, according to Miccoli, the strict analysis of the sources shows a concordant perception of the witnesses, but since there is no direct testimony from the subject, Francis, there is not the same historical certainty as to whether he subjectively lived the experience of the stigmata as they understood it.

However, Miccoli insists that a strict *denial* that Francis subjectively had this experience also finds no textual basis. Therefore, he states, those who do strictly deny it must do so only on the basis of a philosophical prejudgment that what is beyond the empirical is not possible. It would not be an historical judgment but a philosophical one, since at the current state of the question there is no historical proof for the position.

On the contrary, in fact, even though we lack the strict historical certitude for positing that Francis lived this reality as one with a supernatural cause, "the character of the witnesses that we have at our disposal renders it highly probable that the experience was effectively lived by Francis."[8]

Miccoli ends his article with an interesting theory about

what might be said further about Francis's experience, not so much on the basis of historical certitude drawn from direct testimony, as much as on reasonable conjecture based on indirect and contextual testimony. I will return to that type of theory in Part Three.

II. Evaluation of the Second Critical Theory

1. Respecting the Sources and Recognizing Basic Harmony

Miccoli's readings of the primary sources seem more founded on the original authorial intentions and so serve to highlight some of the shaky foundations on which Frugoni has made her readings.

The reading of *The Rubrics of Leo* with an eye to determining just precisely what it says on the level of the *littera* enjoys the sobriety that comes from the simplest reading possible. It is now difficult to sustain the theory that Leo's autograph weakens the idea of the physical stigmata of Francis.

Likewise, I have to agree with Miccoli when he says that the non-stigmata seraph sources, as in *Assisi Compilation* 118 and *Coming to England*, are doubtfully trying to subvert the other version of the story. It is true they are not promoting the stigmata, but they are not for that reason subversive.

And Miccoli's reading of *1 Celano* supports the one I gave earlier in response to Critical Theory One, but it also adds very good theories about *1 Celano*'s value as a primary source, though we will have to return to the question of Thomas's use of witnesses.

The resulting claim that the primary sources are essentially harmonious on the fact of the stigmata is likewise a strong one. At the very least, Miccoli is correct on this point: the witnesses claim to have experienced the truth of the stigmata.

2. Questions Remaining Open

The work of Giovanni Miccoli, therefore, begins the work of solving many of the issues raised by Frugoni's exegesis. Still, much remains, especially on the question of the cause of the wounds. That is, if the witnesses all agree that there were five Christ-like wounds on Francis's body and the witnesses seem trustworthy, the next question is whether the phenomenon was of natural or supernatural origin.

It is a question that can be asked another way: if it is established that there is agreement, and therefore foundation, for the "fact" of the stigmata, can it also be established that the circumstantial elements connected to the fact by some witnesses (e.g., the seraph and implied supernatural intervention) are equally founded (i.e., traceable to Francis's own witness)?

So, whereas on the one hand Miccoli establishes that *The Rubrics of Leo* represent "direct testimony," because Leo was "in those months and in those years at the side of Francis,"[9] on the other hand—if I understand correctly—this testimony is not "direct enough," so to speak, to posit that Francis shared with him details of his experience, for example, of the seraph or of the nature of the reception of the stigmata. In this way, this primary documentary source, like the others, would attest to the experience of the witness, though not necessarily to the experience of Francis, and so we can be certain only about the former.

Thus, to insist on more than the mere experience of the witnesses would require certainty or strong likelihood that the various circumstantial elements of the stigmata story are traceable to Francis's own testimony. We would need to be able to say, for example, not just what Leo intends by his words, but that he is claiming to know something directly from the mouth of Francis or perhaps from a companion who so knew it.

The same question that is here asked of *The Rubrics of Leo*

is to be asked of *1 Celano* and, I would add, *Assisi Compilation* 118. Namely, are the circumstantial elements (e.g., the opening of the Gospel book, the prayer for God's will, the vision of a seraph, etc.) historical? Do they represent the actual experience of Francis? These are all questions that must yet be addressed.

---

1 Giovanni Miccoli, "Considerazioni" (cited in Chap. 1, in my discussion of the authenticity of *The Letter of Elias*).

2 G. Miccoli, "Considerazioni," 20-23; 28-33.

3 G. Miccoli, "Considerazioni," 29-32.

4 G. Miccoli, "Considerazioni," 23-28.

5 G. Miccoli, "Considerazioni," 24.

6 G. Miccoli, "Considerazioni," 33.

7 G. Miccoli, "Considerazioni," 34-35.

8 G. Miccoli, "Considerazioni," 35.

9 G. Miccoli, "Considerazioni," 21.

Chapter 10: **THIRD CRITICAL THEORY: FACT OF THE STIGMATA, INVENTION OF THE SERAPH**

I. Third Critical Theory

Professor Jacques Dalarun, the noted French medievalist, offered an important contribution to our problem at the May 2005 session of the International Congress for Medieval Studies at Kalamazoo, Michigan.[1]

I will summarize his view. Dalarun sees three written sources upon which all the subsequent ones are built: *The Letter of Elias*, *Mira circa nos*, and *1 Celano*. In this case, *Assisi Compilation* 118 and *The Rubrics of Leo* would be placed among those subsequent sources that only build on the aforementioned three. As for *1 Celano* specifically, which finally creates the stigmatization story on which all later ones will be based, Thomas has at his disposal *The Letter of Elias*, *Mira circa nos*, and some oral witnesses for the descriptions of the wounds. And since all of this testimony comes together in the consensus that Francis indeed had five wounds on his body at the time of his death, then such must be true. However, as for the story surrounding the *origin* of the wounds, there is little information, if any, and so Thomas composes an episode according to what is available in order to complete his legend. The real question, then, is not if Francis had the wounds, but whether they were perhaps of human origin.

1. The Witnesses Speak, Hence the Fact[2]

Dalarun, building on the presentation of Miccoli, says that two aspects of Thomas's version assure that there were such

wounds on Francis's body. First, since the legend must somehow result from a canonization process, Thomas certainly uses information from certified witnesses, and indicates those witnesses when possible.[3] Now apparently, Thomas has many more witnesses of the wounds from after Francis's death compared to before, and of the few from before, only two for the side wound. Still, witnesses he does indeed have, and, concludes the scholar, "two or three years after the funeral, in a legend written for the broadest circulation, it would have been absurd to give a false report about Francis's wounds, while a lot of people could have denounced the forgery."[4] So, from the point of view of the concordance of witnesses—and this is not unlike Miccoli's point—an historian must conclude that, upon death and for some period before, Francis bore five wounds on his hands, feet, and side.

Second, Dalarun suggests that Thomas's description of the wounds is also an authenticating feature since there could be no other explanation for such deviation from his written sources. That is, Thomas contradicts Elias when he deviates in the description of the wounds. And, likewise, since the canonization Bull did not mention the wounds explicitly, Thomas is contradicting Gregory IX too. Thus Thomas pits himself against two authoritative positions. Therefore, the only good explanation for this is that Thomas must have been certain that his version was true (which presumes also that Thomas has witnesses insistent on the fact).[5]

2. Francis is Silent: The "Great Secret"[6]

Though the witnesses may speak about the fact of the wounds, Francis is silent about not only their existence but also their origin. This is what Thomas seems to indicate, and Dalarun sees it to be a vital fact for interpreting the information at our disposal.

Thomas is indeed explicit: Francis worked hard to hide the

marks not just from strangers but from friars too. The wounds were his "great secret [*praecipuum secretum*]" (*1 Celano* 96:1), as Thomas explains immediately after the first description of the wounds.

Dalarun follows the logic: if Thomas is trustworthy—and he is—then what he says must be true, namely that Francis did not speak of this, his "great secret." And if Francis did not speak of his great secret, then none of the witnesses has any direct knowledge of the events that occurred on La Verna relative to the origin of the marks on Francis's body.

Therefore, Thomas's account of the events of La Verna is not based on witness testimony but instead on a theological-hagiographical elaboration based on the materials he does have at his disposal. He employs his tremendous skill and impeccable awareness of the textual traditions to accomplish the task entrusted to him.

3. Thomas and the Invention of the Seraph[7]

The French scholar suggests that the mental process by which Thomas arrived at his La Verna account can be reconstructed on the basis of his two literary sources, which are *The Letter of Elias* and *Mira circa nos*.

For much of his language, as I showed earlier, Thomas borrows from *The Letter of Elias*. For the other circumstances and particulars of the actual event of stigmatization, however, Thomas might be inspired by *Mira circa nos*. Could it be, for example, that the association with Mount La Verna—a place at which Thomas had heard that Francis lodged around two years before dying—is encouraged when Thomas reads *Mira circa nos* 4, which, alluding to Abraham and Isaac in *Genesis* 22:2, says that Francis offered his flesh to the Lord *super unum montium* ("on one of the mountains")?

And more importantly, it seems that the origin of the seraph should be attributed to Thomas's reading of *Mira circa nos*.

Thomas's mind must move by association from *igne charitatis* [fire of love] in Gregory's Bull to a sermon of Bernard of Clairvaux, certainly known to Thomas, that describes Seraphim as those whom God—Love itself (*ipsa caritas*)—has drawn to himself such that they are so united to him as to truly resemble fire (*instar profecto ignis*).[8] So Thomas moves from the *igne charitatis* in *Mira circa nos* to the *ignis* and *charitatis* that are characteristics of Seraphim according to Bernard,[9] which therefore leads easily to the theophany of *Isaiah* 6, which in its own turn becomes the model for Thomas's account. A man who has six wings like a Seraph appears to Francis, and the experience that impresses itself in Francis's heart expresses itself in his flesh.

This would be a hypothesis of the process by which Thomas was able, via the written sources available and a subtle theological mind, to move from the incomplete story of how the founder had wounds on his body that were not dissimilar to Christ's, to the complete story of Francis's receiving those wounds in connection to a theophanic event.

4. Leo and a Contaminated Memory[10]

The story as told by Thomas of Celano becomes the official one and the essential source and model for all retellings of the stigmata event. This also explains, suggests Dalarun, the two Leonine contributions, *Assisi Compilation* 118 and *The Rubrics of Leo*, in that they cannot help but be influenced by *1 Celano*'s fuller seraph version.

In this way, when Leo, around 1246, composes the episode now found in *Assisi Compilation* 118, he really only sets out to tell the story of something he remembers from his time with Francis on La Verna, a story about a miraculous sign given in the form of birds that come to sing at the cell where Francis is staying. When Leo tags on to the end of the story something about a seraph it is nothing more than a contamination of his memory

from the continual hearing of Thomas's legend over the years. Now not even Leo can think of La Verna without thinking also of a seraph.

The same thing must be said for *The Rubrics of Leo*, explains Dalarun. The memory of Leo is continually evolving, as memories do, and with the passage of even more time—perhaps many years—Leo places his red annotations on the little parchment and adds mention of the other element he had left out of *Assisi Compilation* 118, namely the stigmata.

So, if *The Rubrics of Leo* offer either first-hand knowledge or testimony gained from being on La Verna with Francis, and if his detail-filled version of the story (with Lent of Saint Michael, location, stigmatization, seraph, and thanksgiving praises) is original, why does he not give the information to Thomas in 1246 with the other new remembrances that were handed over for the eventual compilation of the new version of the legend? In other words, why is there not the fuller version of the story in *2 Celano* 49, which recounts the story of the *Chartula*? Or why not in *2 Celano* 197, which tells of the devotion of Francis to Michael the Archangel? *The Rubrics of Leo* must have been written at least after 1246 or 1247, says Dalarun, and more likely after *Major Legend*.

If Leo's two written sources are contaminated by other sources, what can finally be pinpointed as his original contribution? That is, what are the real events he experienced and now passes on? According to the author, the elements would be the following: Between the summer and fall of 1224 Leo is at La Verna and receives the little autograph parchment of Francis. At that time Francis probably explains to Leo how he liked to make a "Lent" in honor of Saint Michael and how this time he received a special sign in the form of the songs of the birds. Meanwhile, there is no reason to think that Leo knew at this time of the five wounds that Francis bore; only later, being influenced by the

regular reading of the official legend, did Leo begin to associate the events in his mind. First, during the composition of stories in or before 1246, he connected La Verna, the Lent of Saint Michael, and, in a discreet way, the vision of the Seraph, while later, in *The Rubrics of Leo*, he completed the process by placing all the elements together with the stigmatization. This is Dalarun's position.

5. The Origin of the Wounds?[11]

Dalarun does not insist on a solution for the actual origin or nature of the marks on Francis's body. However, he does hint at a possible direction of thought, the mention of which will serve to anticipate the hypothesis I will present in the next chapter:[12] perhaps the wounds are of human origin, as might be implied by *Mira circa nos.*[13] Could it be, Dalarun asks, that the papal Bull makes a discreet reference to the stigmata? (I cited the passage in Part One.) The significance of this would be that if this is indeed a reference to the stigmata, Francis's holocaust is being presented as the result of classical asceticism, therefore of human and not divine origin.

Apparently, explains Dalarun, even Gregory IX had doubts for some time, not so much about the fact of the wounds, but about their miraculous origin. So, while the Bull makes a vague reference to the marks, it avoids the use of the words "stigmata" or "miracle." It is not until 1237 that Gregory makes his belief explicit in several papal Bulls. And this matches well with the story that appears later in Bonaventure of how, before the canonization, Gregory suffered doubts about the wound in Francis's side until the saint appeared to him in a dream to reprove him (*Major Legend, Miracles* I:2). Here it becomes clear that "to doubt the wound in the side" simply means to doubt the divine origin of the wounds. The fact that Francis had these wounds was sworn to in the presence of Gregory and cardinals prior to the canonization, as Gregory explains in one of the 1237

Bulls.[14] So the question must not have been about the fact of the wounds but their origin.[15]

II. Evaluation of the Third Critical Theory[16]

There is much to praise about Dalarun's approach, above all his sensible methodology, the likes of which have been described by him and others as "stratigraphic," to borrow geological imagery. Since the field is finally in a position to date fairly accurately the majority of the early documents, it is increasingly possible to locate in each source the layers of their textual tradition, isolate the witnesses, and make some tentative and hypothetical judgments about the real historical event. In other words, Franciscan historiography is much like archeology. Dalarun knows that this is the only way to go forward, at least with the current state of the question. Instead of emphasizing all in Dalarun's presentation with which I agree, however, I will here outline some points of divergence. I am not attempting to solve all the problems that remain, but merely to raise the questions that come from my own research after considering his position.

My study will show, for example, (1) that Gregory may not be as incredulous as is often said and that perhaps quite the opposite is true; it seems that Gregory's language in *Mira circa nos* 4 is just as likely a subtle allusion to the seraph event as that Thomas invents it on the basis of Gregory's subtle language. I will also suggest (2) that the silence of Francis concerning the events on La Verna is not as absolute as it seems at first; rather, Francis had a special group of friends that did know his secrets, one of whom in particular was the confidant for the "great secret." (3) As for the contributions of Leo, I will give arguments that they are to be taken as original witnesses and certainly not to be considered influenced by *2 Celano* or *Major Legend* because I believe we are now able to date *The Rubrics of Leo* to before the Letter of Greccio.

1. Rereading *Mira circa nos* on Gregory IX's Incredulity

Much has been made, by Dalarun and by others, of the silence of Gregory IX concerning the stigmata of Francis. Some have said that Gregory is silent in *Mira circa nos,* but later, once he realizes the expediency of the new characteristic feature of the saint, he begins to promote it with various papal Bulls dated nearly a decade after the canonization. In this scenario, even Bonaventure would be embarrassed about the silence of Gregory and so would be happy to include (or perhaps invent) a story he has heard about the resolution of Gregory's doubts (*Major Legend, Miracles* I:2). Meanwhile, Dalarun offers a variation on the theme, keenly seeing in *Mira circa nos* 4 a possible allusion to the wounds, which are still, however, not the miraculous stigmata but probably something else like marks resulting from physical asceticism. Either way, Gregory is incredulous.

I suggest a fresh look at *Mira circa nos*, in which any direct mention of the stigmata would have been entirely inconsistent with the tone of the Bull, hence making the silence nothing to be marveled at and so irrelevant to the discussion.

The fact of the matter is that the Bull almost completes itself without the mention of a single historical detail of Francis's life! I am more inclined to compare, mutatis mutandis, *Mira circa nos* to *Major Legend* than to other biographical sources, in the sense that both are quick to jump over the letter of the events, so to speak, in order to get immediately to their spiritual meaning. In reality, if the Bull were the only introduction to Francis someone had, that person would neither know, for example, where Francis was from (neither city nor country), nor whether he was layman, priest, or bishop. The only strict historical facts that can be gleaned from the document would be that Gregory knew the saint personally, and that the saint died on the fourth of October. It is not even mentioned that Francis founded a new, thriving religious order.[17]

I wonder, therefore, if we are not sometimes guilty of reading back into Gregory the later debates about the stigmata without warrant. The magisterial article of Vauchez cited earlier is our touchstone and shows the rise of early medieval detractors of the stigmata and the flurry of papal defense. And from that article it seems clear that the context for the argument is above all the question of the new minoritic Order and its role in the Church and the world. In other words, the stigmata of Francis were placed at the center of an ideological and political debate over the legitimacy of the Order. But the more the Minors emphasized the stigmata of Francis to legitimize themselves, the more it turned into glory seeking, and so all the more did the detractions flourish; it was a kind of vicious circle. So the origins of the detractions seem much less motivated by problems with credulity or evidence than by displeasure with the new Order, which seemed not only to be inserting itself everywhere, but also holding itself up as superior.

This context certainly goes a long way to explain the increasing need to note additional witnesses (e.g., Br. Bonitius at the Chapter of Genoa, mentioned earlier) and to emphasize the stigmata evermore in hagiographic writing (e.g., *3 Celano*). And so, perhaps it also explains the later story, which appears for the first time in Bonaventure, about Gregory's having doubts concerning the side wound resolved in a dream. What more authoritative way to resolve the debated issue than to say that the pope himself doubted but was shown the truth by the very saint? I think we must always remember that this—forty years later—is the first time we ever hear anything said positively about Gregory's having had doubts. So, if Bonaventure does have a good source for the story, which is very difficult to say, I think we should at least trust the chronology he gives, namely that the scruples are before the canonization and not after.[18] But I frankly lean towards saying that the whole thing is anachronistic.

Additional support for this last point about trusting Bonaventure's chronology comes from one of the documents Dalarun mentions, which is seldom included in these discussions. In *Confessor Domini* (5 April 1237) Gregory states unequivocally that he and his brother cardinals not only heard witnesses concerning the stigmata while conducting the process for canonization, but in fact decided to canonize Francis precisely because of that special miracle (*ex ipso specialem causam habuimus*).[19] This is strong testimony, the lateness of which seems irrelevant unless we were to have good reason to question Gregory's honesty or memory, which I do not see. In sum, Gregory here attests to the fact that (1) there were multiple trustworthy witnesses to the stigmata testifying before him and before his cardinals prior to the canonization; (2) they considered it miraculous (since it is mentioned among "his other miracles"); and (3) this miracle was considered a principle reason for the canonization.

I am inclined to say that the much-cited silence of Gregory on the stigmata in *Mira circa nos* may be a kind of straw-man argument. I will return to the question of Gregory's incredulity later.

2. Thomas and the Invention of the Seraph?

Concerning Dalarun's source-critical analysis of Thomas's seraph event, I suspect it might be a bit too difficult to prove philologically the link between the particular sermon of Bernard and Thomas's elaboration of the La Verna event. But Dalarun is correct: Thomas certainly incorporates contemporary understanding of seraphim into his presentation. And if we could be more or less certain that Francis told no one of a seraph apparition, then Dalarun's might be the best guess at how Thomas arrived at his telling of the story.

The idea of seraph appearances may have been more of a commonplace in Francis's day than we are able to know. It could be, for example, that the contemporary story from the life

of Mary of Oignies (d. 1213) is not the anomaly that it seems to be.[20] If so, Thomas's literary application of a kind of *topos* would be less incidental than it seems at first glance.

But, with the current state of our knowledge, the whole episode seems quite unusual, almost too unusual to be created only on a string of textual associations that begin with two or three words in the papal Bull. I am not sure that there are other examples of hagiography (certainly not of such integrity) that work in this manner. It is not impossible; I merely state here that it seems to be a fragile argument for which more evidence is needed.

3. Gregory IX: Doubter or Witness?

As far as this line of reasoning goes (and considering the portrait of *Mira circa nos* I created above), I think that it is equally plausible to suggest that Gregory IX, in *Mira circa nos* 4, has in mind the new and extraordinary miracle of the stigmata but felt it out of place to make direct reference to it when he ought rather to be establishing Francis amongst the biblical models of sanctity. Why should we not say that he employs words like those of Bernard's sermon (consciously or unconsciously) because he is thinking of the seraph that he had heard appeared to Francis but is not sure that this is the appropriate context to speak of it directly? The Bull does not otherwise speak of any of the *littera* of Francis's life, why do so here? Therefore, could we not hypothesize that *Mira circa nos* 4 is perhaps discreet evidence of the existence of early testimony to the seraph apparition, the same testimony to which Thomas would soon be privy when he would make his own interviews (even with Gregory) and receive documentation from the canonization process? This hypothesis is not less valid. And since it better respects the integrity of the sources, I tend to prefer it.

4. Was Francis Silent?

Dalarun is right, of course, that no theories about possible

sources for knowledge of a seraph vision (or any kind of divine intervention, in fact) matter at all if Francis never spoke of it. But the texts concerning Francis's "great secret" deserve greater attention. I will cite the passage and then comment. After the La Verna event and the first description of the stigmata, Thomas writes:[21]

95:9 Studiosissime namque abscondebat haec ab extraneis, celabat cautissime a propinquis, ita ut et collaterales fratres et eius devotissimi secutores haec per multum temporis ignorarent.	95:9 He hid those marks very carefully from strangers, and concealed them very cautiously from those close to him, such that even the brothers at his side and his most devoted followers for a long time did not know about them.
[. . . .] 11 Sed et ne humanus favor datam sibi gratiam furaretur, modis omnibus quibus poterat haec abscondere satagebat.	[. . . .] 11 Rather, in every way that he was able, he was diligent to hide these marks, lest human favor rob him of the grace given him.
96:1 Mos etenim ipsius erat raro aut nulli praecipuum revelare secretum, timens specie praecipuae dilectionis ex eorum revelatione, sicut solent facere praedilecti, pati aliquod in data sibi gratia detrimentum.	96:1 It was his custom to reveal rarely or to no one his great secret, fearing that by his special friends revealing it (as such usually do so as to be esteemed) he would suffer some loss of the grace given him.

First, I would simply note that the text does not say that Francis never revealed the wounds nor that he never spoke of them to anyone at all. Yes, it does stress his great desire to keep them secret. It does say that he succeeded "for a long time." But, to be precise, the actual words of Thomas are that Francis made it a custom to reveal the secret "rarely or to no one." If *raro* is not here an adverb but a dative of *rarus*, then it would be "to the rare one or to no one." This too seems plausible, especially since stylistically a dative *raro* would fit nicely with the dative

nulli. Thomas's expression is rendered well by the editors of the Italian-translation volume who say, *"Si era fatto un programma di non manifestare quasi a nessuno il suo straordinario segreto."*[22] Thomas would be employing a nice rhetorical turn of phrase that essentially means "very, very rarely," but does not mean "never."

Even more, still going by the letter of the text, Thomas does not say that Francis never spoke to any one at all about the fact that he had these wounds, nor that he never told anyone at all how he received them, but only that he was not at all fond of showing them. To say it another way, the only certain thing said positively by Thomas here is that Francis did not like to show the stigmata, his special secret, not even to those closest to him. But it is not said that never once did he tell perhaps a special companion something about them and their origin. Indeed, a literal reading of the text shows that he *did* reveal them, only rarely.

Next, the context of Thomas's discussion seems important, since it does show Francis having certain friars inside his circle of secrets. For the very next lines tell the unusually realistic and frank anecdote of how Francis had a pre-arranged sign taught to his brothers, such that if he suddenly wanted to cut short a conversation with seculars he need only make the sign, and the brothers would dismiss those people (*1 Celano* 96:3). I mean to say that here, in the next line or so after describing Francis's "great secret," Thomas is describing how there are a group of special brothers privy to Francis's secrets. Yes, Thomas also says that Francis hesitates to reveal his special secret (*praecipuum secretum*) even to his special friends (*praecipuae dilectionis*) (*1 Celano* 96:1), but he does not say "never."

Of course, this passage does not say *positively* that Francis did speak to anyone in particular about his La Verna experience, which leads back to the question of witnesses.

5. The Great Secret of Leo: On Thomas's Witness

Perhaps Dalarun's point is better expressed like this: since there is no witness that can claim Francis told him something of the stigmatization event, then the idea of the "great secret" has to be created (maybe as an extension of the real episode I have just mentioned from *1 Celano* 96:3). Dalarun does go on to explain that it is a bad sign when Thomas does not mention his witness because it is customary for him to do so when he is able. But other experts on the legend have a somewhat different emphasis.[23] So what then are the facts concerning Thomas and his use of witnesses?

In another work, Dalarun makes a fine analysis of Thomas and his use of witnesses, explaining how a careful examination of the text of the legend reveals certain times that Thomas seems to be relying on Francis's writings for his retelling, other times where he is relying largely on a *topos*, while many other times he apparently has the use of direct testimony.[24] As for this use of direct testimony, Dalarun cites many examples in which we can easily imagine that the individual or group of people involved in the story must have been the source. Sometimes there is a name associated with the witness, but in fact so many other times there is not. At any rate, I think that Dalarun would say that in the case at hand some mention of a testimony (or at least some apparent involvement of one) should be discernible somewhere in the La Verna event but is not.

Yet, is this accurate? While Dalarun is correct that there is no indication that the theophanic apparition of the man-seraph or the appearance of the marks on Francis's body are actually witnessed by any one, Thomas nevertheless explicitly does say that Francis shared something of his secret with someone. In the very first reference to the stigmata, at the beginning of Book II, in a kind of preface to the La Verna event that follows some paragraphs later, Thomas mentions clearly that what follows

has been shared with a certain, unnamed person: "But there is hidden here some secret [*arcanum*]; here is concealed some awesome mystery, one we believe is known to God alone, and revealed in part by the same saint to a certain person [*et per ipsum sanctum ex parte cuidam revelatum*]" (*1 Celano* 90:8).[25] I have to conclude that Francis makes his great secret into the great secret of someone else too, someone from his inner circle, perhaps Leo.

In accord with this, I point out that the next paragraph, which now begins Francis's retreat from the busyness of the crowds to a place of solitude (which we soon discover is La Verna), makes it known that a certain "very few companions [*socios valde paucos*]" (*1 Celano* 91:3) do accompany Francis. So, even though Francis seems to be alone at the moment of the seraphic vision, he is nevertheless still with a certain small group of his brothers in those days on that mount. And I think that Thomas leaves it to be understood that one of those friars is entrusted with something of Francis's secret and is at least in some general way the source for the episodes that immediately follow.

And even though the confidant is left anonymous, this seems to me quite consonant with Thomas's project, even in comparison to the different case where the names of Elias and Rufino *are* revealed as witnesses for the side wound (*1 Celano* 95:5-8). Whereas on one hand Thomas has special need of a very concrete witness for a concrete, physical fact (the side wound that confirms the reality of the likeness of Francis's wounds to Christ's), on the other hand Thomas wants to leave mysterious something of the invisible, interior, and spiritual experience connected to the origins of that same physical phenomenon. Therefore, he says he has a witness, yes; but perhaps out of respect for the ineffability of the event, he does not want to say more. He does not want to tarnish Francis's mystical experience by giving the impression that Francis freely chatted about it to whomever.

After all, Thomas believes that Francis "had learned through experience that one cannot be a spiritual person unless one's secrets are deeper and more numerous than what can be seen on the face" (*1 Celano* 96:4).[26]

In addition, is there not good reason to surmise that the witness wanted to remain anonymous,[27] did not want to be the single name mentioned in the official and public legend as the repository of special secrets of the founder? And why not also think that he who had kept Francis's secret for so long during Francis's life, out of loyalty to what was entrusted to him, still hesitated to reveal what had also become his own secret, and expressed that hesitation by requesting anonymity?

And does the anonymity not concord also with the fact that, a little later in the text, the encomium to the "four pillars" (*columnae quatuor*, the special friars to whom Francis entrusted his care in his last two years) deliberately omits their names? Thomas explains it: "I omit their names for the present, out of regard for modesty, which is a close friend of these spiritual men" (*1 Celano* 102:4). I imagine that this phrase could be applied also to explain the anonymous witness to whom Francis revealed something of his secret. And for that matter, this witness might well be one of those four pillars.[28]

When Dalarun offers his hypothesis of Thomas's literary invention of the seraph, he explains well and clearly that it is not as if to say that Thomas is trying to mislead; instead Thomas is in some manner writing according to the literary genre and by the means at his disposal.[29] I would agree with this analysis if it were not for what I noted above, that Thomas does indeed signal his anonymous witness. I do not know precisely what the content of the secret revealed to the certain confidant was, but I do know that it relates to the mysteries surrounding the stigmata. So if I move too quickly to doubt the elements of Thomas's narrative, I might indeed risk calling Thomas a liar.

6. For an Earlier Dating of The Rubrics of Leo

This hypothesis of a repository of Francis's secrets within his intimate circle brings us back to the question of the written Leonine sources, which Dalarun has said seem to be contaminated sources, increasingly so with time, such that *The Rubrics of Leo* are very late and therefore most complete. In order to better evaluate this reading, I would like to address the tricky and persistent problem of the dating of the rubric autograph, which I briefly described in Part One, Chapter 4.

Dalarun's arguments on the late dating of *The Rubrics of Leo* are essentially drawn from the early twentieth-century German scholar Josef Merkt.[30] Merkt's argument is simple: writers like Thomas of Celano are obviously making use of Leo's oral testimony for a long time, but it is not until the later source of Bonaventure (1260-1263) that all of the elements also found in Leo's rubrics appear together in a single written source. Therefore, the autograph gloss certainly could not have been made before that time, and it is highly unlikely that Leo had this full version in mind before then, since otherwise there would be some traces of it elsewhere owing to his influence.

With the more precise knowledge we have today of the story of the sources, Dalarun is able to pinpoint the problem all the more. He asks: when Thomas sets again to writing around the end of 1246 with the new companion sources in hand, why does he not include all the elements currently found in Leo's gloss?

Further, something extremely interesting to me is that Dalarun also points out how we can see *The Rubrics of Leo* to have taken elements from two separate stories Leo told or wrote during the time of the composition of the 1246 *Florilegium*.[31] This would show how later, when he sets himself to writing the gloss, Leo begins to conflate all these elements. Here is what the text

looks like with the exact parallels of *Assisi Compilation* 118 in bold, and the ones of *MS Little* 154 underlined:

> [1] Beatus Franciscus duobus annis ante mortem suam **fecit quadra / [2] gesimam** in loco **Alverne ad honorem beate Virginis matris dei et beati / [3] Michaelis** arch**angeli** a **festo Assumptionis sancte Marie Virginis usque ad festum sancti / [4] Michaelis** septembris. **Et facta est** super eum manus **domini**. Post **visionem** et allocuti / [5] onem **Seraphym** et impressionem stigmatum Christi in corpore suo fecit has laudes ex alio / [6] latere cartule scriptas, et manu sua scripsit, gratias agens Deo de beneficio sibi / [7] collato. Beatus Franciscus scripsit manu sua istam benedictionem mihi fratri Leoni.

Dalarun's discovery is nothing short of remarkable, easily one of the most important insights for the stigmata debate in decades. For, while Dalarun uses it to show Leo's conflation of memories, I suggest rather that he has provided us with the means of discovering something certain of the dating of *The Rubrics of Leo.* I have first a philological demonstration, then a conclusion to make from it.

My first point is that I think Dalarun's synoptic comparison shows not a conflation of memories but a certain textual dependency. In other words, if we presume for the moment that *The Rubrics of Leo* are made after the *Florilegium*, I would posit that Leo has the *Florilegium* in front of him when he glosses the *Chartula.* Proof of this is that, without these texts, Leo's language would show some influence of the now common language of *2 Celano* or *The Major Legend*, but it does not. The philological evidence shows where the strong, textual dependency is, and it is not on these. I will make two synoptic charts to illustrate the point.

Here is a chart highlighting common elements of the episode about the friar who wanted something written from the hand of Francis:

Rubrics of Leo	*MS Little*	*2 Celano*	*Major Legend*
. . . fecit h**as** **laudes** ex alio [6] latere **cart**ule scriptas, et **manu sua scripsit**, gratias agens Deo de beneficio sibi [7] collato. Beatus franciscus **scripsit manu sua** istam **benedictionem** mihi fratri Leoni.	[154] . . . desiderabat habere aliquem recreabile **scriptum manu sua** de verbis Domini, maxime quia erat tunc tribulatus maligna et gravi temptatione . . . [2] Et dixit . . . Franciscus: Da michi **cart**am et atramentum, quoniam volo scribere quedam verba Domini et ejus laudes, quas meditatus sum in corde meo. . . . [3] Ivit b. Franciscus et **scripsit** illa verba et ill**as** **laudes** et in fine **scripsit suam benedictionem** illi, dicens ad eum: [4] Accipe hanc cartam	[49:4] Quadam enim die vocat eum beatus Franciscus dicens: "Porta mihi **chart**am et atramentum, quoniam verba Domini et **Laudes** eius scribere volo, quae meditatus sum in corde meo." [5] Allatis protinus quae petierat, **scri**bit **manu** propria **Laudes** Dei et verba quae voluit, et ultimo **benedictionem** fratris, dicens: "Accipe tibi **chart**ulam istam . . ."	[XI:9:5] . . . unus e sociis magno desiderio cupiebat habere de verbis Domini aliquod **scriptum manu** ipsius breviter adnotatum. [. . . .] [XI:9:9] Portari namque sibi iussit a fratre praedicto atramentum et chartam, Laudesque Domini iuxta fratris desiderium propria **manu scripsit** et ultimo **benedictionem** ipsius, dicens: "Accipe tibi **chartul**am istam . . ."

I observe three philological phenomena. First, *The Rubrics of Leo* and *MS Little* have in common that the *laudes* are modified by a demonstrative pronoun (*has* / *illas*); the change from *illas* in *MS Little* to *has* in *The Rubrics of Leo* is normal since the former speaks of "those" praises on "that parchment" in question, while the latter speaks of "these" praises on "this parchment" on which

the author is writing. In comparison, neither *2 Celano* nor *Major Legend* modifies *laudes* with a demonstrative pronoun.

Second, *The Rubrics of Leo* and *MS Little* have in common the personal pronoun *sua* modifying *manu*, but the others do not: *2 Celano* has *propria* and *The Major Legend* uses *ipsius* once and *propria* another time.

Meanwhile, I do not see anything that *2 Celano* or *The Major Legend* have in common with *The Rubrics of Leo* that is not also in *MS Little*.

Next I chart the common elements regarding the Lent of Saint Michael.

Rubrics of Leo	*MS Little*	*2 Celano*	*Major Legend*
Beatus	[118:1] . . . ivit	[197:5] Bea-	[IX:3:3] . . . ob
Franciscus	beatus Francis-	tum vero	devotionem
duobus annis	cus ad heremi-	Michaelem,	ipsorum ab
ante mortem	torium montis	eo quod	Assumptione
suam **fecit**	**Alverne;** [2] . . .	animarum	Virginis glorio-
quadra[2]**g-**	voluit ibi	reprae-	sae quadraginta
esimam in	**facere quadra-**	sentandarum	diebus ieiunans
loco **Alverne**	**gesimam ad**	haberet	orationi iugiter
ad honorem	**honorem**	officium,	insistebat. . . .
beate Virgi-	**sancti Michae-**	saepe dicebat	[VIII.10.6] Cum ad
nis matris	**lis.** [3] Iverat	excellentius	eremum per-
Dei et beati	autem illuc	honoran-	venisset **Alver-**
[3] **Michaelis**	ante **festum**	dum. [6] Nam	**nae** propter
arch**angeli**	**Assumptionis**	**ad hon-**	quadragesimam
a **festo**	gloriose **virgi-**	**orem sancti**	celebrandam
Assumptio-	**nis Marie**, et	**Michaelis**,	in honorem
nis sancte	numeravit dies	inter **fest**um	Archangeli
Marie Vir-	a **festo sancte**	**Assump-**	Michaelis. . . .
ginis usque	**Marie usque**	**tionis** et	[XIII:1:4] . . . post
ad festum	**ad festum**	**festum** eius,	labores multi-
sancti [4]	**[sancti]***	quadragenam	modos perduc

Michaelis septembris. Et facta est super eum manus Domini.	**Michaelis**, quod essent quadraginta dies, [4] et ait: "**Ad honorem** Dei et **beate Virginis** Marie, matris eius, et **beati Michaelis**, **angel**orum principis et animarum, volo hic facere quadragesimam."	dierum devotissim	tus est in locum excelsum seorsum, qui dicitur Mons **Alvernae**. [XIII:1:5] Cum igitur iuxta solitum morem **quadragesimam** ibidem ad honorem sancti Archangeli **Michaelis** ieiunare coepisset . . .

In this case I make the following observations. First, in *The Rubrics of Leo* and *The Assisi Compilation* Francis "makes" (*facere*) a Lent, but in *2 Celano* and *The Major Legend* Francis would "fast for forty days."

Second, in *The Rubrics of Leo* and *The Assisi Compilation* there are very similar expressions where Francis honors not only the Blessed Virgin but also Blessed Michael Archangel. But in *2 Celano* and *The Major Legend* those two devotions are not mentioned together.

Next, in both *The Rubrics of Leo* and *The Assisi Compilation* Francis makes his Lent precisely *a festo . . . sancte Marie . . . usque ad festum sancti Michaelis*. But in *2 Celano* it is rather *inter festum Assumptionis et festum eius*, while once in *The Major Legend* Francis is merely said to fast for forty days from the Assumption, and in another place he is said to fast for forty days in honor of Saint Michael Archangel.

Finally, I do not see any literal parallels between *The Rubrics of Leo* and *2 Celano* or *The Major Legend* that are not held also in common with *The Assisi Compilation*.

In my opinion, all of this amounts to philological certainty of a strict textual relationship between *The Rubrics of Leo* and the *Florilegium*. I think there are two hypotheses that would explain this, one that *The Rubrics of Leo* were written contemporaneously to the *Florilegium*, the other that they were written before.

At the very least—and this is the first hypothesis—Leo must have glossed the *Chartula* during the days of the composition of the *Florilegium*, specifically at the same time as the writing of the two episodes in question. What we know of the history of the *rotuli* of Leo does not suggest that there were any copies to be found after they were consigned to the Minister General in 1246, nor that the copy (perhaps the original) known to be at Assisi, according to certain witnesses in the latter part of the thirteenth century, was easily or often accessed. I suppose we could try to imagine Leo returning to the Sacro Convento in his old age, asking for access to the old scrolls, and being inspired to gloss the *Chartula* as a result. But to me it seems much more plausible that he did everything at the same time, when he still had the scrolls in front of him, and the spirit in the air was one of recording memories,[32] whether or not he ever showed that record to Crescentius, to Thomas, or to anyone else, or simply kept it for his continued personal use. So, this would be a hypothesis of an intentional use of the recently written texts by the same author.[33]

The other scenario, to me more likely, is that Leo had glossed the little parchment sometime before participating in the drafting of the *Florilegium*, and they were those little phrases on that relic that, nostalgically reread often over a period of time (weeks, months, or years), influenced his language when he dictated or wrote the two stories we now know in *MS Little* 154 and *Assisi Compilation* 118. This, then, is a hypothesis of a probably unintentional but literal use of phrases from *The Rubrics of Leo* in the later *Florilegium*.[34]

In light of this, I propose that the strict *terminus ante quem*

for *The Rubrics of Leo* is the date of the Greccio letter; and the strict *terminus post quem* is the canonization of Francis (as I noted in Part One). Therefore, *The Rubrics of Leo* are broadly but certainly dated July 16, 1228-August 11, 1246. Beyond that we can only speculate.

One reasonable speculation would be that Leo makes the gloss during the wave of new recordings of memories that seems to begin unofficially in 1241 with *The Anonymous of Perugia* and receives special sanction at the Chapter of Genoa in 1244.

But to me it is also reasonable, as Miccoli mused, that it was the canonization of Francis, which effectively transformed the parchment into a relic, that occasioned Leo's notation.[35] For the sake of argument, I will operate as if *The Rubrics of Leo* are to be dated after *1 Celano*, but this too, frankly, is arbitrary.

7. The Value of Leo's Testimony

If my dating is correct then Dalarun's concerns about the Leonine stories that find their way into *2 Celano* without the fuller stigmata event details of later accounts are much less significant.

The question is no longer why *2 Celano* 49, concerning the friar who wanted something written from Francis's own hand, does not say anything about the seraph or stigmata if those events really happened together, but rather why Leo did not recount it that way when we know that he clearly did associate all those things together already early on. And the answer can now be very simple: that particular "flower" was meant to emphasize not the mysterious events of La Verna but something else, namely Leo's personal temptation and Francis's spiritual care for him. In other words, *The Rubrics of Leo* are about Francis, but *2 Celano* 49 / *MS Little* 154 is about Leo. In Leo's mind the latter was also a story worth telling in its own right; it was a story that had not yet been told.

Similarly, the question is no longer why *2 Celano* 197,

concerning Francis's devotion to Michael the Archangel, does not mention the seraph or the stigmata, but why Leo decides not to mention them in the same breath in that recounting. The answer must be that Thomas or the source simply wants to emphasize something else, a specific devotion—which is consistent, in any case, with Thomas's thematic presentation in Book II of that work.

So Thomas includes in his latest work the relevant new information he has learned from the *Florilegium* (i.e., about the brother who wanted something written by Francis to dispel temptation, and about the devotion of Francis to St. Michael), but he apparently does not see any need to treat again the stigmatization event of Francis *per se*, and certainly not merely for the purpose of adding that the context was a "Lent" of St. Michael (the only really new piece of information that would be drawn from *The Rubrics of Leo* by then). Of course, this point only matters if Thomas was ever actually shown the *Chartula*, something to which no one in fact attests. After all, Thomas's source for *2 Celano* 49 is not Leo directly but the *Florilegium*.

Therefore, if the date of the gloss of Leo is pushed back to the fervent period of collecting memories in the early and mid 1240's (if not earlier), then we must recognize its status as original witness. This is especially true since it is written not only by a very close companion of the saint, but by a companion who says he received the very artifact on which he recorded his memories at the very place and time in which the alleged event took place. It is further supported since the gloss shows strong signs of independence from the official version. For example, Leo makes no allusions to the circumstances of the stigmatization, speaking, for example, of a mere seraph, and not of a "man-seraph" or a crucified one, a point I will return to later when I discuss the state of the question.

Several questions still remain unanswered. I will return to some in the next and final hypothesis, others in my summary of the state of the question and final reconstruction.

---

1 J. Dalarun, "Great Secret," cited earlier. This article is brief, but anyone who takes the trouble to retrace the author's research will see how unexpectedly dense it is, and how careful is the work that went into it.

2 J. Dalarun, "Great Secret," 12-13.

3 The author develops this point in the book: J. Dalarun, *Misadventure*, 109-111. I will return to Dalarun's treatment of witnesses in my evaluation of his hypothesis.

4 J. Dalarun, "Great Secret," 12.

5 J. Dalarun, "Great Secret," 13-14. Cf. J. Dalarun, *Misadventure*, 129-130.

6 J. Dalarun, "Great Secret," 14-15.

7 J. Dalarun, "Great Secret," 14-15, esp. n. 30-32. Dalarun is not the first to speculate on the origin of the seraph in Thomas's account. An important earlier article, emphasizing the theological place of the seraph in *1 Celano*, is: J. A. Wayne Hellmann, "The Seraph in Thomas of Celano's *Vita Prima*," in *That Others May Know and Love: Essays in Honor of Zachary Hayes, OFM, Franciscan Educator, Scholar*, edited by Michael F. Cusato, O.F.M.—F. Edward Coughlin, O.F.M. (St. Bonaventure, NY: The Franciscan Institute, 1997), 23-41 (This article develops an idea previously announced in J. A. Wayne Hellmann, "The Seraph in the Legends of Thomas of Celano and St. Bonaventure: The Victorine Transition," in *Bonaventuriana. Miscellanea in onore di Jacques Guy Brougerol, ofm,* a cura di Francisco de Asís Chavero Blanco (Roma: Edizioni Antonianum, 1988), 347-356). Another unique approach to making sense of the presence of the seraph in Thomas's narrative is M. Cusato, "Of Snakes and Angels," esp. at 29-53.

8 S. Bernardus Claravallensis, "Sermo XIX," in *Sermones super Cantica canticorum* 1-35, Sancti Bernardi Opera I, ed. J. Leclercq, C. H. Talbot, H. M. Rochais (Roma: Editiones Cistercienses, 1957), 108-113, at 111. The passage reads: "But not those that are called Seraphim, namely, those whom God—Love itself [*ipsa caritas*]—has so drawn to Himself and has absorbed and snatched up into the same ardor of holy affection that they seem to be one spirit with God, truly in the likeness of fire [*instar profecto ignis*] that inflames the air, so that it seems not to be merely on fire, but to be made fire itself [*non ignitum, sed ignem fecisse cernitur*]. And thus those ones that cannot be numbered [the Cherubim] love particularly to contemplate the love in God that never fails. All, therefore, receive even their names from that in which they seem to be pre-eminent: for the Cherubim are called the fullness of knowledge, but the Seraphim are called burning or inflamed [*Seraphim vero incendentia vel incensa dicuntur*]." Translation (modified) cited from O. Schmucki, *The Stigmata*, 202.

9 In fact this general way of envisioning the seraphim is a consistent feature of medieval theology ushered in by Pseudo-Dionysius. Cf. *Angelic Spirituality: Medi-*

eval Perspectives on the Ways of Angels, translated and introduced by Steven Chase, preface by Ewert H. Cousins, The Classics of Western Spirituality (New York: Paulist Press, 2002).

10 J. Dalarun, "Great Secret," 21-25.

11 J. Dalarun, "Great Secret," 18-20; 25-26.

12 Dalarun's reflections are apparently inspired by those of Richard Trexler, whose hypothesis is my Critical Theory Four.

13 J. Dalarun, "Great Secret," 9-12.

14 *Confessor Domini*, in *BullFranc* I, 214.

15 Further demonstration that there was general concern to dispel rumors of the wounds' being of human origin is found in other texts, such as Alexander IV's Bull *Benigna operatio* (29 October 1255). *BullFranc* II, 85-87; *FA:ED* II, 780-781: "We wish at least to set before your eyes those gratifying insignia of the Lord's Passion which should be frequently recalled and greatly admired, and which the hand of divine operation impressed upon the body of this saint [*Sancti corpore manus caelestis operationis impressit*] while he was still alive. . . . After he had died, a wound in his side, which was not inflicted or made by man [*non inflicta humanitus*], was clearly seen in his body." See also *A Life of Saint Francis by an Anonymous Monk of a German Monastery*, 79-80 (in *FA:ED* III, 837-871; *Legenda monacensis*, in *AnalFranc* X, 694-719).

16 I express my deep gratitude to Professor Dalarun for reading with attention a draft of this critique of his article while in the midst of his many and immense (!) projects, and for responding with care and kindness, as is usual for him. His comments were extremely helpful, and I have tried to learn from them and strengthen my arguments accordingly when I could, while I apologize if weaknesses remain.

17 Instead of giving the "facts" we would expect, the Bull strings together biblical references ranging from the most revered patriarchs to the most obscure judges. Gregory wants us to know that at the eleventh hour Francis was sent forth like Shamgar who slew six hundred Philistines, Samson who slew many thousands of Philistines, and Abraham who left even his Father's house; yes, Francis rose like Jacob, as the Lord commanded. And rather than being content to cling to Rachel's embraces alone (benefiting only himself with beautiful but sterile contemplation), Francis went down to Leah's forbidden bedroom (to bear fruit for all). He rushed headlong into the camp of the Midianites (those who were disregarding Church teaching), forcing its submission to Christ. As for Francis's practice of virtue, he disregarded the baggage of worldly possessions and offered his own flesh as a holocaust (as we saw); like Jepthah he offered this "only-begotten daughter." Of course he also received the seven-fold gift of the Spirit and was aided by the eight Gospel beatitudes, but the Church would not presume that her judgment on these things alone was sufficient for enrolling a man among the list of saints: many numerous and outstanding miracles confirm God's wishes. Sabatier made this same point (cf. Paul Sabatier, *The Life of St. Francis of Assisi*, 441), and Bihl later confirmed it, comparing this Bull of Gregory to other ones he wrote in a similar style for Saints Dominic (1234) and Elizabeth (1235). See Michael Bihl, "De stigmatibus," 400.

18 "Antequam crucis signiferum catalogo Sanctorum ascriberet, scrupulum quemdam dubitationis in corde gerebat de vulnere laterali," (*Major Legend, Miracles* I:2:2).
19 "Quo ad nostram, & Fratrum nostrorum deducto notitiam, & cum ceteris ejus miraculis per Testes fide dignissimos probato solemniter, & ex ipso specialem causam habuimus, quod Confessorem eumdem de dictorum Fratrum, & omnium Praelatorum consilio, qui tunc apud Sedem Apostolicam existebant, Sanctorum Catalogo duximus adscribendum . . ." (*BullFranc* I, 214).
20 "So inflamed had she been by an exceeding fire of love that she had risen above the pain of her wound and, in this ecstasy of mind, she had seen one of the seraphim standing close by her." *The Life of Marie d'Oignies by Cardinal Jacques de Vitry*, second edition, translated with introduction and notes by Margot H. King (Toronto: Peregrina Publishing, 1989), no. 22 (p. 36-37); cf. *Acta Sanctorum*, Iunius, V, 1867, 542-572, at 552.
21 Translation modified.
22 *Fonti Francescane. Nuova edizione. Scritti e biografie di san Francesco d'Assisi. Cronache e altre testimonianze del primo secolo francescano. Scritti e biografie di santa Chiara d'Assisi. Testi normativi dell'Ordine Francescano Secolare*, a cura di Ernesto Caroli (Padova: Efr—Editrici Francescane, 2004), 314.
23 One speaks of how noteworthy it is that Thomas *does* mention Elias and Rufino by name in reference to the side wound considering how few are the occasions in which Thomas specifies friars by name. Cf. R. Michetti, *Paradosso*, 268.
24 J. Dalarun, *Misadventure*, 109.
25 Translation modified. *Cuidam* is omitted in a thirteenth-century MS of Italian Minoritic origin (Falerone), and is replaced with *quadam* in a MS of French Cistercian origin (Longpont). Cf. *AnalFranc* X, 69.
26 And it is also likely that Thomas knew Francis's *Admonition* XXI: "[1] Blessed is the servant who, when he speaks, does not disclose everything about himself under the guise of a reward and is not quick to speak, but who is wisely cautious about what he says and how he responds. [2] Woe to that religious who does not hold in his heart the good things the Lord reveals to him and does not reveal them by his behavior, but, under the guise of a reward, wishes instead to reveal them with his words. [3] He receives his reward and his listeners carry away little fruit." The collection of Francis's *Admonitions* is found in: Franciscus Assisiensis, *Admonitiones*, in *Scripta*, 352-377; Francis of Assisi, *The Admonitions*, in *FA:ED* I, 128-137.
27 Cf. R. Michetti, *Paradosso*, 269, n. 100.
28 I have reached conclusions very similar to Michetti's, with whose excellent study one should be proud to be in agreement: "Thomas does not miss the opportunity, therefore, to inform, *en passant* but unequivocally, that the saint confided in a faithful person at least a part of his most intimate secrets—who could not but be Leo, in light of what we know; but such mention, while reinforcing all the more the historicity of the event of the stigmata with the indication of an anonymous witness (anonymous for us and for the vast ecclesiastical public of such a legend, but certainly not for the confreres of its author), does not for that reason mitigate at all the indecipherability of the divine plan. A silent witness, one might affirm,

that is almost intentionally hidden within the folds of the prose, but unique and precious, because capable of recounting not the materiality of the stigmata, but the explanation of part of the mystery, that is, the truth of Francis" (R. Michetti, *Paradosso*, 269).

29 Cf. J. Dalarun, "Great Secret," 15: "I don't want to say that Thomas was a liar. He did his job like we do ours nowadays. But he knew—and we must know—that each time that he or his brothers spoke of the stigmata, each time that we, historians or theologians, speak about them we are in contradiction, according to Thomas himself, with Francis's clear and absolute will. This is a violation of a secret that he wanted to share only with God."

30 J. Merkt, "Die Wundmale," 44-47. I thank my friends who helped me with this German text. Merkt divides the witness of Leo into two kinds, the one we can know indirectly and the one we can know directly. His arguments about the indirect ones would sound familiar here because Frugoni more or less presents them in her comments on the passages from *Coming to England, Assisi Compilation* 118, and Salimbene's chronicle. Earlier I agreed with Miccoli's criticism of Frugoni's reading, and it applies equally to Merkt. Merkt's comments on Leo's "direct" witness pertain to the *Chartula*, which I explain presently.

31 J. Dalarun, "Great Secret," 24, n. 81.

* This *sancti* is omitted in: (1) Perugia Cod. 1046; and (2) Sarnano Biblioteca Comunale, E., no. 60. However, both Bigaroni and Brooke include it in their respective editions.

32 This is consistent with everything we know of the period, beginning from the certain datum of the request from the 1244 Chapter of Genoa for memories to be recorded and sent in, and including other speculative data such as why the author of *Anonymous of Perugia* would be motivated to write his work even before the 1244 Chapter, as well as the motivation for the making of Assisi cod. 338, which includes the earliest collection of Francis's writings, and is possibly datable back to these very years. Cf. Luigi Pellegrini, "La raccolta dei testi francescani del codice assisano 338. Un manoscritto composito e miscellaneo," in *Frate Francesco e i suoi agiografi*, Saggi 8 (S. Maria degli Angeli—Assisi: Edizioni Porziuncola, 2004), 371-423.

33 It is, in other words, a true intertextuality, but without explicit indicators that it is a citation. This is the type of intertextuality sometimes called by philologists an "implicit citation." Cf. Giovanni Pozzi, "San Francesco 'di seconda mano,'" in *Verba domini mei. Gli* Opuscula *di Francesco d'Assisi a 25 anni dalla edizione di Kajetan Esser, ofm*, Atti del Convegno internazionale, Roma, 10-12 Aprile 2002, a cura di Alvaro Cacciotti (Roma: PAA—Edizioni Antonianum, 2003), 279-327.

34 This is what philologists call a "reminiscence," which is normally considered a type of intertextuality, but stands at the border of "interdiscoursivity," the term used to describe the case of a prior text being imbedded in an actual text not through direct text-to-text relation but through an indirect one (for example, where the prior text is known to the current author not as part of the original text but simply as part of common discourse).

35 G. Miccoli, "Considerazioni," 22.

Chapter 11: **FOURTH CRITICAL THEORY: SELF-MUTILATION, INVENTION AND HIDING OF THE STIGMATA**

I. Fourth Critical Theory

A provocative article by Richard Trexler (d. March 8, 2007), which appeared in 2002, gives the version of the theory I will present here.[1]

Before detailing Trexler's argument I offer a brief overview of it. Contrary to common belief, Elias did not actually announce miraculous stigmata, if *The Letter of Elias* is read carefully. It was a little later that such an idea was conceived, and it received its official expression in *1 Celano*, where Thomas implies that God was the agent of the wounds (while still later, Leo adds that the seraph was used as God's intermediate cause). Thomas also adds the element of "two years before," changing Elias's "not long before death," so as to create time for there to have been more witnesses before Francis's death. Much effort had to be put in to this fraud, especially in light of the doubts of many, including Gregory IX.

Elias and others knew that the marks on Francis's body were self-inflicted wounds of mortification, no different from those of many other ascetics contemporary to Francis. This is why the oft-repeated claim that before Francis there were no known "stigmata" must be abandoned.

Soon, though, Elias must have realized the expediency of having a founder who was not just a flagellant like others, but miraculously stigmatized. This is the explanation for the controversial and mysterious events surrounding the translation of

Francis's body in May of 1230, where Elias was desperate not to allow anyone to see the corpse, lest the fraud be discovered.

1. Francis and His Contemporary Stigmatics[2]

Trexler says that Francis's stigmata must be understood in light of the practice of voluntary self-flagellation that appears as if from nowhere around the beginning of the second millennium. He gives many examples, of which I will repeat a few. The examples, he will conclude, show that by the time Francis is born "the presence of passion stigmata on the bodies of holy men had long been a hagiographic and devotional convention."[3] The appearance of stigmata would not be a new miracle but a commonplace.[4]

The first group of Trexler's examples all share the fact that the Scripture verse of Paul *ego enim stigmata Domini Iesu in corpore meo porto* (*Gal* 6:17) is employed to describe flagellation marks.

A well-known instance of these proto-flagellants,[5] found in St. Peter Damian's writings, is that of Dominic "Loricatus" (d. 1060). Dominic, whose governing value is personal penance in expiation for personal sin, is said by Peter to have carried the stigmata of Jesus on his body, not only having painted (*depinxit*) on his forehead the standard of the cross (*vexillum crucis*), but also impressing it (*impressit*) into all his members. Really, Peter adds, Dominic had made his whole life into a Good Friday.[6] Though it is difficult to be sure exactly what these statements mean and how literally or figuratively they are to be taken,[7] it seems that Peter is referring to the way Dominic's dead body, because of his practice of self-flagellation, resembled that of Christ crucified. Not only had he perhaps literally painted the cross on his forehead—which Trexler says was practiced by the *militia Christi*—but he had also pressed wounds *into* his flesh, on all his members, perhaps above all the four or five "main" Christ-like wounds.

About a century later, the life of St. Stephen of Obazine

(d. 1159) also uses the word stigmata in a clear way to speak of the wounds resulting from the saint's daily flagellation. And not long after Stephen, Jocelin of Furness wrote in 1185 a fictitious life of a seventh-century saint called Kentigern. This saint would whip himself continuously on Good Friday, such that—again—he was "carrying about the stigmata" on his body. Jocelin even uses the expression (apparently metaphorically) that Kentigern "crucified himself along with the Crucified,"[8] once again showing the connection between these practices and the Passion of Christ in the minds of these medieval people.

Two further examples overlap chronologically with Francis and are quite vivid representations of physical self-abuse out of devotion to the Passion. First is the early beguine Mary of Oignies, who mutilates her flesh and does so specifically because she was "invigorated by the wounds of Christ" (*Christi vulneribus vegetata*).[9] Second is a case in 1222 of two lay persons who call themselves "Jesus" and "Mary" and who dramatically reenact the Passion when the man has himself crucified, perforating his hands, feet, side, and head, which left scars. The two receive an ecclesiastical condemnation at Oxford (Trexler hypothesizes that it is not for overzealous imitation of the Passion but other actions).[10] At any rate, the point is that four years before the death of Francis there are dramatic and physical reenactments of the Passion.

These examples should show, according to Trexler, the historical-devotional context into which Francis's wounds must be placed. When Elias uses the word "stigmata," he uses it according to contemporary parlance.

2. Re-reading Elias's Letter: The *Miraculi Novitatem*[11]

Having established the historical context in which Francis's stigmata are situated, Trexler moves on to discuss the documentary sources for them, concentrating on Elias's encyclical letter.

Trexler posits that a re-reading of *The Letter of Elias* shows

that Elias never says that Francis received the wounds by means of supernatural intervention. This, combined with the description of the wounds as punctures from the outside, shows that initially Francis's stigmata are understood to be voluntarily self-inflicted wounds, like those of his contemporaries, in imitation of Christ and devotion to his Passion.

The *miraculi novitatem* announced by Elias, suggests Trexler, comprises two aspects, neither of which are the stigmata, per se, or their appearance. These two aspects correspond to two mini-sections of *The Letter of Elias*: 5/15-5/19 and 6/20-6/22. The first describes Francis "not long before death," and the second describes how his appearance changes after death.

First, Elias does announce the news of a miracle, but the miracle is not the presence of wounds, but—in the first place—the remarkable way the dying body of Francis resembles Christ. That is, the *miraculi novitatem* was that Francis, through his wounds, appeared identical to Jesus and made Jesus appear, in a manner of speaking, to those present because of his action. No mention is made of the origin of the wounds, least of all of a divine origin of them. Elias leaves the obvious unsaid: Francis's wounds are the result of his vigorous asceticism, in keeping with contemporary devotion, and consistent with "Francis's own self-mutilating past."[12]

Then, the nature of the novel miracle has a further aspect, explained in *Letter of Elias* 6/20-6/22, namely, the transformation of Francis's body from its crucified state to a beautiful and dazzling one, like the body of Jesus after the Resurrection.

This is the great news that Elias has to offer. Other, misinformed readings begin later with Thomas of Celano and snowball into hugely different stories, says Trexler.

3. Elias and the Cover-Up[13]

Trexler proposes that Elias had to hide the body of Francis once and for all in order to sustain the recently invented

stigmata story.[14] In other words, even though it was not his initial intention, Elias did not mind the radical shift that Thomas of Celano created when introducing God instead of Francis as the agent of the wounds or when indicating the very visible presence of the wounds on Francis's dead body in order to leave it understood that his body was in just that state when it was buried. Some were not pleased with the implications, however, and from the beginning dispute arose over these allegedly miraculous wounds.

Certainly much effort would be needed to perpetuate the fraud, and the evidence of Elias forcing the reality, writes Trexler, is the controversial translation of Francis's body, scheduled to coincide with the May chapter of 1230. If there was dispute over the reality, the *translatio* would have been the perfect opportunity to settle it, but what occurred instead raises questions of "foul play" and is therefore central to the question of Francis's stigmata.

As for sources regarding the events of that day, the earliest is a papal letter in reaction to it, *Speravimus hactenus* (June 16, 1230). Along with this, though, Trexler suggests that the commentary of seventeenth-century chronicler Luke Wadding, accompanying his edition of that Bull, seems to be based on early accounts we no longer have.[15]

We learn from Wadding that the processional translation of the body had been in preparation for some time, and the pope had assisted in those preparations, both by sending gifts and representatives and by giving the proper permissions to the friars to carry out the rite and have their chapter coincide with the translation, etc. However, even though the Order was commissioned to carry out the solemnities, the rulers and people of Assisi presumptuously seized the body (*rapientes illud in superbia*), not allowing the friars to properly venerate the saint (*non passi a Fratribus praedicto corpori debitam venerationem exhiberi*). By force

of arms (*vi et armis*), with guards and military means (*multis custodibus, et valida militum manu*), the laity took the lead role in the show in order to prevent that the body be reduced in its parts (*minueretur*) or stolen away (*surriperetur*).[16]

Speravimus hactenus was quickly issued and Assisi was punished: the whole city was placed under interdict until reparation would be made and General Chapters of the friars could no longer be held there.

Some friars, Wadding notes, have unjustly blamed the punishment on some role played by Elias. But probably, Wadding tries to guess, Elias simply acted in such a way as to make sure the body got into the church and out of view so no one would know where it was placed.

Meanwhile, Thomas of Eccleston, probably writing about twenty five years after the event, implies a different story, mentioning that friars were very upset that Elias had arranged the translation of the body three days before the Chapter convened (*Coming to England* XIII), apparently meaning that the body was transferred secretly before the public ceremony, which therefore would have been the celebration of the transfer of an empty casket.[17]

Whatever was really behind what happened that day, one thing for Trexler remains clear: the viewing of the body on May 25, 1230 that would have been the one chance to verify the stigmata of Francis and the dazzling, supple skin that Elias announced in his letter was not allowed to happen. And no possibility of it was allowed after since no one knew where exactly the body was anyway. And when in fact the sarcophagus was finally unearthed in 1818 the contents were "so nondescript and the few grave goods accompanying the skeleton indeed so anachronistic as to leave the question open if these remains are those of Francis."[18]

There are two hypotheses, according to the historian, as to

why the viewing of the body did not occur that day. First, the fear of either losing the sarcophagus and its contents to theft or the body being decimated by relic seekers. But this theory fails to explain why not even the friars would be allowed to view the body once in the church. Getting the body safely into the church was one thing, and that happened successfully. But the real question is why the body was not allowed to be viewed once inside, and, moreover, why the body was hidden away such that it could not be venerated.

The second hypothesis, which Trexler proposes as the best hypothesis to explain our current knowledge, is that the casket was not allowed to be opened either because it was empty or because it was occupied by a body that did not resemble the Francis that had to be seen. Perhaps the wounds Francis inflicted on himself had healed, or perhaps Elias had invented the whole thing so as to promote the cause of the saint and the Order, something then exaggerated all the more by Thomas of Celano, something that could not now be uncovered. Elias conceived the idea, Thomas processed it, and then the body was made to disappear.

II. Evaluation of the Fourth Critical Theory

My response to Trexler's theory will concentrate on (1) his reading of *The Letter of Elias* on the nature of the *miraculi novitatem*; (2) the proposal that Francis practiced a flagellation that left stigmata on his body; and (3) the suspicion of Elias's deceptive hiding of Francis's body.

1. The Nature of the *Miraculi Novitatem*

At issue is the meaning Elias intends for the *miraculi novitatem*. Trexler suggests, as I showed, that instead of meaning that God is at the origin of Francis's stigmata, Elias describes a twofold miracle, namely that Christ seemed to "appear" in Francis when he was dying, and that after his death Francis's body was

transformed from its mutilated state into a dazzling one. However, I read the letter differently.

On the level of the pure letter of the text, Elias proceeds in this way: First, he says that he is announcing a great joy and the news (or novelty) of a miracle, adding that it is a thing unknown since Christ (*Letter of Elias* 5/15-16). Elias's next phrase would seem by all reckoning, then, to be that aforesaid new miracle, and it is this: Francis appeared crucified (5/17a), having five wounds (5/17b), which are truly the wounds of Christ (5/17c). And to clarify this statement Elias immediately gives the detailed description of the five wounds (5/18-19). So I note: Elias does not modify his "he appeared crucified" with a statement about how it seemed to onlookers that Christ was now present; instead he simply announces and gives the detailed description of the five wounds. The miracle is that Francis appeared with these five wounds, not that Christ appeared in Francis. I do not think that this first, "grammatical" level of meaning in the text can be bypassed.

Furthermore, since others in the Christian tradition (at least since the time of Peter Damian) had also appeared with the five wounds (humanly produced), the mere fact of the wounds cannot be the *miraculi novitatem* that Elias intends to announce. There must be something more, something about the wounds that makes them miraculous. Trexler is correct that Elias does not say it, but I cannot think of what else it could be other than the origin. And the text supports this because these wounds are not like those of the other stigmatics of Francis's day; instead these are truly (*vere*) the wounds of Christ (*Letter of Elias* 5/17). Whatever else such a statement may mean, it must indicate that Elias thinks God is in some manner at their origin.

Maybe in this sense Trexler is correct: the miracle Elias communicates is that Christ's very own wounds appear on Francis. But, again, the letter of the text is the starting point: Elias does

not say that the stigmata of Christ *seem*, in the eyes of onlookers, to be on Francis. He says that the wounds that did appear on Francis *are* the wounds of Christ ("vere sunt stigmata Christi," *Letter of Elias* 5/17). So Elias announces that Francis had miraculous wounds on his body.

Having addressed Trexler's reading of *Letter of Elias* 5/15-19, I address now his reading of 6/20-22, which posits that Elias means also that the new miracle is the transformation of Francis's body from its miserable appearance to a shining and beautiful one, probably meant to recall the resurrected body of Jesus. Elias cannot mean, as Trexler suggests he does, that the *miraculi novitatem* also consists in this glorious aspect of Francis's dead body because that would not be a novel miracle. Quite the opposite, this is a *topos* repeated time and again in hagiographic literature,[19] originating with the *Vita S. Martini* by Sulpicius Severus. Elias references it intentionally and with the certain hope that his readers or hearers would notice. After all, the life of Martin of Tours was the single most influential and diffuse *vita* of a saint-bishop in the Middle Ages.[20]

On both counts, then, I find Trexler's attempt to reread *The Letter of Elias* forced. Rather, Elias intends by his letter to say that at his death Francis had five miraculous, Christ-like wounds on his body, and that he was a saint because he was like St. Martin.

I. Francis the Flagellant?

The link that Trexler makes between the self-mutilating flagellant stigmata tradition and Francis is circumstantial. The only essential connection is the use of the biblical word *stigmata* by Elias, which I believe to have shown intentionally breaks from former categories by its insistence on the novelty of what has occurred in Francis.

Citing briefly Merkt and Hampe, Trexler offers just two references to Francis's documentary dossier and then goes on to

speak matter-of-factly of "Francis's own self-mutilating past."[21] What would be needed instead would be a more careful analysis of the sources that would show (1) Francis having a practice of self-flagellation and (2) Francis's motivation for that practice being devotion to the Passion.

This is not the place to present the full results of a study of the general idea of mortification in Francis or the early fraternity, but suffice it to say that, apart from that which naturally comprises an itinerant life of voluntary poverty, external mortification does not figure into the core spirituality of the early Franciscan fraternity,[22] and the reason seems to be precisely Francis himself tempering the brothers' zeal in this regard. Here follows a brief analysis of relevant passages.

First, situated in a larger section of *1 Celano* describing the life of the early fraternity (*1 Celano* 38-44), it is said that if the friars ever failed in moderation they would correct it through severe fasting, and that when they wanted to combat "the burning of the flesh" they would treat themselves very harshly, even unto stripping themselves on ice, or covering "themselves in blood from gashing their bodies with sharp thorns [*ac totum corpus spinarum aculeis compungentes effusione sanguinis irrigare*]" (*1 Celano* 40:7-8).[23] This episode does not speak much to our question, mainly because the motivation for this self-mutilation is not devotion to the Passion but rather the fight against concupiscence, a fact emphasized by Thomas since he employs a *topos*, the story of St. Benedict throwing himself into a thorn bush for the same motivation.[24] And anyway, the episode and activity is rather anomalous in the sources.

Generally, when there is mention of physical mortification within the early fraternity, the activities implied are fasting from food and sleep or accepting the difficulties of daily life,[25] not anything more dramatic. In fact, it seems that when other types of more violent—one might say "less natural"—forms of

mortification are brought up it is only to say that Francis was displeased about it. In the *Anonymous of Perugia*, for example, it is said that Francis would:

> . . . reprove them [the friars] for the great austerity which they brought upon their bodies, for the brothers were then exerting too much effort in fasts, vigils, and bodily mortification [*corporalibus exercitationibus*] in order to repress within themselves every urge of the flesh [*ut cuncta in se carnis reprimerent incentiva*]. [. . . .] When he heard and saw this, blessed Francis reprimanded them . . . and ordered them not to act excessively (*Anonymous of Perugia* 39:1, 3).

But again, even here, the motivation of such penance is control of the "flesh" and not devotion to the Passion. Similarly, in *Assisi Compilation* 50, after the very vivid and realistic story of Francis having all the brothers arise in the middle of the night to show fraternal solidarity to a friar who had overdone his fasting and needed a gentle lesson on discretion, the narrators[26] take the opportunity to mention how Francis had gone so far as to command at a chapter that no brother wear anything next to the skin except the tunic because some were discovered with "iron rings and breastplates and the roughest hair shirts" (*Assisi Compilation* 50:18-19). Once again, I must conclude that those types of activities that externally harm the body do not agree with the authentic spirituality of the early fraternity; and when they are nevertheless present (as deviations), still they are neither motivated by imitation of nor devotion to the Passion.

More to the point, though, is what the early sources reveal about the practices of Francis himself, the founder of the early fraternity. I have already made clear his discretion with the friars and his stern warnings for them to be reasonable with their mortifications. But sometimes the sources say that Francis makes a double standard for himself, abusing himself far beyond what he allows in the others. Is this rhetorical or factual? And if factual,

does it support Trexler's theory? I will examine the relevant passages from the sources.

First, in a section of *1 Celano* on Francis's austerity (*1 Celano* 51-54), it is said that "toward himself he had become like a broken vessel, burdened by no fear or concern for his body" (*1 Celano* 53:2). It is hard to make much of this one: it is a passing statement included in a list of other activities concerning Francis's poverty in food, sleep, and reputation.

Or, again, when Thomas later speaks of the mounting illnesses of Francis (in the pages following the stigmatization), he explains that since Francis "had over many years chastised his body and brought it into subjection, he suffered infirmities often" (*1 Celano* 97:2). Like the last one, this is a passing statement on the austerity of Francis and does not seem related either to flagellation or devotion to Christ's Passion. Instead, it borrows its language from a passage of St. Paul, the context of which is Paul saying that he wants to imitate the athlete who trains in order to control himself (*"se abstinet,"* 1 Cor. 9:25).

Chronologically, the next relevant passage is from *Three Companions* 14. The important thing about this one is that Francis's devotion to the Passion[27] is mentioned in explicit connection with his mortification practices.[28] The pericope is a kind of coda following the story of the speaking Crucifix at San Damiano, after which time Francis always "melted when remembering the Lord's passion" and "carried the wounds . . . in his heart." And, consequently, from that moment forward, he "inflicted his flesh with such mortification[29] [*tanta se carnis maceratione afflixit*] that, whether healthy or sick, the excessively austere man hardly ever or never wanted to indulge his body." He was so hard on himself that when later dying he confessed "that he had greatly sinned against 'Brother Body'" (*Three Companions* 14:1-3). I note that even in this case, where Francis's motivation for his mortification is clearly devotion to the Passion, the form of the

penitential activity that he is said to practice is very general, and there is no implication of flagellation. One would have hoped for Thomas to use any one of the verbs *flagellare*, *verberare*, or even *caedere*. Instead, he uses *affligere maceratione*.[30]

The only other text I have been able to find that explicitly links Francis's mortification to his Passion devotion is from *Assisi Compilation* 77-78, and it confirms the conclusions just reached.[31] These two paragraphs begin by speaking of Francis's illnesses, which augment after he returns from Egypt, then explain that because of devotion to Christ he does not want to concern himself with treatment of those illnesses, and they then go on to tell the story (that *Three Companions* 14 also tells) of how Francis was crying loudly in the road near the Portiuncula out of devotion to the Passion. Therein is this statement:

> What was bitter to his body he accepted and considered sweet on account of the sweetness and compassion that he drew daily from the humility and footprints of the Son of God. Because of the sufferings and bitter experiences of Christ, which He endured for us, he grieved and afflicted himself daily in body and soul [*cotidie dolebat et pro ipsis interius et exterius se affligebat*], to such a degree that he did not treat his own illnesses [*in tantum . . . quod suis propriis non curabat*] (*Assisi Compilation* 77:5).

The author notes that Francis was "afflicting" himself, employing a word (*affligere*) that is in itself unspecific, such that *Three Companions*, for example, can say both that Francis "afflicted himself in tears [*affligebat se in lacrimis*]" (*Three Companions* 14:9), and that he "afflicted himself with mortification," as we saw above. Here in *The Assisi Compilation*, Francis afflicts himself not just interiorly but also exteriorly, yet the latter is not by means of flagellation, since the text explains that the extreme to which he went was the non-treatment of his illnesses (*in tantum quod suis propriis non curabat*).

Moving on, the text Trexler cites that I have not yet treated is found in *2 Celano* 129. In that episode, after an impressive

lesson by Francis on caring for the body's needs with discernment while still teaching it also to stay in its place, Thomas adds that this is the teaching that Francis for his part did not follow, considering that "he tamed his innocent body with flogging and privation [*flagellis et penuriis*], multiplying wounds on it for no reason [*multiplicans ei vulnera sine causa*]" (*2 Celano* 129:5-6).[32] Interesting though it is, this passage on its own has to be rejected as a source, unfortunately, because *Assisi Compilation* 120:1-12 preserves a more ancient version of the episode, from which we can see that the applicable phrases were added arbitrarily by Thomas onto the end of the episode in embellishment.[33]

A better candidate for Trexler's position—the best that I can find—would be one found grouped in *2 Celano*'s section of episodes on the various temptations that Francis endured (*2 Celano* 115-117). It is the story of how the devil, on a certain night at the friars' hermitage in Sarteano, mounted a severe attack on Francis. And after his first mode of attack had failed, he tried to give a very violent temptation to lust. But Francis, as soon as he felt it,

> 116:10 took off his clothes and lashed himself furiously [*chordula durissime se verberat*], saying: 'Come on, Brother Ass, that's the way you should stay under the whip! 11 The tunic belongs to religion: no stealing allowed! If you want to leave, leave!' 117:1 However, when he saw that the temptation did not leave even after the discipline [*propter disciplinas*], though he painted welts all over his limbs black and blue [*tamen iam livoribus membra cuncta pinxisset*], he opened the cell, went out to the garden, and threw himself naked into the deep snow.

As far as I have found in the sources (up through Bonaventure and apart from that found in *2 Celano* 129 dealt with above), this is the only episode that certainly and clearly speaks of Francis flagellating himself, which is somewhat surprising given the presence of such activity in prior and sometimes respectable hagiographical literature, as Trexler showed.

We are not fortunate enough to know Thomas's source for this episode or a more ancient version, but I nevertheless wonder if this passage is not compromised, given its similarity to the last episode treated. I do not think the whole episode is invented willy-nilly by Thomas, especially given the specific topographical detail of the hermitage location (*2 Celano* 116:1) and a reference to a friar witness made at the end of the episode (*2 Celano* 117:7-8). Still, I suspect that these lines on Francis's flagellating himself, so anomalous in the sources, are just an embellishment of the (probably authentic) statement by Francis reported in *Assisi Compilation* 120:10, mentioned above. Francis said that after the body has been treated fairly but still misbehaves, the friar "should punish it like any wicked and lazy beast of burden."

We can note Thomas's method of working here in his descriptive usage of the term *frater asine* ("Brother Ass," *2 Celano* 116:10). I suggest that this term is Thomas's creation; it is an amplification of the phrase of *The Assisi Compilation* that refers to the body as a "beast of burden," *pigrum armentum*. Though later sources will favor the colorful appellation "Brother Ass," which Francis would have given his body to describe its lapsarian aspect, it is an hapaxlegomenon in the corpus of Thomas and never appears in any other source before Bonaventure, who simply borrows the term from Thomas.[34] So, we can see how Thomas is embellishing his source here and how easy it would have been for him to expand the vivid analogy of Francis about "punishing a lazy beast of burden" to say that Francis whipped himself, especially if Thomas knew any of the literature that Trexler cites about such practices.

Yet, even if my intuition about this Thomasian episode is wrong, Trexler's position is nevertheless left with several grave problems: (1) this is the only possible episode in all the reliable documentary literature that would indicate with certainty Francis flagellating himself; (2) it has nothing to do with devotion

to the Passion but a battle against sexual temptation; (3) it gives no indication of a habitual practice of Francis, but is instead presented as a singular extreme reaction to a singular extreme situation, a direct attack from the devil.

Before moving on, I should say something about the writings of Francis himself, though I find in them nothing contrary to what has been said up to this point. Francis, who seems to know the psalms by memory, thinks that the flogging of Jesus was foreshadowed in Ps. 34:15, quoting that text in his Office dedicated to the Passion: "They rejoiced and united together against me. Blows were heaped on me and I knew not why" (*Office of the Passion* V:10).[35] But, instead of giving any indications in his other writings that this act on behalf of humankind's salvation should be imitated, Francis gives more of the lessons on discretion that we have come to expect after the evidence seen above. In his *Admonitions*, for example, he teaches that many "inflict abstinences and punishments [*abstinentias et afflictiones*] upon their bodies" but fail to see the much greater importance of poverty of spirit (*Admonition* XIV). And in his letters to all the Christian faithful[36]—clerics, religious, and lay—, when Francis gives many lessons on what it means to live a converted life he does not recommend anything like flagellation. One place where it might have been appropriate for him to do so would have been *2 Letter to the Faithful* 37-40, where he gives one of his lessons on the necessity of "hating one's body." But the advice he gives on how to do that is (1) to observe the commands and counsels of Jesus; (2) to deny ourselves by placing our bodies under obedience.

Francis does not seem, then, according to the written documentary sources, to be a man that promotes or practices any form of flagellation, certainly not with any regularity, and never out of devotion to the Passion. To therefore explain the five marks on his body at the end of his life by appealing to such a

practice is to make an enormous leap based not on documentary evidence but very loose speculation.

3. On the Mysterious *Translatio* of Francis's Body

Here I treat the theory of the hiding of Francis's body, which would be the hiding also of the non-stigmata. First I will look again at the *translatio* event, and then I will make an observation based on some of the archeological evidence.

I feel no qualms in excusing myself from the burden of trying to solve the riddle of what exactly did or did not happen during the days surrounding May 25, 1230. The worst case scenario based on the actual documentary sources is that Elias would be pronounced guilty of secretly transferring the body of Francis before the official public celebration of the *translatio*, which took place anyway. The only way to make a further step and posit that Elias's *motivation* was the hiding of non-stigmata would be to have other documentary evidence that accuses Elias of such, or at least that proves that Francis never had stigmata. And since on both counts I find such evidence lacking, I have to conclude that Trexler's theory is tantalizing but unfounded. Nevertheless, I can still quickly review the documentary evidence at our disposal and suggest my reading of the sources.[37]

The earliest source we have concerning the *translatio*, as Trexler notes, is the letter *Speravimus hactenus* of a very upset Gregory IX.[38] No "foul play" on the part of Elias or anyone else is at issue here, however. Rather, the Pope's concern is above all sacrilege, or at the least liturgical impropriety. That much is clear from the vivid Old Testament passages invoked. There are 2 Samuel, where Uzzah is smote by God for having touched the ark after the oxen stumbled,[39] and 2 Chronicles, in which King Uzziah of Judah, who presumptuously took upon himself to burn incense in the temple is stricken with leprosy.[40] Certainly the pope is not happy also because those he personally assigned to care for the translation (both Minors and legates of the Holy

See) were pushed aside by local magistrates and citizens. But for all the pope's anger and demands for restitution, he shows no awareness of any deceit.

Is there a source contemporary to *Speravimus hactenus* that accuses Elias of suspicious activity? Luke Wadding, who Trexler thinks has sources now unknown to us, makes mention—though insisting he does not agree—that some blame Elias. No specifics are given, but he says that many accusations beyond the truth have been leveled against the former Vicar of the Order.[41] Wadding defends him: he was probably simply trying to keep the body from being stolen away. But is Wadding's text evidence of an early source that knows more of the story than Gregory was told? I do not believe it is. Though the opening lines from Wadding (about the pomp when Francis's body was raised to the cart amid trumpet blasts at St. George's) seem to be copied from some archival record, much of the rest of the commentary is made up of words borrowed from Gregory's letter, and the lines currently in question are mixed up with those later stories about a fabled medieval church beneath the Lower Church that by now cannot be held to have ever existed.[42]

The earliest mention of Elias's disagreeable behavior at the *translatio*, then, is in Thomas of Eccleston's chronicle, finished probably around the beginning of 1258.[43] None of the prior sources make mention of any suspicious behavior on the part of Elias in this regard.[44] We would expect Jordan of Giano, or, later, Salimbene de Adam to say something about it since they make other complaints against Elias, but they too are silent. In the 1370's, Arnald of Sarrant can only repeat what Thomas of Eccleston had said without adding anything new.[45]

I tend to agree with Donal Cooper who thinks that the accusation of Elias hiding the body in any way and for any motive is poorly founded.[46] The accusation comes late and seems to be seen through the lens of the controversies that surround Elias's

later years.[47] After all, two years after the translation, the General Chapter freely chooses to elect Elias as Minister General, nor is any real motive (other than a disagreeable relationship with John Parenti) offered by Thomas of Eccleston or the author of *Chronicle of the Twenty Four Generals*. Furthermore, even though Elias was in charge of the building project, it seems highly unlikely that he could have prepared a burial place that no one else knew about. Besides, in the end, the body was not hidden at all:[48] though arriving there was not easy, the excavators of 1818 found the body exactly where it was expected to be: very, very deep but directly below the high altar in the Lower Church.

But even if we were to say, for the sake of argument, that Elias was guilty of what he had been accused of in *Coming to England*,[49] does this lend support to Trexler's conclusions? He said there would be two alternative hypotheses to explain the fact: one that Elias had to perpetuate the great fraud of the stigmata, the other that Elias was trying to protect the body from theft or decimation. The latter theory Trexler dismisses out of hand since it does not explain why the friars could not be allowed to view the body once inside.

I see the matter differently than does Trexler. If Thomas of Eccleston is correct, then the reason why the viewing could not be allowed is because an empty sarcophagus had been taken in procession, the real transfer having already happened privately. In this case the question is not why the viewing was disallowed but why the secret *translatio* had been made. If, on the other hand, no secret transfer had happened, an explanation is required for the strange events of May 25 that provoked such anger in Gregory IX and prevented the friars their proper ritual, which included one last viewing of the body.

The response I give to both scenarios is the same: there was grave concern for the preservation of the relics. Trexler rejects this theory, but I see overwhelming evidence for it.

Concern to protect Francis's body and keep it as an Assisian relic goes back to the beginning. Francis, who asked explicitly to be carried back to the Portiuncula (located well outside the Assisian city walls) in order to die (*1 Celano* 108:11-12), probably would have liked for his body to stay there. And the friars too surely would have wanted the same. Thomas of Celano, though, explains that the people and the clergy of Assisi came down to Santa Maria degli Angeli and took his body to the city to bury him there instead.[50] Jordan of Giano later explains that there was already at that early time fear that the body would be taken away, and he even names the rival town of Perugia as the principal threat.[51] This may seem to be an exaggerated paranoia, until we learn that two hundred years later the Perugians are still in pursuit of the body. For immediately following the sack of Assisi in 1442 led by the hired Italian mercenary leader Nicolò Piccinino, the Perugian leaders formally requested Pope Eugene IV to authorize the transfer of Francis's body to their city.[52]

And none of this fear and precaution seems at all surprising when seen in the context of medieval devotion to relics and the hysteria they seemed to create, as is notable in contemporaneous examples.[53] In Padua, hardly one year after Francis's *translatio*, there is an incredible ado over another Minorite body, that of Anthony. Anthony dies by chance at the friary in Arcella (a neighborhood in the northern part of the city), which was established to care for the monastery of the Poor Ladies next door. Before the friars have a chance to move the body to their friary on the southern side of the city (where the Basilica now stands), armed guards from the northern suburb of Capo di Ponte surround the building to prevent it. It is not until the fifth day after his death that the friars and other citizens are able to attempt to move the body down to its final resting place, but the bridge that they make to cross the river into town (because they are afraid to take the bridge in Capo di Ponte) is hacked to pieces

by the inhabitants from the northern part of the city. Only narrowly is a bloody battle avoided between the inhabitants that then came from the southern part armed to fight for the body. With drastic intervention of the city magistrates, the body is finally transferred.[54]

Another saint with Minoritic associations, who also dies that same year, is Elizabeth of Hungary. In her case, the holy body does in fact suffer at the hands of maniacal relic seekers, who swoop upon her, cutting off pieces not only of her tunic, but also her nails, hair, ears, and breasts.[55] Nor should it be forgotten that Assisi had its very own tradition of relic wars. For, in the early eleventh century, the body of the town's patron, St. Rufinus, becomes a point of vivacious dispute when it is finally brought to Assisi after many centuries of lying where it had fallen in martyrdom. It is Peter Damian, in his sermon *De Sancto Ruffino Martyre*, who describes for us a literal tug-of-war that ensues over the relics when a group of citizens refuses to allow the bishop to enshrine the relics in his cathedral.[56]

With all of this evidence, direct as well as circumstantial, I suggest that whether Francis's body was really transferred on May 25, 1230, by an armed procession of laity that refused to allow the proper rites to unfold, or whether it had been secretly moved some days before, it is clear that the involved parties had good reason to fear for the safe and continued custody of the relics. There is no need to imagine other scenarios to explain these events.

I would simply add one minor piece of archeological information to this discussion in order to show further why Trexler's theory of a desperate need to hide Francis's body is unsustainable.

When Francis was finally unearthed after almost 600 years, he was found in an ancient, used, stone sarcophagus that had itself been form-fitted in a custom-built iron cage, clearly designed not to hide the body but to allow viewing of it.[57]

Though a travertine slab had been laid over the top of the whole as an additional cover, it was neither the original lid (which seemingly had been lost) nor the actual lid, but simply additional protection. With the form-fitting iron cage the sarcophagus had a kind of permanent lid, at least one that could not be removed quickly and without metal workers. But that "lid" was composed of forty-four iron bars spanning the width and sixteen spanning the length of the sarcophagus, creating a see-through grate comprised of small holes of varying sizes (the largest being 3.72 cm).[58] The design of the sarcophagus, then, was intended for viewing Francis's body.

We do not have any records attesting to such viewing, but we do have some circumstantial indications that lead in that direction. First, the mere fact of the caged sarcophagus means that at least the workers who constructed the iron cage and laid the travertine slab saw Francis's body. Next, it is highly likely that it was this very same caged sarcophagus construction that was located also at St. George for nearly four years prior to being moved as is to the new basilica,[59] making it therefore likely that prior to the transfer there was some moment or period in which the body was able to be viewed through the grated lid.

I see the following indications as support for this theory. First, though many of the details of the first burial at St. George are obscure and remain unresolved, I do see in the reference of Henri d'Avranches to a "tomb of pure stone" an allusion to our sarcophagus.[60] Also, this arrangement is the obvious explanation for the artifacts discovered in 1818 inside the sarcophagus with the skeleton: the twelve coins, the ring, and the beads were probably tossed in through the grate by devotees of the saint.[61] Moreover, the medical doctor who examined Francis's skeleton at the time of exhumation asserted that the body had been placed in that same sarcophagus before decomposition had begun.[62] And finally, we do know that such an arrangement of viewing a saint's

corpse through a grated coffin was used at times, for example, in the case of Margaret of Cortona, for whom there is still a watercolor copy of a medieval fresco depicting precisely that.[63]

III. Conclusion to Chapters 8-11

Before I summarize the state of the question and develop my own hypotheses, I will briefly and in broad strokes summarize the more essential elements we have seen so far in Part Two.

What I have called Critical Theory One, that of Chiara Frugoni, took up many elements from a century-old school of historiography, but freshly synthesized them and expressed them to a much more developed field of Franciscanism, encouraging them to be considered anew in light of all that we now know. She proposed that if there were wounds on Francis's body, it was only with Elias's letter that they came to be viewed as Christ-like and miraculous. Thomas had no choice but to tell the story, but tried to temper it with a truer one, the one kept alive by the companions of Francis, the one that shows hints of survival here and there in writing and art throughout the first decades after Francis's death. That truer story was told by Francis to his companions and was about how he received a special grace to overcome his inner trials, which he described in terms of a vision or a dream of a visitation from some kind of seraph.

In a second theory, which is very much a direct response to Frugoni, Giovanni Miccoli reread the sources in a way more sensitive to their intended meanings, as I believe the scholars of the field would generally agree. As a result, he recognized that one basic datum is not in doubt: all the early witnesses—and certainly not just Elias—claimed to have directly known wounds on Francis's body that were in the form of Christ's five crucifixion wounds. That subjective experience, then, cannot be seriously called into question by historical means. But what this means about the objective experience of Francis, said Miccoli,

remains open, since we do not have the testimony of Francis.

This last point is rightly exploited by the scholar whose thesis I have called Critical Theory Three. Jacques Dalarun wrote that Francis was said to be strictly silent about this whole phenomenon, and therefore anything that the early writers do say would be theological or hagiographical elaboration, rather than historical data. Perhaps Thomas's presentation, then, which did not come from Francis, was an elaboration of the wording of *Mira circa nos*, which used language normally employed to describe the burning love of seraphim, to which Christians should all aspire. This would be merely an hypothesis, though a much needed one, since there are no other foundational sources to go on, given that the three sources of Leonine origin are only re-elaborations of Thomas's story, evidenced by their growing, changing memory of what happened. Meanwhile, since Miccoli is right that it is impossible to doubt that Francis had wounds on his hands, feet, and side that everyone witnessed, there remains also an open question on their true origin, and perhaps, again, *Mira circa nos* gives the interpretive key, namely that the wounds were the result of human asceticism. This last point is consistent with the basic direction taken (not for the first time in Franciscan historiography, but the most thoroughly) by the author of the fourth critical theory, who said that Francis is merely another one of the many medieval flagellants, whose self-inflicted wounds were sometimes called *stigmata* by those who wrote about them.

But, in dialogue with Critical Theory Three, I said that the three Leonine sources in question are not to be considered a growing and conflating memory, because the one that contains all the elements is in fact the earliest, as philological analysis (in conjunction with our knowledge of the "Franciscan Question") proves. And, more importantly, it is very reasonable to go a step beyond this and assert that the information contained in that

source is something the author, Leo, was claiming to have heard from Francis himself, because Thomas actually does assert that one of Francis's special companions was told personally something about the special secret.

And, in response to Critical Theory Four, I showed that the idea (in this case represented by Richard Trexler) that Francis inflicted the wounds on himself is unsustainable by textual means; critical analysis of the sources puts on the shakiest ground the idea that Francis *ever* flagellated himself, and even more that he did so out of devotion to the Passion. Likewise, the old hypothesis, refurbished by Trexler, that the body of Francis was hidden in order to hide the non-stigmata is extremely difficult to support since even the worst critics of Elias do not claim it, archeological evidence does not sustain it, and there are very acceptable explanations for any of the otherwise unusual happenings on the day of the *translatio*.

---

1 Richard C. Trexler, "The Stigmatized Body of Francis of Assisi. Conceived, Processed, Disappeared," in *Frömmigkeit im Mittelalter. Politisch-soziale Kontexte, visuelle Praxis, körperliche Ausdrucksformen,* Herausgegeben von Klaus Schreiner (München: Wilhelm Fink Verlag, 2002), 463-497. Trexler, more than the other historians herein presented, is consciously and very much the inheritor of the first modern critics of Francis's stigmata, especially of the German school. While distancing himself from some of their positions and developing them in significant ways, he still remains indebted to them, especially to those of Josef Merkt.

2 R. Trexler, "Conceived, Processed, Disappeared," esp. at 472-485.

3 R. Trexler, "Conceived, Processed, Disappeared," 478.

4 I believe the first to try to explore this avenue of approach was N. Tamassia, *Francis and His Legend*, 115. After him was J. Merkt, "Die Wundmale," Chap. 1. In this same general camp was K. Hampe, "Die frühesten Stigmatisationen," 1491-1493, which suggested that Francis inflicted the wounds on himself during an ecstasy.

5 Flagellation will later come into fashion, even unto the appearance of lay confraternities that publically process while collectively practicing the devotion, a phenomenon that occurs for the first time in 1260 at Perugia. Cf. André Vauchez, *La spiritualità dell'Occidente medioevale*, terza edizione ampliata (Milano: Vita e Pensiero, 2006), 149-151.

6 *Vita venerabilis viri Dominici Loricati*, in *PL* 144, cols. 1012-1024, at 1024:

"Dominicus autem noster stigmata Jesu portavit in corpore, et vexillum crucis non tantum in fronte depinxit, sed cunctis etiam undique membris impressit. . . . Tota haec vita facta est sibi parasceve crucis. . . ."

7 Cf. Giles Constable, "The Ideal of the Imitation of Christ," in *Three Studies in Medieval Religious and Social Thought* (Cambridge: Cambridge University Press, 1995), 145-248, at 202-203.

8 "In parasceve vero incredibili cruciatu cum crucifixo semetipsum crucifigebat. Et plagis virgarum, et nuditate, et crebris genuum flexionibus, vix aliquando sedens stigmata vulnerum Christi in corpore suo circumferens, cum nimia cruce cordis et corporis, diem cum nocte continuando ducebat" (Alexander Penrose Forbes, *Lives of S. Ninian and S. Kentigern. Compiled in the Twelfth Century*, The Historians of Scotland 5 [Edinburgh: Edmonston and Douglas, 1874], 189).

9 I mentioned her earlier in my evaluation of Dalarun's idea of Thomas's invention of the seraph. Here is the larger passage, curious and striking for many reasons: "As if inebriated and from the fervor of her spirit, she began to loathe her flesh in comparison with the sweetness of the Paschal Lamb [*prae dulcedine Agni Paschalis carnes suas fastidiens*] and in her mistaken fervor, she cut out a large piece of her flesh with a knife [*frustra non modica cum cultello resecavit*], which, because of her modesty, she buried in the earth. So inflamed had she been by an exceeding fire of love [*quia nimio amoris incendio inflammata*] that she had risen above the pain of her wound and, in this ecstasy of mind, she had seen one of the seraphim standing close by her [*unum de Seraphin in hoc mentis excessu sibi adstantem aspexit*]. When some women were washing her corpse after she had died, they were amazed when they found the places of the wounds but those who had known of this through confession understood what they were" (*Life of Marie d'Oignies*, 36-37).

10 Cf. the testimony of Walter of Coventry in *Councils and Synods, with Other Documents Relating to the English Church*, vol. 2, pt. 1, edited by F. M. Powicke and C. H. Cheney (Oxford: Clarendon Press, 1964), 105.

11 R. Trexler, "Conceived, Processed, Disappeared," 485-490.

12 R. Trexler, "Conceived, Processed, Disappeared," 486.

13 R. Trexler, "Conceived, Processed, Disappeared," 490-497.

14 This theory is not entirely new either. It goes all the way back to Ernst Renan, "François d'Assise," in *Nouvelles études d'histoire religieuse* (Paris, 1884), 345-348; cited in Rosalind B. Brooke, *Early Franciscan Government: Elias to Bonaventure*, Cambridge Studies in Medieval Thought—New Series 7 (Cambridge: Cambridge University Press, 1959; first paperback edition, 2004), 141-142. After him soon came other theories about the deceptive role Elias probably played in the invention of Francis's stigmata (possibly even branding them on the dead saint's body) and the hasty burial of his body to hide the evidence: K. Von Hase, *Franz von Assisi: Ein Heiligenbild*, 143-202.

15 *Annales Minorum seu trium Ordinum a s. Francisco institutorum*, tom. II [=*AnnalMin* II], auctore Luca Waddingo, editio tertia (Quaracchi, 1931), 261-262. The more recent edition of Gregory's Bull is found in *BullFranc* I, 66-67; the differences from Wadding's version are miniscule, except for one: the Wadding edition (at least in the 1931 printing) dates the Bull "[a.d.] XVI Kalendas Junii,"

which would have the pope writing his Bull on our May 17, several days before the translation of the body. *BullFranc* gives the correct "[a.d.] XVI Kalend. Julii," our June 16.

16 From Luke Wadding's commentary that precedes the Bull itself (*AnnalMin* II, 261).

17 "From this chapter a solemn delegation was sent with the minister general to Pope Gregory to obtain an exposition of the Rule . . . They told the pope what great scandal Brother Elias had caused because the minister general had revoked his decree so that not all the brothers could come to the chapter who wished; and also how he became indignant about this and had the body of St. Francis translated before the chapter convened [*et insuper quod indignatus ex hoc priusquam fratres convenissent, fecisset translationem fieri*]. The pope, already greatly moved by all this, became very angry toward him, until he heard of the unusual life he was leading at the hermitage."

18 R. Trexler, "Conceived, Processed, Disappeared," 494.

19 Of note is the example found in the life of English Cistercian St. Aelred (d. 1167). Cf. Walter Daniel, *The Life of Ailred of Rievaulx*, translated from the Latin with introduction and notes by F. M. Powicke (Oxford: Clarendon, 1951), 62, 76-77. The curious thing about this example is that we also have the *apologia* in which the hagiographer—who had been present at the death of Aelred—later defends his description of the dead body of the saint against a certain skeptic. Interesting commentary on this is found in T. Heffernan, *Sacred Biography*, Chap. 3.

20 Cf. André Vauchez, *Sainthood in the Later Middle Ages*, translated by Jean Birrell (Cambridge: Cambridge University Press, 1997; paperback edition, 2005), 288. Recourse to the texts reveals clear parallels. Francis's members are not rigid as is usual for dead men; the witnesses say Martin's lifeless body seems already like a glorified man's. Francis appears very beautiful, shining marvelously; the face of Martin also shines clearly. The limbs of both are moveable, almost like those of a boy. Thomas of Celano will notice the parallels and tease out even more Martinian similitudes (cf. *1 Celano* 112:9-12).

21 R. Trexler, "Conceived, Processed, Disappeared," 486.

22 Vauchez seems to be correct when he says that Francis, Dominic and the early mendicants incorporated traditional forms of asceticism but very notably demonstrated and emphasized the importance of moderation in such. He says that, unlike in some later moments in mendicant tradition, their penances were a means to an end and not the end itself (A. Vauchez, *Sainthood*, 340-341).

23 This is one of the two episodes Trexler cites.

24 Cf. *AnalFranc* X, 32, n. 9: "Auctor hic respexisse videtur vitam S. Benedicti: S. Gregorius, *Dial.*, II, 2: '*nudum* se in illis *spinarum aculeis* . . . proiecit . . . *toto* ex eis *corpore* vulneratus exit' (*PL* 66, col. 132)."

25 E.g., *Assisi Compilation* 56:34: "They used to mortify the flesh not only by fasting, but also by many vigils, by cold, nakedness and manual labor." The choice of phraseology here is of course influenced by the language of Paul and his own difficulties (cf. 2 Cor 11:27).

26 "Nos . . . qui cum ipso fuimus . . ." (*Assisi Compilation* 50:20).
27 A surprisingly rare topic in the earlier sources. *1 Celano* 84:3 and *Assisi Compilation* 77-78 are the only other clear and original statements about Francis having a special devotion to the Passion that I can find. *2 Celano* 10-11 only echoes *Three Companions* 14-15; even Thomas's section in the *Vita secunda* on Francis's special devotions (*2 Celano* 196-203) has only a simple few words on Francis's devotion to the cross, and then only as an attempt at explaining the meaning of the stigmata (*2 Celano* 203).
28 This will be one of only two such passages that I have found.
29 The *FA:ED* editors render it "fasting," which I think is too specific, although they have reason for using that word, taking the sense of the larger context since *Three Companions* 14:9 specifies that Francis not only afflicted himself with tears but "also did so by abstaining from food and drink."
30 The noun *maceratio* in its origin refers to a soaking that is meant to soften, and the English cognate verb *macerate* corresponds, essentially meaning "to soften, weaken, or break down." Generally, the Latin word is simply translated into English with the vague "to mortify," even though there is also a later Latin word for that too. Thomas of Celano, for example, uses both *mortificare* and *macerare* (and corresponding nouns) in his corpus, but very infrequently, and with more or less the equivalent, vague meaning of "subduing the 'flesh,'" and never means physically attacking the body. For *maceratio*, one should see *1 Celano* 11:3; *1 Celano* 40:8a. For *macerare*: *1 Celano* 130:1; *2 Celano* 21:4; *2 Celano* 115:5; *2 Celano* 134:1. Of these, *1 Celano* 130:1 is the only usage of *macerare* implying any external damage to the body; it speaks of a layman praying at Francis's tomb who was mortifying his body with a hairshirt, *cilicio macerante*. For *mortificatio*: *1 Celano* 42:9. For *mortificare*: *1 Celano* 41:4; *1 Celano* 43:1. As for *Three Companions*, there are two uses of *maceratio*: the present one and *Three Companions* 17:5, which is a mere borrowing from *1 Celano* 11:3. The single usage in Bonaventure is a borrowing of *2 Celano* 134:1 (*Major Legend* VI:3:7). I have not figured *Mira circa nos* into my current presentation but can briefly say something about it here in this context, since it is the earliest use of *macerare* in the Francis dossier. It is the passage we saw in the last chapter from *Mira circa nos* 4 where Francis is said to have offered his flesh as a holocaust. He does so by hunger, thirst, cold and nakedness, many vigils, and mortifying himself with fasting (*jejuniis macerando*); or perhaps better, the American editors read *macerando* as governing all of the previous ablative-of-means nouns, such that Francis mortifies himself—*macerando*—by each of these means—*fame, siti, frigore*, etc. (*FA:ED* I, 567). Either way, the portrait of Francis painted here is once again one of a traditional saint performing traditional ascetical practices, and no intimation of flagellation.
31 It is hard to know if *Assisi Compilation* 77 belonged to the *Florilegium* or not. On one hand, the episode is not found in *2 Celano*, which would seem to negate the possibility. However, since it seems that it could be a unit with *Assisi Compilation* 78, which is roughly parallel with *Three Companions* 14 (a passage that does find its way into *2 Celano*), perhaps Thomas of Celano simply did not find it necessary to make use of it.

32 Translation modified.

33 This is not uncharacteristic for Thomas. Normally he condenses his sources, but he sometimes adds a brief panegyric tag at the end of an episode. Cf. J. Moorman, *The Sources*, esp. at 113-115. Here are the texts:

Assisi Compilation 120	*2 Celano* 129
[7] He said: "In eating, sleeping, and other necessities, the servant of God must satisfy the body with discernment, so that Brother Body cannot grumble, saying: [8] 'Because you do not satisfy me, I cannot stand up straight and persevere in prayer, or rejoice in tribulations, or do other good works.'"	[1] The saint also said on one occasion: "Brother Body should be cared for with discernment, so that it won't raise the storm of acedia. We must take away from it the occasions for complaining, [2] so it won't get weary keeping vigil and staying reverently at prayer. Otherwise it will say: [3] 'I'm dying of hunger. I can't hold up the load of your exercises.'
[9] He also used to say: "If a servant of God . . . has satisfied his body well enough and as decently as he could, [10] but Brother Body wants to be lazy, negligent, and sleepy in prayer, vigils, and other good works, then he should punish it like any wicked and lazy beast of burden [*pirgum armentum*] . . ."	[4] "Now, if it grumbles that way after it has gobbled down a sufficient ration, then you will know that lazy ass [*pigrum iumentum*] needs a good kick, and the reluctant donkey is waiting for the stick."
[11] If, however, Brother Body cannot have its needs fulfilled, [etc.]	[5] This was the only teaching in which the most holy father's actions were not in harmony with his words. [6] For he tamed his innocent body with flogging and privation, covering it with wounds for no reason. [etc.]

34 The more authentically Franciscan phrase—and perhaps a witness to a healthier anthropology—is the term "Brother Body," which is used many times, beginning with the advent of the companion sources. Cf. *Three Companions* 14:3; *Assisi Compilation* 108:22; *Assisi Compilation* 120:7, 10, 11; *2 Celano* 126:3; *2 Celano* 211:12.

35 Franciscus Assisiensis, *Officium Passionis Domini*, in *Scripta*, 70-107; Francis of Assisi, *The Office of the Passion*, in *FA:ED* I, 139-157.

36 Franciscus Assisiensis, *Epistola ad Fideles* I, in *Scripta*, 174-179; Francis of Assisi, *Earlier Exhortation to the Brothers and Sisters of Penance (The First Version of the Letter of the Faithful)*, in *FA:ED* I, 41-44. Franciscus Assisiensis, *Epistola ad Fideles* II, in *Scripta*, 186-201; Francis of Assisi, *Later Admonition and Exhortation to the Brothers and Sisters of Penance (Second Version of the Letter of the Faithful)*, in *FA:ED* I, 45-51.

37 For introductory indications and further bibliography on the burials of Francis first at St. George and then at the Basilica of St. Francis one can begin with Pasquale Magro, "Tomba di san Francesco," in *Dizionario francescano*, col. 2065-

2086; 2598. Then, the thorough and lengthy study of Gatti is indispensible: Isidoro Gatti, *La tomba di s. Francesco nei secoli*, Il Miracolo di Assisi 6 (Assisi: Casa Editrice Francescana, 1983). Recently bringing fresh eyes to more or less the same bibliography are two very fine contributions: Donal Cooper, "'In loco tutissimo et firmissimo': The Tomb of St. Francis in History, Legend and Art," in *The Art of the Franciscan Order in Italy*, edited by William R. Cook (Leiden: Brill, 2005), 1-37; and Rosalind Brooke, *The Image of St Francis: Responses to Sainthood in the Thirteenth Century* (Cambridge: Cambridge University Press, 2006), 454-471. On the events surrounding the translation of Francis's body, one perspective is offered by Gratien de Paris, *The Foundation and the Evolution of the Friars Minor in the Thirteenth Century: A History*, 3 vols., translated by Stephen Paul Laliberté, private printing, vol. 1, 55 (original: *Histoire de la fondation et de l'évolution de l'ordre des Frères Mineurs au XIIIe siècle* [Paris, 1926-1928]; 2nd edition: Roma: Istituto Storico dei Cappuccini, 1982); and Rosalind B. Brooke, *Early Franciscan Government*, 138-142.

38 I thank Richard Bailey, Cong. Orat., for his help with the Latin text of the Bull and Wadding's accompanying account. I cited these earlier when presenting Trexler's position.

39 "Iratusque est indignatione Dominus contra Ozam et percussit eum super temeritate, qui mortuus est ibi iuxta arcam Dei" (2 Reg 6:7).

40 "Iratusque Ozias tenens in manu turibulum ut adoleret incensum minabatur sacerdotibus. Statimque orta est lepra in fronte eius coram sacerdotibus in domo Domini super altare thymiamatis" (2 Par 26:19).

41 " . . . cui plura ultra veritatem imposita" (*AnnalMin* II, 261).

42 I find D. Cooper, "Loco tutissimo et firmissimo," 17-23, definitive on the matter of the medieval crypt church. The text from Wadding is: "Fortasse in eo laboravit Elias, ut non pateret rapinae corpus, et ut ab omnium auferretur oculis ea arte, ut nulli innotesceret locus, in quo recondebatur, nec cuniculus, aut ostiolum, per quod descendebatur ad Ecclesiam subterraneam" (*AnnalMin* II, 261).

43 *Coming to England* XIII: "The first minister general after Blessed Francis was Brother Elias [to 1227] who had been a notary at Bologna. Brother John Parenti succeeded him [1227-1232]. . . . In the chapter held at the time of the translation of St. Francis's remains, the partisans of Brother Elias . . . wanted to make him general in opposition to the ministers provincial. Wherefore they carried him on their arms from his cell to the door of the chapter room, and there, after they had broken down the door, they wanted to put him in the place of the minister general. When the good Brother John saw this, he stripped himself before the whole chapter; and thus finally they were confounded and gave up after a very great disturbance. . . . The people, however, thought that the discord arose because the body of St. Francis had been translated already on the third day before the fathers had convened."

44 The earlier mentions of the translation are *Julian Speyer Vita* 75-76; *Umbrian Choir Legend* 11; *3 Celano* 48; *3 Celano* 109.

45 *Chronica XXIV generalium Ordinis Minorum*, cum pluribus appendicibus inter quas excellit hucusque ineditus *Liber de laudibus s. Francisci fr. Bernardi a*

Bessa, edita a patribus collegii s. Bonaventurae, in *AnalFranc* III (Quaracchi: Ex Typographia Collegii S. Bonaventurae, 1897), 212.
46 D. Cooper, "Loco tutissimo et firmissimo," 8-9.
47 By now we have a more balanced picture of Elias, not a figure free from controversy, but neither the villain he was made into by many, from early Spirituals to modern historians like Sabatier. Cf. G. Barone, *Brother Elias Revisited*, already cited.
48 Cf. R. Brooke, *Image of Francis*, 471.
49 Brooke's would be a good argument for this position. For her *Speravimus hactenus* is written before the whole truth had come out, and perhaps Gregory learned more a little later when the delegation reached him after the controversial Chapter meeting that took place in those days. Thomas of Eccleston is reliable, and so his testimony should be trusted. Gregory imposes penalties not just on the laity of Assisi but also on the Basilica and the Order, so there seems to be some implication of wrongdoing also on the part of the friars. Etc. Cf. R. Brooke, *Early Franciscan Government*, 138-142.
50 "Mane autem facto convenit multitudo civitatis Assisii cum universo clero, et tollentes sacrum corpus de loco in quo obierat, cum hymnis et laudibus, clangentibus tubis, ipsum ad civitatem honorifice portaverunt" (*1 Celano* 116:2). This concords well with another early narrative: "When blessed Francis lay gravely ill in the palace of the bishop of Assisi, in the days after he returned from Bagnara, the people of Assisi, fearing that the saint would die during the night without them knowing it, and that the brothers would secretly take his body away and place it in another city, placed a vigilant guard each night around the palace's walls" (*Assisi Compilation* 99:1).
51 *Jord. Giano Chronicle* 50: "Francis departed to the Lord at St. Mary of the Portiuncula. And though our Blessed Father Francis wished to be buried in that church, the people of the district and the citizens of Assisi, fearing that he might be snatched away violently by the Perugians because of the miracles God had deigned to work through him in life and after death, bore away his body and buried it with honor in the church of St. George near the walls of Assisi where he had first learned his letters and where he later first began to preach."
52 The Pope responded that, on the contrary, every assurance would be made to keep the body of Francis safely in its proper resting place at Assisi. Niccola Papini, *Notizie sicure della morte, sepoltura, canonizzazione e traslazione di S. Francesco d'Assisi e del Ritrovamento del di lui corpo* (Firenze, 1822), 188-192; cited in I. Gatti, *La tomba*, 114-115.
53 Cf. I. Gatti, *La tomba*, 85-86.
54 *Vita prima di s. Antonio, o "Assidua" (c. 1232)*, introduzione, testo critico, versione italiana e note a cura di Vergilio Gamboso, Fonti Agiografiche Antoniane 1 (Padova: Messaggero, 1981), n. 18-24. English translation: *Life of St. Anthony "Assidua" by a Contemporary Franciscan*, introduced by Vergilio Gamboso, O.F.M. Conv., translated by Bernard Przewozny, O.F.M. Conv. (Padova: Messaggero di Sant'Antonio Editrice, 2006).
55 L. Waddingus, *AnnalMin* II, 306: "Videre tum erat, ut certatim advolan-

tes, pro se quisque reliquiarum aliquid, vel de capillamento nudi verticis, vel de unguium praesegminibus, vel de mamillarum capillis [or "papillis"], vel de auricularum summitatibus, vel de laciniis abjectae vilisque tunicae decerpere, et quod audacius erat, praesecare festinarent; adeptasque portiunculas maximi putarent, saepiusque deosculatas reverenter acervarent."

56 *PL* 144, col. 693-699, at 694-695.

57 Images are reproduced in I. Gatti, *La tomba*, fig. 3, 13, 15, 57.

58 I. Gatti, *La tomba*, 41.

59 This is another reason why it is very improbable that Elias (and party) could have moved Francis's body without everyone knowing of it. The construction was huge and weighed hundreds of pounds.

60 " . . . et in ecclesia sepelitur / Assisii, Sanctus quae dicta Georgius exstat: / Puro de lapide fit honorifice sibi tumba" (*The Versified Life of Saint Francis*, XIV:29b-31). For other indications in the early sources that might help to clarify details of the first burial one may see *1 Celano* 116:5; *1 Celano* 118:1; *1 Celano* 121:1; *1 Celano* 123:5; *1 Celano* 126:8; *1 Celano* 127:2-3. On whether or not visitors would have found at St. George the body inside a giant wooden *arca* (as would seem to be the case from *AnnalMin* II:261, "elevata a terra magno cum clangore tubarum, aliorumque instrumentorum capsa lignea, in qua sanctum corpus occludebatur" and some early iconographical tradition), I find strong the arguments contra in R. Brooke, *Image of Francis*, 466-467.

61 This kind of devotional practice finds parallel in the vita of St. Anthony, cited earlier, where the people who could not draw close enough to see the body while it was being guarded before final burial "would throw at random through the windows and doors their embroidered girdles and money-belts, rings and necklaces, keys and other ornaments. Still others, attaching these same articles to long poles, would reach within so that they might have them back, sanctified by contact with the most revered body" (*Beati Antonii vita prima seu Legenda "Assidua,"* 21:12). Francis himself, in the early days of his conversion, throwing money through the altar screen at the old St. Peter's in Rome, is reported to have asked, "Since the Prince of the Apostles should be greatly honored, why do they make such meager offerings in the church where his body rests?" (*Three Companions* 10:3). On the items found in the sarcophagus I refer to I. Gatti, *La tomba*, 266-268, and fig. 24, 26. Trexler's skeptical comments on the nature of the items found are odd and not supported by the evidence.

62 " . . . prima che cedesse alla corruzione, giacché altrimenti non si sarebbe trovato né lo scheletro composto; né le ceneri, avvanzo delle carni e dei panni sfacelati, [sarebbero] rimaste al naturale nel luogo di loro caduta" (Giosafat Rossi, *Memorie storiche della vita del Serafico Patriarca S. Francesco di Assisi e del ritrovamento delle di lui Sagre Spoglie* [Assisi, 1824], 150; cited in I. Gatti, *La tomba*, 42).

63 R. Brooke, *Image of Francis*, 468, plate 75 (reproduction from Joanna Cannon and André Vauchez, *Margherita of Cortona and the Lorenzetti* [University Park, PA: Penn State University Press, 1998,] 250).

Chapter 12: A PROPOSED RECONSTRUCTION OF THE EVENT

Now that I have completed my assessment of the recent secondary literature, I am in a position to outline the current state of the question and propose a reconstruction of the La Verna event. I will begin by reviewing, one last time, each of the sources.

I. The Letter of Elias

The encyclical letter, which may really be two letters, is authentic. Even if it might have suffered in its transmission, there is no substantive reason to think that the portion of the text that regards the stigmata has likewise suffered, especially given its obvious use by Thomas of Celano and Julian of Speyer separately.

In the letter, Elias announces what few knew before Francis's death: by some kind of divine intervention (the specifics of which are not given) Francis, towards the end of his life, bore wounds on his body that were like the five wounds of Christ's crucifixion.

Elias does not say in his letter how he knows any of this, but apparently he later tells Thomas of Celano that he had personally seen the side wound while Francis was alive (*1 Celano* 95:6), which would explain his ability to describe the side wound with the specific indication that it bled (*Letter of Elias* 5/19). Plus, Elias was certainly present among the many witnesses of the wounds after Francis's death, which makes sense also of his ability to offer vivid descriptions of the other four wounds. As for that description, the fact that it is later modified by Thomas of Celano, though not necessarily completely contradicted by him, in my opinion authenticates both testimonies (not that both are

correct, but that both are real, early witnesses). I mean that such a process is plausible, bespeaking verisimilitude: the first witness describes what he remembers seeing (perhaps being a little careless about it), while when others are asked, they say that the first description was on the right track but needs more precision; they choose a more "clinical" approach, as someone has described it.

What remains an open question is why Elias says nothing about the circumstances in which the wounds appeared. It could be merely that Elias did not see it as part of the exigency of the announcement, though the problem with this hypothesis is that the letter certainly dabbles in things hagiographical, so the thought that he was waiting for an eventual official hagiographer to deal with it is weakened. Another possibility is that Elias was simply caught up in the moment and did not think carefully of everything that should be included. On the one hand, I find this more convincing than the last hypothesis, since one can imagine the pressure and emotion of such a grave moment of passage, especially for the one charged with guiding the nascent Order. But, on the other hand, I also think that the sheer novelty of the miracle being announced would have demanded at least some more explanation. I lean toward a third possible explanation for the omission: Elias did not know the circumstances yet; no one had told him. This would concord with the information Thomas later reveals, namely that Francis did not talk freely about this topic, nor did he like for his special companions to do so (cf. *1 Celano* 96:1-2).

II. THE CANONIZATION BULL, *MIRA CIRCA NOS*

The canonization Bull does not mention the stigmata explicitly, but this is not to be considered evidence that Pope Gregory IX believed that Elias or someone in the Order invented the thing, especially since he later explains that witnesses had testified in his presence about the stigmata, and this aided the decision to

canonize Francis. Besides, Gregory's style of canonization Bull does not seem to admit of such details anyway.

Since the stigmata had been one of the confirming pieces of evidence for Gregory's decision to canonize Francis, it is difficult to believe that he did not have the wounds in the back of his mind when he discreetly wrote about Francis offering his flesh as a holocaust to the Lord on a certain mountain and thus being crucified with Christ. After all, certainly the same people who soon recounted to Thomas of Celano that the stigmatization event was related to the La Verna Mountain explained the same thing to Gregory. The aforesaid being the case, those who have noticed in the same passage of *Mira circa nos* terms always associated in the middle ages with seraphim, *ignis* and *charitas*, very well could be on to something.

III. *1 Celano*

But, while Elias did not have all of the details, and Gregory hesitated to speak openly of them, Thomas did not have thc luxury of remaining silent. It was his assignment to put all of the pieces together. Certainly Gregory told him as much when he commissioned the *vita*.

Thomas, then, gathers witness testimonies.[1] We have some indications, although not as many as we would like, of who they are and which testimonies they offer. Eyewitnesses of the wounds after Francis's death are the local friars, the citizens of Assisi, and the Poor Ladies at San Damiano. Eyewitnesses of the wounds themselves before Francis's death are not clearly named, except for Elias and Rufino who are witnesses to the side wound.

Those personally knowledgeable about the general fact of the stigmata and about something of their origins, however, at least include a certain unnamed person (*quidam*) whom Francis personally told. It is very likely that this person is one of the four special companion "pillars," and likely also that it is Leo

specifically. The arguments for it being Leo are: (1) the certainty of Leo's proximity to Francis in those days, known because of *The Rubrics of Leo* and *MS Little* 154; (2) Leo's claim to know Francis's intention for writing *The Praises of God*, an intention connected to the stigmata; and (3) later assertions that Leo was the "confessor" of Francis, and so probably also a kind of confidant.[2]

I would add something (not directly related to *1 Celano*) that I have not emphasized thus far: Bonaventure's legend, written between 1260-1263, rarely contains new information, and generally truncates and reworks its sources, the Minister General does go to the trouble of offering a name never previously associated with the stigmata event, namely Illuminato (*Major Legend* XIII:4:3). It is not apparent to me that the particulars of the account merit serious historical trust (because of the tone of the account, the method of Bonaventure, and the almost forty-year distance from the event). But what does interest me very much is the use of a particular name, the name of a friar who is still alive,[3] whom Bonaventure very likely interviewed (cf. *Major Legend*, prol., 4:1-2), and who is listed among the weighty authorities to which Leo, Rufino, and Angelo had recourse when gathering their "flowers" (*Three Companions* 1:3-5)." It should be considered certain, therefore, that in 1260 Illuminato is claiming to have been told personally by Francis details about the stigmatization event. And even if I hesitate to accept the details of his account as it has been transmitted to us in *Major Legend*, I can see no reason to disbelieve the assertion of him claiming to have been entrusted with Francis's great secret, nor do I see reason to doubt the veracity of his basic claim. I do not know if this makes Illuminato the *quidam* of *1 Celano*, or if it involves him in the telling of the story that becomes *Assisi Compilation* 118, or if it simply puts him in the group of special companions that perhaps shared memories with each other and perhaps went to

Thomas with their memories when he was writing the first *vita*. But what is clear is that there is an authority of no small stature who is putting his name down as a personal confidant of Francis on this matter, and this should not be passed over, however late the testimony.

Things begin to become more complicated when we try to determine not whether Thomas had sure witnesses stepping forward to testify about the miraculous phenomenon, but what precisely they told him and where it fits in to his narrative. I think Frugoni is on the right track when she tries to glimpse in the narrative Thomas's effort to reconcile different testimonies, for example that of Elias and that of the companions. Based on all that has preceded this point in my study, my hypothetical proposal of Thomas's use of sources would be charted in this way:

1 Celano	Content	Source
91-93	Francis's retreat and discernment about how to bring his project to completion	"Socii pauci" (91:3) / the four pillars (102:3)
94	The seraph apparition and appearance of the wounds	"Quidam" (90:8): Leo or Illuminato
95:1-4	The first description of the wounds	*Letter of Elias*, but with additional testimony, possibly from friar witnesses at the deathbed (even Thomas himself?)
95:5-8	Witnesses to the side wound while Francis was alive	Elias (95:6) and Rufino (95:7-8)
95:9-96:6	The solicitude of Francis to hide the wounds, the friars' protection of him from those with whom he did not wish to speak	fratres et filii qui secum morabantur (96 :3) ("Socii pauci" / the four pillars)

112:1-9	The arrival of the citizens at Francis's deathbed, the mourning of the friars, the appearance of Francis as someone just taken down from the cross	*Letter of Elias* plus oral testimony (perhaps Elias or possibly even Thomas himself)
112:10-12	The description of Francis's dead body	*Letter of Elias*; *Vita S. Martini*
113:1	The second description of the wounds	*Letter of Elias*, modified by new testimony from friars who were present at the deathbed

To be able to establish this much is an achievement. However, there still remains a critical gap, namely in our knowledge concerning how precisely Thomas *used* those sources, at least the ones that were oral or otherwise have left no written trace.

This point leads back to the three written Leonine sources I have emphasized: *The Rubrics of Leo*, *Assisi Compilation* 118, and *MS Little* 154. That is, if it is true that Leo was a likely informant for Thomas, and if it is likewise true that these three written sources associated with him represent witnesses that are textually and ideologically autonomous from *1 Celano*, then, despite the fact that these written sources are made after *1 Celano*, there should be at least something, however minimal, that they can tell us about the original story told to Thomas. I will begin with *The Rubrics of Leo*.

IV. *THE RUBRICS OF LEO*

The intention of the gloss is not to testify to the veracity of the stigmata or clarify the details of the related events, but to contextualize the writings of Francis on the parchment, thus identifying the value of it for whomever one day would have care of it. Nevertheless, even though his primary intention is not to correct Thomas's version, Leo effectively adds the following data to the

then known version: (1) the further specification of the dating to the "Lent of St. Michael"; (2) the seraph not only appears to Francis but also speaks to him; (3) after the event Francis writes a little prayer to give thanks to God for the favor (the twofold favor of seraph vision and stigmata) granted him; and (4) he drew at the same time a picture of a Tau-shaped cross on Golgotha (apparently) and humankind being saved by it.

And these additions are to be considered of primary-source value, for the following reasons. First, since the intention of the gloss is simply to describe the content of the parchment, Leo's rubrics have no apparent polemical or apologetic intention with regard to the stigmata. I realize that if Leo made the rubrics after 1237 (something not at all certain), when a series of papal defenses of the stigmata began, then he is writing at a time when assertion of original witness might be viewed as apologetic. However, even if this is the case, it does not seem that Leo showed the rubrics very often if ever, given that he wrote them before *2 Celano*, but no influence of them can be discerned before *The Major Legend*.[4] Plus, the text is written by someone who was at La Verna during the days in question, and is probably the informant (*quidam*) of Thomas, as I have argued. And above all, this informant for the first legend—who, yes, certainly knows that legend from that time forward—shows no signs of dependency on it. For example, he does not take any of the other elements from *1 Celano*'s narrative about the seraph: he does not also call the seraph *vir*, nor say that he was crucified. For these reasons, therefore, a *"post hoc, ergo propter hoc"* argument (still arbitrarily supposing that *The Rubrics of Leo* are written after *1 Celano*) is insufficient for removing this source's value as an autonomous and primary source. Nor can we argue anymore that the lateness of the text seems to disqualify it, since it is at least as early as the wave of companion literature in the 1240's, and possibly much earlier.

The importance of the preceding point is not just relative to the new information that *The Rubrics of Leo* bring, but also to the *datum* held in common with *1 Celano*, namely that the appearance of the stigmata are to be associated somehow with a vision of a seraph. Leo is asserting that he knows (i.e., was told by the author) that the intention of *The Praises of God* is to give thanks for the seraph and the stigmata both. For Leo, these two things are to be considered somehow part of a single *beneficium*. Thus, *The Rubrics of Leo* are to be considered an autonomous, primary witness for this seraph-stigmata association, and so we cannot attribute the seraph's invention to Thomas of Celano.

I have to underline a point of crucial significance that has emerged: if Francis has communicated to his confidant in a manner that makes him think that the two mystical events of La Verna are to be grouped together into a single one, we must always respect that and be very careful not to separate their place in Francis's experience merely because there was some temporal separation. Francis's subjective experience was of what we should call "the grace of La Verna" or "the La Verna event," not of unrelated, discrete moments bearing no internal connection. This is no surprise. Certainly he experienced it this way, because real life is this way. There is for us a danger of letting abstract historical data sometimes cloud over such obvious realities. Francis was the same man at each moment of this one retreat in which he was experiencing the ongoing action of the one God in his concrete situation. It is indeed our duty as historians to isolate events in order to analyze them, but let us not lose sight of the fact that it is equally our obligation to discover the *connections* between them, which is precisely what it means to do history.

V. *THE ASSISI COMPILATION*

One thing now needs more attention: the simple seraph (i.e., not a man-seraph or a crucified seraph) of *The Rubrics of Leo*.

The question is whether Leo's is merely a form of abbreviated speech or if it is instead evidence that he does not think of the seraph as Thomas described it since that is not how he first heard the story. If the latter is the case, then it seems we have pinpointed one way in which Thomas has elaborated his source, changing the original story.

The only way I know to explore answers to this is to move on to the other related source that apparently comes from Leo's own pen, the one that becomes our *Assisi Compilation* 118. As I showed earlier, there is an evident philological relationship between *The Rubrics of Leo* and *The Assisi Compilation*, the most likely explanation for which being that the author of *The Rubrics of Leo* later wrote or dictated *Assisi Compilation* 118.

I think we must begin by determining precisely what these two sources, *1 Celano* and *The Assisi Compilation*, have in common and where precisely they differ. I chart the elements of each narrative, noting what they have in common in the left column.

Common element	*1 Celano*	*Assisi Compilation*
Retreat on La Verna	Retreat from the crowds [to La Verna] with a few companions (91:1-3).	Francis goes to La Verna to make the Lent of St. Michael (118:1-4).
Prayer to know God's will for him	Prayer to know what more God wants from him (91:4-92:4). Plan to open the Gospel book in order to be shown how to bring to fulfillment what he had earlier begun (92:5-8).	He prays to know if it is God's will that he remain there or if he should go out preaching (118:5-8).

Receives a sign that answers his prayer	Opening of the book three times to the foretelling of the Passion, understanding that he would enter the kingdom through many trials and difficulties (93:1-4).	Birds come and go from his cell as a sign, which gives him a great consolation. The Lord tells him that it is a sign that the Lord will do good for him there and give many consolations (118:9-12).
Vision of a seraph that brings great consolation	Apparition of a man-seraph, crucified and with six wings (94:1-2). Francis rejoices and is delighted by the look the seraph gives him, but is sad because of the bitter suffering of its passion. He does not understand what the vision means for him (94:3-6).	The Lord's prophecy comes true since he later has a vision of a seraph that gives him consolation for his whole life, which he told his companion about (118:13-14).
Many trials on La Verna from demons	—	But there were also trials from demons, he told his companion, for which reason he later complained that the brothers would have more compassion on him if they knew, and that he was unable to satisfy them sometimes (118:15-17).
Wounds appear on his body	While trying to understand the vision that has ended, wounds like the ones he saw on the man-seraph appear on his body too (94:7).	—

First, it seems very significant that these independent narratives have the commonalities that they do: Francis goes to La Verna on retreat, prays to know God's will, receives a sign in answer to his prayer, then has a vision of a seraph that gives him great consolation. These things—in the same order, no less—both narratives assert. I suggest that these concordant elements are to be considered historically certain.

Next, each narrative has one major element missing that the other includes. First, I have already shown that the missing stigmata in *The Assisi Compilation* are nothing to be alarmed about since *The Rubrics of Leo*, previously written by the same person, include them. Second, *1 Celano*, for its part, is missing the element from *Assisi Compilation* 118:15-17 about the demonic trials Francis also suffered on La Verna. Here, though, I would not emphasize the divergence too strongly. For it seems in fact that Thomas has subsumed these very particular struggles of Francis into the more general struggles of Francis at that time (e.g., his struggles to know God's will and the drama surrounding the opening of the Gospel book to the Passion narratives). This is a literary technique that Thomas is effectively utilizing. In Part Three, the specifics of Francis's struggle will return in an important way.

A final point to address—and it is the most difficult one—is that within the common elements I have noted between the two narratives, which I have said are in their substance historically certain, there are real and significant deviations. Even a cursory glance will notice the differences in the content of the prayer for God's will, the type of sign Francis receives in answer to that prayer, and the details about the seraph.

When faced with these divergent elements, three questions arise: (1) does the divergent version as it is currently found in *The Assisi Compilation* truly represent the version of the *Florilegium*, that is, of the three friars Leo, Rufino, and Angelo? (2) If

so, does it therefore also represent a version of the story closer to what Thomas of Celano was told when he was preparing the first legend? (3) If it does, should *The Assisi Compilation* version be considered more or less the story that the companion friars learned from Francis (though without mention of the stigmata)?

To the first question, I do think that *Assisi Compilation* 118 probably represents the version that was composed by Leo, Rufino, and Angelo. My first reason is the philological dependency on *The Rubrics of Leo* in some of its parts, which I showed earlier to be best explained by positing that the same author is involved in both texts. My second reason is based on the synoptic comparison with the same episode in *Major Legend* that I made in Part One, which shows that Bonaventure had then the episode that we have now, at least in large part.

The second question is much more difficult to answer, but I give a provisory yes that *Assisi Compilation* 118 is closer to the original version of the story Thomas was told but modified in the retelling. The main reason is that I cannot see any other reason for the companion friars in 1244-1246 to deviate from the official version in the *vita*, saving polemical motivation, of which I see none in this episode.

The final question is the most difficult to answer: Does the version in *The Assisi Compilation* represent the version of Francis? Here, there is no certain way to verify. And it is easy to place doubts, beginning from the failsafe appeal to the vacillations of human memory. And yet, similar to my previous point, I have difficulty seeing how the human memory would move from the known, official version of the story to the one here present. One would rather expect an embellishment on the official version, but that is not what this one is. I have to conclude that, in broad strokes, this is the picture Francis painted for the companions, which they then told to Thomas.

VI. The Official Version and Its Historicity

This hypothetical conclusion that I have made raises questions about the version of Thomas. Are its elements disqualified as historical facts when they differ from the substance of *The Assisi Compilation* version of the La Verna event? To attempt to answer this question (treading very lightly, since, I would emphasize, we are very much on the level of hypothesis) we must take each differing element individually.

The first element (following the chart I have made above) is the prayer of Francis to know God's will for him. In *1 Celano* Francis is first said to be praying to know what more is being asked of him, how he could follow Christ more perfectly (91:4-92:4); then, more specifically, Francis is said to be asking what he can do to bring to completion what he had earlier begun (92:5-8). But in *Assisi Compilation* 118:5-8 it is a much simpler question directed to the specific moment: should Francis stay on La Verna in retreat or go out and preach? I would explain this discrepancy by saying that Thomas is actually in agreement with *The Assisi Compilation*, but in a generalizing or globalizing way. That is, in these paragraphs, Thomas wants to speak less about this very particular story and more about how it fits into the universal story of Francis. It is almost a kind of narrative synecdoche. I say this because Thomas thinks that the particular story is true; he knows that Francis certainly had this question about whether or not he was sent to preach or to pray.[5] But instead of repeating the simple, particular incident about how Francis is at this moment on La Verna perhaps feeling guilty for not being out preaching, Thomas frames it in more universal terms saying something else that is also true: Francis is praying about how to fulfill the original inspiration he had had. Only, Thomas does not give the specific details of it here. He does not say that at issue here is the original inspiration to not live only for oneself in prayer, but for the salvation of souls in preaching.

This synecdoche is also the means to explain the discrepancy in the second element of the story, namely the sign that Francis receives in answer to his prayer. In Thomas we find Francis opening the Gospel book at random and receiving a sign that way, but the authors of the *Florilegium* tell us about how Francis received a special sign in the form of birds coming and going from his cell. Certainly the complete disappearance of this element in the *vita* is what made the three friars be sure to include this story in their collection of stories in 1246. But again, I suggest that Thomas felt he was only taking the historical particular of this La Verna story and globalizing it to explain better the meaning of the last two years of Francis's life. So, no, I suspect that at this particular moment Francis did not practice the so-called *sortes Apostolorum*, but rather that Thomas uses this hagiographical commonplace[6] to many ends: (1) Thomas is making a general application of the particular fact of Francis receiving a sign from God while on La Verna; (2) by introducing these Passion prediction narratives, Thomas is beginning to build towards the climax of his story, the stigmatization account; and (3) Thomas is, by the content of the Scripture passages received in these *sortes*, in fact beginning to describe the real situation told to him by the "four pillars" of how Francis suffered also *interiorly* in these last years, something confirmed in other passages of *1 Celano*, Book II, as I will have occasion to show later.

The third element of discrepancy pertains to the vision of the seraph and is strongly related to the final element, the wounds. Both sources agree that there was such a seraph vision, but *1 Celano* describes that seraph not like the ones described in Scripture, but as being a kind of combination of seraph and crucified man; meanwhile, *The Assisi Compilation* says nothing about that. Frankly, I would not be concerned about this discrepancy if it were only in *The Rubrics of Leo*, which is not necessarily interested or capable of entering into all types of particulars. However, if

we take the longer narrative of *The Assisi Compilation*, considering the widespread awareness of the official version of the story, I would say that it is odd not to have some hint—any hint at all—of the unusual features of the seraph. Nor can I see any other reason for the author(s) to describe the seraph so simply, thus changing the story, except that this is how it was first told. This is especially the case since hagiographical episodes never devolve in their retelling but always develop, which is certainly true with the stigmatization of Francis. If there is one thing that Frugoni's work has shown definitively, it is that this story evolves, and in two directions. First, the appearance of the stigmata and the appearance of the seraph become ever more intertwined, such that what Thomas only implied becomes explicit, namely that the latter is the efficient cause of the former. Second, the seraph becomes ever more Christ-like: Thomas could speak of a seraph-like-man on a cross, but Bonaventure did not hesitate to speak matter-of-factly of *Christ* looking kindly at Francis (*Major Legend* XIII:3:6). In *The Assisi Compilation*, though, both elements, stigmata and Christ, are missing entirely. I have explained why I believe we have no choice but to forgive the first omission, but I have yet to find an explanation for the second, though perhaps there is one yet to be discovered.

Given the current state of the evidence, then, how would I explain Thomas's version? It is not difficult, and other scholars have already hinted at it. Thomas is putting all of the elements together, using his honest interpretation of the meaning of them, making a coherent story out of the sources he has. Thomas wants to show the divine origin of the wounds, and he does so by the literary technique of putting them on the seraph vision (which is also of divine origin), since he does not have other details about the appearance of the wounds, and since he knows Francis himself also associated them in some manner. I do not mean that Thomas invented the idea of the miraculous

nature of the wounds. No, that idea goes back to Francis, as is clear from what Leo relates in his autograph rubric. I only mean that Thomas does not know any more than that and so takes these two elements, the seraph and the stigmata, and weaves them together skillfully.[7] The consistency between the two—a true consistency, since they are both from God, both part of the *beneficium*—is then re-emphasized by Thomas when he imputes to the seraph the features of the crucifixion.

The fourth element of discrepancy is precisely the wounds, and so we have reached the heart of the analysis. The stigmata are not only present but central in *1 Celano*, while they are completely absent in *The Assisi Compilation*. On the one hand, I have said, because of *The Rubrics of Leo*, that the absence of the stigmata in *The Assisi Compilation* is no indication that the author of that episode does not think that the stigmata are factual. On the other hand, I have also said that *The Assisi Compilation* version probably represents in some way a version more like Thomas's source than does what finally appears in the finished *1 Celano*. This means that the author of *The Assisi Compilation*, who does believe in the facticity of the stigmata, must think that the seraph aspect of the La Verna story could be told devoid of the stigmata without compromising either. From this I must conclude that, while Francis was able to think of the two great graces of La Verna together as a single *beneficium*, there was nevertheless enough temporal separation between them to allow speaking of one without the other. The story of the consolation of the seraph was a story in its own right, while the connection between that and the wounds on his body was perhaps something only told in confidence to Leo. And, perhaps because it was their secret, a custom developed among the companions of telling the seraph story by itself.

And so there remains a tension: the two salient events of the La Verna retreat—the appearance of the seraph and the

appearance of the wounds—are inseparable and yet separable. What does this mean practically on the level of real historical facts? I propose that Francis grouped the two events together, giving thanks for them as a single grace because they were two events that he experienced in the same days of retreat and as from the same God. That is, upon reflection, Francis's perception was that the two events together made up the grace that God was giving him in those days. But at the same time, I have to say that the events were temporally distinct, such as to allow Francis to have told the story of the seraph appearance as a different story from the one of the appearance of the Christ-like wounds. Therefore, when Thomas combines the two elements, both historically factual, he is trying to explain theologically the meaning of these extraordinary events, not necessarily relate them as they strictly unfolded.

VII. An Historical Reconstruction

Everything that I have said up to this point, then, would add up to the following skeletal outline of the La Verna event of 1224.

Brother Francis, with some special companions who spent those last years with him, went to La Verna in the autumn of that year, ostensibly with the intention of honoring the Blessed Virgin and St. Michael (and so between their two feast days), but also with the need to rest away from the crowds of seculars, and away from some elements of the Order too, as we will later see when I try to expound more on Francis's personal experience.

While there during those weeks, Francis wondered if he actually was just pampering himself with rest, if he should not really be out preaching as he had felt convicted to begin doing fifteen or twenty years earlier. But a strange thing happened: birds began to come and go from his cell, one at a time, singing little songs to him. He knew it was a sign from God; it was permission to stay, and an indication that God had special things in

store for him during that sojourn. This gave him great consolation, he told his companion. He was very grateful, probably, especially because of how much he really did need the physical as well as emotional and spiritual rest; there were many things he was suffering, outwardly and inwardly.

Two things happened during the days that followed, two separate events, but Francis always thought of them as a single grace, as he later told Leo. And he also told Leo, or someone else, some other details about them, but those details likely have remained to this day largely unrepeated. Those two gifts, which were a single grace, were an apparition of a seraph, which gave Francis special consolation for the rest of his life, and the appearance of five wounds on his body that were in the same pattern as the ones on the crucified body of Jesus.

Francis was so grateful for these two things that he asked Leo to bring him some paper so he could write a little pastiche of praises of God. We actually still have that very piece of parchment today, almost eight hundred years later. The reason why we have it is because at some point thereafter Francis decided that his companion needed a blessing, and so he wrote one on the other side of the paper and gave it to that brother (adding a little drawing that depicted the saving mystery of the cross of Christ). It happened that, even though Francis did not know it, Brother Leo was having his own struggles in those days and had become convinced that something written by the hand of Francis would ease his suffering. It must have worked, and he kept that little paper with him, even later using it as a relic in intercessory prayer for others. He also decided along the way that he should notate it well to preserve for posterity the precise indications of just what that little parchment contained, because despite its size, it contained quite a lot.

Brother Francis did his best to keep the wounds to himself for the next two years, but at least two of the friars managed

to confirm that the wounds in his hands and feet were not just coincidentally in the form of the crucifixion marks of Jesus, since Francis also bore in his side a wound like the one made from a lance in the side of Jesus by the Roman soldier. But when Francis died, not only did all the friars see the wounds, but practically the whole city of Assisi, and the cloistered nuns as well. Once everyone got a good look at the wounds in his hands and feet they were able to see that they were very peculiar, almost as if there were nails present, but nails formed of the man's flesh. Francis's great secret, one half of his La Verna grace, was divulged and soon became the distinguishing feature of the humble man.

---

1 And he must have done so quickly, since, as I mentioned, Thomas's legend is completely finished and approved seven months later. This also means that there is not as much time for inventing memories as is sometimes suggested. The final version of the stigmatization story may grow much by the time of the *Fioretti* or even *Major Legend*, but the gestation period for the nascent story is much too brief to suggest dramatic hagiographical maturation.

2 *Liber de laudibus S. Francisci fr. Bernardi a Bessa*, I:1:16. This late thirteenth-century work is found in *AnalFranc* III, 666-692; now also in *Fontes*, 1253-1296; English translation: *A Book of the Praises of Saint Francis by Bernard of Besse*, in *FA:ED* III, 31-74.

3 Cf. Omer Englebert, *Saint Francis of Assisi: A Biography*, a new translation by Eve Marie Cooper, Second English edition revised and augmented by Ignatius Brady, O.F.M., and Raphael Brown with introduction, appendices, and comprehensive bibliography covering modern research (Chicago: Franciscan Herald Press, 1965), *Appendix VII: Companions*, 434.

4 This presumes, of course, that the indications in *Major Legend* XIII:3:7-8 about the seraph who spoke to Francis are taken from *The Rubrics of Leo*, but in fact the ostensible source for the information is Illuminato, who could have either known the information from Francis himself, from Leo orally, or from *The Rubrics of Leo*.

5 When the little band of penitents had just returned from Rome the first time in 1209, arriving in the Spoleto valley they were asking this very question. See *1 Celano* 35:5-6.

6 Cf. *AnalFranc* X, 70, n. 14.

7 Some of Frugoni's analysis along these lines may be correct. For example, she notes how the wounds appear on Francis's body in Thomas's account as an explanation for the vision, which Francis had been otherwise unable to understand. This would explain why Thomas has to silence the seraph, since a speaking seraph would leave fewer unanswered questions. Cf. C. Frugoni, *L'invenzione*, 156.

PART THREE: GUESSING FRANCIS'S EXPERIENCE OF THE STIGMATA

Chapter 13: **FRANCIS AS FOLLOWER OF CHRIST**

I. How to Discover Francis's Experience

If we know the basic facts of the La Verna retreat of 1224, what value would such knowledge have if we cannot also discover something of what these things meant to Francis, the one who lived them? History, after all, is not piles of raw data dug up out of the past. No. For the Christian, at least, it is what the events mean.

In this case, our interest is first of all in what the events meant in the life of the real man Francis. Therefore, I do not want to know first and foremost the meaning of the stigmata according to Thomas of Celano, for example, though that is interesting too for other reasons. Before I care to understand what the stigmata meant or mean in the mind of any hagiographer or theologian, or to the Order, to the Church, or to Christians of every time and place, I want to discover how they were experienced in the spiritual life of the subject in question. This is all the more important (and delicate) in the case of Francis of Assisi because he was the first one to have experienced them.

Of course, while such a project may be supremely valuable, it is difficult to realize, to say the least. For, although we may have the first-person sworn testimony of certain modern-day stigmatics,[1] we have nothing of the sort for Francis, for whom the stigmata were indeed a "great secret." This author, therefore, is the first to recognize the foolhardiness of this study. In point of fact, better scholars than I have already articulated the reasons for discontinuing the research precisely at this juncture. Grado

Giovanni Merlo, for example, wanted to forestall objections to his own paper by explaining the problem clearly:

> I could raise the objection against myself that I have neglected to illustrate the spiritual and mystical dimension of the stigmatization. It is easy to respond to the objection by saying it is true. However, this has not been of my own choosing: I think that it is impossible to deal with this dimension since the sources reveal only the spiritual and mystical meaning attributed to the La Verna event by the hagiographers. The "writings" of Brother Francis are silent in this regard; and we should think of the fact that the same "writings" are silent as well—and not by chance—concerning the painful sicknesses that frequently afflicted the Assisian and only got worse in the last two years of life. How can we pretend to enter into a "fact" so mysterious and private as the identification of Brother Francis with Jesus Crucified without there being a protagonist to supply us with his own personal testimony?[2]

Merlo's assessment is not less valid today than when he first made it. Still, I wonder if it is not worth the trouble to search for some manner of valid approach that would somehow yield reliable data, even if we know that the results are doomed to be incomplete and provisory.

Since there are no direct ways forward, we have to move indirectly. We have to begin by formulating a clear picture of Francis's spiritual self-understanding, one that is not based on clichés but solidly founded on his writings, which scholars by now recognize as the ultimate authentic touchstone. If this can be done, then we will have a chance of reasonably surmising how the stigmata experience fits in.

Fortunately, we do have some reliable pieces of data to aid us. First, from without Francis, we know now that we can rely on the lines Leo wrote on the *Chartula* to give us something from the heart of Francis himself. And, related to this, we have a prayer Francis composed, Leo tells us, in direct response to receiving the stigmata, even if the prayer itself does not otherwise

say so. Furthermore, we know enough about the biographical events of the last years of Francis's life to know what his personal situation was like when he went up to La Verna. We know that he was suffering severe trials. Context is of crucial importance to understand the real events of a man's life, for it is the background upon which the picture is painted, and so is inseparable from it.

II. Francis, *Alter Christus?*

Certainly, it is true that part of the meaning of Francis for us is that he appeared as "another Christ." All Christians are in a manner meant to come to resemble Christ more and more, and these miraculous wounds remind us of that. But what about for Francis? Did he seek to be conformed to Christ? And, if so, did he imagine himself as having achieved it on La Verna? We do often think of it this way. The *Considerations on the Stigmata*, appended to some manuscripts of the *Fioretti*, capture the idea:

> And he prayed in this way: 'My Lord Jesus Christ, I pray You to grant me two graces before I die: the first is that during my life I may feel in my soul and in my body, as much as possible, that pain that You, sweet Jesus, sustained in the hour of Your most bitter Passion [*che in vita mia io senta nell'anima e nel corpo mio, quanto è possibile, quel dolore che tu, dolce Gesù, sostenesti nella ora della tua acerbissima passione*]. The second is that I may feel in my heart, as much as possible, that excessive love with which You, O Son of God, were inflamed to endure willingly such suffering for us sinners.'
>
> And remaining for a long time in prayer, he understood that God would grant it to him, and that it would soon be conceded to him to feel those things as much as is possible for a mere creature.
>
> Having received this promise, St. Francis began to contemplate with intense devotion the Passion of Christ and His infinite charity. And the fervor of his devotion increased so much within him that he was being utterly transformed into Jesus through love and compassion [*che tutto sì si trasformava in Gesù, e per amore*

> *e per compassione*]. And while he was thus inflaming himself in this contemplation, on that same morning he saw coming down from Heaven a Seraph with six resplendent and flaming wings. As the Seraph, flying swiftly, came closer to St. Francis, so that he could perceive Him clearly, he noticed that he had the likeness of a crucified man, and his wings were so disposed that two wings extended above His head, two were spread out to fly, and the other two covered His entire body. . . .
>
> And while he was marveling . . . he who was appearing to him revealed to him that this vision was shown to him by Divine Providence in this particular form in order that he should understand that he was to be transformed into the direct likeness of Christ Crucified [*egli doveva essere tutto trasformato in nella espressa similitudine di Cristo crocifisso*], not by physical martyrdom, but by an enkindling of the mind.[3]

But, while certain aspects of this account may have won out in the popular imagination, they nevertheless appear foreign to the earlier sources examined thus far. For example, we see here that before the stigmatization Francis is consciously seeking a physical share in the Passion of Jesus. And, at the time of the stigmatization, Francis is meditating on the Passion of Christ. Moreover, it is revealed to Francis that the seraph vision means that he will be transformed into the direct likeness of Christ Crucified.

I do not say that these elements are inconsistent with stigmatization, generally speaking; comparisons with other stigmatic experiences from the centuries after Francis would prove that to be false. The question, rather, is if these were in fact component elements of Francis of Assisi's experience, which simply cannot be presumed if no reliable documentary evidence will be found for it.

These elements and this La Verna portrait will serve us as we move forward in these chapters. Present in them is an admixture of the real Francis and a Francis that is in the process of a conceptual and theological evolution. A kind of caricature of

the real La Verna event achieves its final crystallization in this account—beautiful and important though it is for many reasons—, and in trying to understand the evolution, we will be forced to identify the authentic features of Francis's experience.

I will move gradually from more general aspects of Francis's spirituality towards the core of his La Verna experience, contextualizing in that way what we really want to know.

III. On the Literalism of Francis

Before we can ask the direct question of whether Francis, as in the episode above, was inclined to desire to participate literally in the physical sufferings of Christ's passion, we can ask more broadly questions about Francis's literalistic approach to the Gospel. Was Francis one to put literally into practice elements of the Gospel—even non-essential ones—in a slavish way? If so, then the picture of one who would practice a literal mimicry of the earthly life of Jesus comes into clear focus as well. And, in that case, Francis would easily think of his stigmatization as a continuation or even divine completion of his own strivings.

To begin with the question of the literalism of Francis, then, Carlo Paolazzi has demonstrated beyond doubt, for example, the saint's rigorous fidelity to the Gospel prohibitions to call no one good but God alone (cf. Luke 18:19), to call no man on earth father (cf. Matt 23:9), and never to call any one but Christ master (cf. Matt 23:10).[4] His study proves that the anecdote of Francis addressing Doctor Bongiovanni ("Good John") as "Brother John" so as to avoid calling anyone but God "good" (*Assisi Compilation* 100:1-4) is no hagiographical elaboration but an authentic reflection of Francis's strict practice. Of the 104 cases in Francis's corpus of writings in which the word *pater* [father] occurs, the 32 in which *bonus* [good] occurs, and the 5 in which *magister* [teacher] occurs, not a single one of them shows neglect for the Gospel precepts in question.[5]

Was Francis, then, an early forerunner to modern fundamentalism? Early friars must have had a question not unlike this one in mind when they sent representatives to Pope Gregory in 1230 to ask for certain clarifications on the *Rule*. Since Francis had opened the *Rule* by saying that the "Rule and Life of the Lesser Brothers is . . . to observe the Holy Gospel" (*Regula bullata* I:1),[6] they needed to know if they were bound under pain of sin to observe all of the counsels of the Gospels and their precepts too. The Pope responded in the negative (*Quo elongati* 4),[7] but what would Francis have said had he been around to clarify? Did he want this type of rigorous attachment to even the "extra" elements of the Gospel?

Questions like these are dealt with by André Vauchez in an illuminating study on Francis's literalism.[8] He recognizes that Francis is undoubtedly interested in the unmitigated letter of the text, such that at times the Poverello seems to think that any kind of gloss on a text might be a barrier between text and reader. That would be why Francis commands that the words of his own *Testament*[9] not be added to or taken away from (*Testament* 35), and that neither it nor the *Rule* ever be marred by a gloss (cf. *Testament* 38).

And yet, while Francis is deeply interested in the unmitigated letter of the text, Vauchez notes that the terminology of *litteraliter* and *ad litteram* never actually enters the lexicon of Francis. Certainly in the biographical sources *sine glossa* goes hand-in-hand with *ad litteram*, as in the polemical episode of *Assisi Compilation* 17. But it is not so in the autobiographical ones. Francis does not go on to say in the above-quoted passage from the *Testament* that since he desires the *Rule* to remain unglossed it should be kept with literal rigor. Instead, the adverbs he chooses to describe the type of observance required are *simpliciter* and *pure*: "But as the Lord has given me to speak and write the *Rule* and these words simply and purely, may you

understand them simply and without gloss and observe them with a holy activity until the end" (*Testament* 39).

In fact, the only time Francis refers in his own writings to the *littera* of the text is to quote St. Paul who says that the letter kills (*Admonition* VII; 2 Cor 3:6). He explains that the letter of the text can be said to kill religious, for example, when they want to know merely the words of Scripture in order to appear wise or to profit in some way. Whereas, he explains, religious are not put to death by the letter when they follow the "spirit of the divine letter" (*spiritus divinae letterae*). He uses the word "spirit" to clarify his position, and it becomes programmatic for him. In this way, when he is describing the reception of new friars into the Order in the *Regula non bullata*, and he explains how they are to sell all their belongings and give all to the poor (cf. Matt 19:21; Luke 18:22), he does not say that they must fulfill the requirements literally but *spiritually* (*Regula non bullata* II:1-4).[10] Similarly, Francis speaks in the *Rule* of those brothers who may have to have recourse to their ministers when they feel they are stuck in a situation that prevents them from observing the rule *spiritually* (*Regula bullata* X:4).[11] Where one might have expected Francis to say *literally*, he says *spiritually*.

Vauchez sums up the problem by saying that Francis practices a "spiritually literal" observance of the Gospel. He means that Francis knows that the letter without the spirit of the letter kills. Simultaneously, though, he knows that the authentic spirit of the text truly resides in the letter, that the spirit and the letter are inseparable, like matter and form.[12] A puppet-like application of the words of Scripture is therefore out of the question for him, even while the letter is indispensable, because instead of getting caught up in the "rind" of the letter, Francis sees deeply into the letter's *ratio*.

This may be why there is not slavish copying of Gospel precepts even while there is obvious concern for following them.

One example is the appearance in the *Regula non bullata* of the prescriptions Jesus gives to those he sends on mission. Whereas Jesus makes sandals and a second tunic contraband (cf. Luke 10:4; Matt 10:10), Francis drops those two items from his own list and includes only knapsack, purse, bread, money, and walking stick (*Regula non bullata* XIV:1), and he explicitly allows the friars to have two tunics, if they wish (*Regula non bullata* II:13; *Regula bullata* II:14).

It seems, we can say in conclusion, that Francis's radical Gospel following, which indeed pays close attention to the letter of the text, never wants to fall into a blind literalism, but hopes instead to follow the profounder *meaning* of the letter. This has obvious implications for how we must conceive of Francis's brand of following Christ, particularly when often faced with the caricatures of a saint who practiced an external mimicry.

IV. Francis: Imitator or Follower?

But even though a meaningless literalism is not at issue with regards to Francis's interpretation of the Gospel, was there not still some intention to imitate Christ in literal ways? I will show in this section that it is better to speak of Francis as one who desired to "follow" Christ because that language is his own, while the language of imitation implies aspects that are not so clearly part of his experience. I will also specify the content of Francis's idea of "following" and show how it helps to clarify his experience of Christ and ultimately also the La Verna event.

There is no doubt that early members of the Order saw parallels between the lives of Francis and Jesus. Thomas of Celano points out several and even tries to highlight those parallels with well-placed Scriptural allusions.[13] In his own writings, Francis certainly shows solicitude for doing what Jesus did. He explains in the *Rule*, for example, that the motivation for the special Lent of Benediction is that it was a period already consecrated

by Christ's fast (*"quam Dominus suo sancto ieiunio consecravit," Regula bullata* III:6).[14] Or again, he encourages the brothers not to be ashamed of needing to beg alms since Jesus "was poor and a stranger and lived on alms" (*Regula non bullata* IX:3-5; cf. *Regula bullata* VI:2-3). Along these lines, Clare reports these words from a last will that Francis wrote for the Poor Ladies of San Damiano: "I, little brother Francis, wish to follow the life and poverty of our most high Lord Jesus Christ and of His most holy Mother and to persevere in this until the end; and I ask of you, my ladies, and I give you my advice that you live always in this most holy life and poverty" (*Last Will for the Poor Ladies*, 1-2).[15]

This last example actually begins to bring us to the heart of the matter, because with it we come upon the key for understanding Francis's own manner of thinking: if he were to be asked to define this aspect of his spirituality he would not speak of "imitating" (*imitari*) but "following" (*sequi*) Christ.[16]

Both are biblical words, but the latter is favored by the Gospels to the complete exclusion of the former,[17] while the opposite is true for the writings of St. Paul.[18] Could it be that Paul, who was not a disciple during Christ's earthly life, could not conceive of "following" (*akolouthon*) Christ as did the Twelve, but instead sought to "imitate" (*mimeisthai*) his life and sentiments? Francis, like the Gospel writers, never uses *imitari* or *imitatio*.[19] The only time the word appears in his corpus is in a rubric later added as a title to *Admonition* VI, *De imitatione Domini*. This later addition is not a surprise, really, since the word quickly comes into use in the Franciscan family. But the latest editor of the writings sees the inconsistency of this and justifiably replaces the rubric with *De sequela Domini*, "Following the Lord."[20]

1. Story of an Evolution: Follower to *Alter Christus*

An excursus on the story of a language shift is necessary here in order to see the full implications of what is at stake. I will

briefly show how the conception of Francis grows in the course of about a century, passing from follower to imitator to conformed one to *alter Christus*.

Thomas of Celano may not strongly favor the word *imitari* when he first sets to writing, but he does use it. In fact, when he alludes to 1 Peter 2:21, "that you might follow in his footsteps [*ut sequamini vestigia eius*]," he replaces *sequi* with it: "His highest aim . . . was to follow the teaching of our Lord Jesus Christ and imitate His footsteps [*vestigia imitari*] completely" (*1 Celano* 84:1). And Thomas later will call Francis a "true imitator of Christ [*Christi verum imitatorem*]" (*2 Celano* 216:2). Clare uses exactly the same two expressions, surely having learned them from Thomas.[21] Bonaventure will speak of Francis having imitated the actions of Christ in his life to thus be conformed to him in his passion.[22]

With Bonaventure, this theme, which is present before but not central, begins to develop theologically. The usage of the word *imitari* is shifting. In most of the earlier cases it seems to have been a synonym for *sequi*, whereas later it begins to mean the path toward "identification" or "conformity." However, as Théophile Desbonnets has pointed out, it will still be a few decades before the theme becomes pivotal and develops strong overtones of the theme of literal observance, so dear to the Spiritual-Franciscan party. It is with the *Mirror of Perfection* that the shift becomes definitive, where the compiler "systematically changes the word *sequi* to *imitari* in the texts that he otherwise transcribes *ad litteram*."[23]

And the linguistic shift does not end there, at imitator. For Francis, who is the perfect imitator of Christ, arrives by his perfect imitation at perfect *conformity* to Christ (obvious above all in his stigmata). Only some ten or twenty years after the compilation of *Mirror of Perfection*, the *Acts of Blessed Francis* is able to make its programmatic opening phrase read: "One must first

of all know that our blessed Father Francis was conformed to Christ in all his deeds" (I:1).[24] Some of the ways that Francis was conformed to Christ are listed: as Christ had twelve apostles, Francis had twelve companions; as one of Christ's apostles hanged himself, John of Capella did the same; as Christ's apostles were admirable to all, so too were the holy companions of Francis, etc. (cf. *Acts of Blessed Francis* I:2-4).

Now, with the full arrival of the concept of conformity, the way is finally prepared for the theme of Francis as *alter Christus*, a term used for the first time in *The Acts of Blessed Francis and His Companions*. For example, Chap. VI, on the Lenten fast of St. Francis, explains:

> Because Francis, that very real servant of Christ, was in some ways another Christ [*alter Christus*] given to the world, God the Father made this fortunate man conformed [*fecit esse conformem*] in many things to Christ, his Son, as was apparent in his venerable band of holy companions, in the wonderful mystery of the stigmata of the Cross, and the holy fast of forty continuous days.[25]

With this we have arrived at the apex of the friars' conception of Francis. Desbonnets summarizes the lexical and conceptual evolutionary process we have seen:

> Francis, in accord with the spirituality of his century, preaches the *sequi vestigia Christi*. The Stigmata make him "conformed to Christ." To follow the footprints of Francis is, then, to follow someone who has become "another Christ." It is possible, then, like Francis, to become "another Christ," i.e., ultimately to imitate Christ.[26]

2. To Follow the Footsteps of the Lord

We are now in a position to return to the main thread of this discussion, namely that Francis did not conceive of himself as an "imitator" of Christ in the newer, developed sense of the term, but as a "follower" of Christ, the latter, to repeat, being a word he learned from the Gospels and from 1 Peter. What precisely

did Francis mean when he used the term *sequi*, and what might that teach us about his experience of God and of the stigmata?

Of the sixteen appearances of *sequi* in the writings of Francis,[27] thirteen are relevant to this discussion. Of these, two are direct citations of Jesus' words from the Gospels, five are direct citations or variations of 1 Peter 2:21, and the remaining six are original but in the spirit of these latter.

1 Peter 2:21 reads, "To this you have been called, because Christ also suffered for us, leaving you an example that you should follow in his footsteps."[28] The author is exhorting slaves suffering unjustly at the hands of their masters to bear patiently their situation. The phrase as it appears in the Vulgate seems to have resonated deeply with Francis, for he uses *sequi vestigia eius* and variations thereof frequently in his small corpus of writings, as follows: (1) in *Regula non bullata* I:1, Francis uses the phrase to complement and fill out the command of Jesus to "follow me" and as a precursor to the statement in *Regula bullata* I:1 that the Rule of the Friars Minor is to observe the Holy Gospel;[29] (2) when the Petrine phrase appears in *Regula non bullata* XXII:2, it is a careful application of the original context of 1 Peter, namely an encouragement to bear unjust persecution in the manner of Christ;[30] (3) *Letter to Leo* 12[31] seems to use the phrase as it had been used in *Regula non bullata* I:1, namely as a euphemism for "the life of the Friars Minor," which in this case means something like "Gospel discipleship"; it is noteworthy that the Lord's "footsteps" and "poverty" are conjoined;[32] (4) *2 Letter to the Faithful* 13 is relevant since the example and footsteps of Jesus, which Francis here says we must follow, are synonymous with the Father's will that Jesus be offered on the cross for the people's sins;[33] a careful look at the passage also reveals how Francis conceives the *sequi vestigia eius* as an entry into the life of the Trinity: in this case, for example, to follow the footsteps of Jesus is to enter into the will of the Father; in fact,

in (5) *Letter to the Order* 51-52, our final example, the *vestigia* of Jesus mark precisely the pathway that leads to the Father.[34]

A look at the other relevant *sequi* passages (those without *vestigia*) completes the picture: (1) as in *Letter to Leo* 12, *Regula non bullata* IX:1 sees "following the Lord" to mean following in particular the earthly poverty of Jesus, and here is added also "humility"; it is another passage consistent with the original meaning of 1 Peter 2:21, namely, it is an exhortation that says, "Christ accepted these things, so we should as well";[35] (2) Francis's last written words to the Poor Ladies of San Damiano are along similar lines;[36] (3) *Admonition* VI:1-3 explains that true followers of the Good Shepherd follow one who suffered on the cross to save his sheep, and so they must likewise follow him during times of tribulation and other suffering;[37] and (4) several passages use *sequi* to mean "obey," as in "to do the Lord's will."[38]

In summary, what emerges from an analysis of the *sequi vestigia eius* passages and the other *sequi* passages in Francis's writings are two themes. The first, inspired by the Petrine passage addressed to slaves, takes the form of an exhortation to notice that the paths Christ took during his earthly life were often sorrowful and imbued with poverty and suffering; and therefore, those whom Jesus has asked to follow him should expect that following in his footsteps will lead at times down similar paths. The second theme concerns how following in the footsteps of Jesus is to enter into the life of the Trinity, specifically by embarking on a path that is guided by the Father's will and leads to him. The first theme is simply a faithful application of the original biblical context, while the second is original to Francis and bespeaks, I would say, something important in his personal experience and meditation.

The first theme is interesting because it both shows that Francis undoubtedly thinks about or meditates on the earthly suffering and hardships of Jesus and reveals his peculiar manner

of conceiving his own such trials. Whereas one day Christian spirituality will be able to speak of "participation" in Christ's suffering, Francis does not. He could have spoken of wanting to "imitate" Christ's sufferings, "participate" in his passion, or even "make up in his own flesh what is lacking in Christ's sufferings" (Col 1:24). Instead, he speaks only of following a master, who was a suffering one, wherever he might go, which means also down paths of suffering. The difference is subtle because the end result probably looks the same; it is mostly the interior perspective and motivation that is different.

Meanwhile, the second theme is important because it too clarifies our picture of Francis's subjective stance towards Christ. His activity of meditating on Christ is obviously central to his basic *propositum*: he proposes a life of following in the footsteps of Christ, who was poor and who suffered. Still, this aspect does not stand on its own, isolated from a conscious relationship with the Trinity. Francis does not focus on Christ to the exclusion of the other persons of the Trinity. On the contrary, Francis focuses on Christ *so as* to enter into relationship with the Trinity. I would say that this is a key difference between the concept of imitator in question and Francis's concept of follower. And this also greatly clarifies the portrait of Francis's devotion, especially in light of common conceptions. While it had for so long been so often said that there is no better word to describe Francis than Christocentric,[39] more recently it has become fashionable to correct this and say that there is instead in Francis's spirituality a primacy of the Father.[40] In fact, both statements are reductive. It is better if we explain that Francis consciously cultivates a relationship with the whole Trinity, his relationship with one person putting him in relationship with the others. Such an outlook of Francis is not some theological precision that he developed later in life, but is instead a clear part of his early experience, evidenced by the fact that the *Forma vivendi* for

Clare and the Poor Ladies, likely traceable back to 1212, already bears this mark. Since the sisters have chosen to live according to the perfection of the Gospel (which is synonymous with following the footsteps of Jesus, as in *Regula non bullata* I:1ff), they have become daughters and handmaids of the Father, and spouses of the Holy Spirit.[41]

We can say in summary, then, that "imitation of Christ" in the later sense of the term (the path of acting out Christ's patterns of life with the hope of one day being identified with or conformed to him) is not characteristic of Francis's self-understanding or expression (even though we might be able to say that the later development is a viably consistent one for his followers). What is instead clearly central to Francis's *propositum* is the Gospel idea of "*following* Christ," which Francis knows will sometimes lead down paths of sufferings and hardship, since Jesus' earthly life did; and Francis believes doing so will be an entryway into a relationship with each of the Trinitarian persons.

V. FRANCIS'S MEDITATION ON THE PASSION

With these last points, I have already begun to anticipate this next section, in which I have to determine the place of the Passion of Jesus in the meditation of Francis.

As I have just said, we do not want to speak of a "primacy of the Father" in Francis's spirituality, nor even a "primacy of Jesus," but instead a mature Trinitarian spirituality where each divine person receives due attention according to the specific role that each person plays in the Christian life of grace. With this balanced perspective of Francis restored, it still should not come as a surprise that just because Francis is one who addresses most of his written prayers to the person of the Father, it does not mean that he never gives direct attention to Christ, and to Christ under the specific aspect of his humanity. No, Francis

is also the one who exhorts his confreres, "Let us all look at the good shepherd, brothers, who suffered the passion of the cross to save his sheep" (*Admonition* VI:1). A brief look at this aspect of Francis's interior life is necessary, therefore, in order to gain still further perspective for understanding what might have been Francis's experience of the stigmata.[42]

We know that Francis had devotion to the cross of Christ. He himself explains in his *Testament* that from early on in his converted life he would pray, "We adore You, Lord Jesus Christ, in all Your churches throughout the world, and we bless You, because by Your holy cross You have redeemed the world" (*Testament* 5). And it is known that Francis adopted the Tau cross even as his own signature.

But when he thought of the cross and the suffering of Jesus, how did he think of them? Was his meditation a "mysticism of the historical event," to borrow the terminology of one scholar?[43] Was it a practice of considering in an affective manner the concrete, historical details of the Passion?

I will limit myself to one simple point, which is this: those times that Francis does speak in his writings of the historical particulars of the Passion of Jesus, he does not do so with the affective emphasis that will later become indicative of Franciscan devotion,[44] nor does he pray to receive a participation in the Passion. Rather, Francis shows, I would say, a devotion to the Passion of Christ based more on a profound understanding of its meaning than on the emotions its consideration can produce. Here I briefly look at the texts.

In *2 Letter to the Faithful* 8-12, Francis recalls the suffering of Jesus in the Garden, including the specific, moving detail of his having sweat blood. But he does not remain only on the level of graphic description, but moves on to explain the important soteriological point that Jesus was doing the Father's will, and that this made his self-sacrifice salvific for us.[45] Similarly, the

same letter is able to exhort every creature to praise "him who suffered so much for us" (*2 Letter to the Faithful* 61).

As for *Admonition* VI, mentioned earlier, rather than "thinking about individual events of the historical passion," Francis is considering "the work of salvation in its wholeness."[46]

In *Regula non bullata* XXII:1-2, Francis speaks of Judas's betrayal of Jesus. Since his point is to expound on Christ's command to love one's enemies, he does not elaborate on all the historical details, for example the kiss.[47]

Then there is the entire Office Francis dedicated to the Passion. In all, there are fifteen psalms that Francis has composed, mostly by weaving together biblical phrases (largely from the Psalms and the Gospels, but other biblical books as well) that had probably been committed to memory.[48] This work confirms what the other sources have shown us, and also adds another element, which is that Francis's sense of Jesus' spiritual suffering is profounder and more important to him than that of the physical. For example, Psalm I (to be said at Compline during the Triduum and other weekdays of the year) paints the picture of Gethsemane rather well; yet, even while the reader can picture the condemnation, the kiss of betrayal, and the arrest of Jesus, more powerful is Francis's expression of the interior, spiritual sufferings of the Savior.[49] In a masterful way, the Psalmist's various words of lament are put onto the lips of Jesus, and his inner experience comes to life. A study of the rest of *Office of the Passion* reveals the same. There is a deep understanding of and devotion to the mystery of the Passion, but not one that bespeaks emphasis on the emotive or affective experience of that mystery.

Francis's own writings, therefore, do not seem to show us someone whose dominant spirituality features affective meditation on the Passion or prayers for participation in it. Rather, it is apparent that Francis had not only the capacity for, but also the

tendency to consider seriously the Passion in its deeper, theological significance.

We must presume that the experience of the stigmatization, which surely is fitted by God into Francis's concrete life and individual personality, does not do violence to his person and outlook, but instead builds on it and brings it to its full and proper fruition.

---

1 The interviews with Pio of Pietrelcina conducted under oath by Apostolic Visitator Raffaello Carlo Rossi in 1921 have recently been published in their entirety; within the Capuchin saint's three depositions is found a brief but frank account of his experience of receiving the wounds he would bear for the succeeding decades. See Francesco Castelli, *Padre Pio sotto inchiesta. L'"autobiografia" segreta*, prefazione di Vittorio Messori (Milano: Edizioni Ares, 2008), 220.

2 Grado Giovanni Merlo, "Le stimmate e la 'grande tentazione,'" in *Intorno a frate Francesco. Quattro studi*, Presenza di san Francesco 39 (Milano: Edizioni Biblioteca Francescana, 1993), 131-156, at 155. Cf. Raoul Manselli, *St. Francis of Assisi*, translated by Paul Duggan (Chicago: Franciscan Herald Press, 1988), 330-331.

3 "The Third Consideration on the Stigmata," in *The Little Flowers of Saint Francis: First Complete Edition, An Entirely New Version with Twenty Additional Chapters, also The Considerations on the Holy Stigmata, The Life and Sayings of Brother Giles*, a modern English translation from the Latin and the Italian, with introduction, notes and biographical sketches by Raphael Brown (Garden City: Image Books, 1958), 190-191, translation slightly modified. For the original see: *Delle Sacre Sante Istimate di Santo Francesco e delle loro considerazioni*, in *I Fioretti di San Francesco*, a cura di P. Benvenuto Bughetti (Quaracchi: Ex Typographia Collegii S. Bonaventurae, 1926), 183-254; now in *Fonti Francescane*, 1233-1272 (nos. 1896-1957). Introductions to the *Fioretti* and the Latin source on which they are largely based, *Actus beati Francisci et sociorum eius*, are found in F. Uribe, *Introduzione alle fonti*, 421-461.

4 Carlo Paolazzi, "Francis and His Use of Scribes: A Puzzle To Be Solved," translated by Edward Hagman, O.F.M. Cap., in *GreyfrRev* 18:3 (2004): 323-341.

5 Paolazzi in fact extends the demonstration to other Gospel-oriented words and concludes: "[I]n Francis's *Writings* the use of ten basic words (*good*, *master*, *father*, *my*, with the corresponding series *your-his-our-their*, plus *praise*), for a total of 1043 occurrences, does not deviate once from those norms for speaking (and thus for writing) that Francis drew from the pages of the Gospels with such religious reverence. Anyone at all familiar with the analysis of texts will agree that such absolute lexical rigor, systematically confirmed by the numbers, can be imagined only in an author who possesses within himself unwaveringly clear ideas . . ." "Francis and His Use of Scribes," 340.

6 Franciscus Assisiensis, *Regula bullata*, in *Scripta*, 322-339; Francis of Assisi, *The Later Rule*, in *FA:ED* I, 99-106.

7 Critical edition: Herbert Grundmann, "*Die Bulle 'Quo Elongati' Papst Gregors IX*," *ArchFrancHist* 54 (1961): 3-25; *Quo elongati of Gregory IX*, in *FA:ED* I, 570-575.

8 André Vauchez, "Francesco d'Assisi e il vangelo tra lettera e spirito," in *FrateFr* 74 (2008): 325-338 (author's translation and elaboration of his "François d'Assise entre littéralisme évangélique et renouveau spirituel," in *Frate Francesco d'Assisi*, Atti del XXI Convengo Internazionale, Assisi, 14 -16 ottobre 1993 [Centro Italiano di Studi sull'Alto Medievo, 1994], 185-198). Now see also, A. Vauchez, *Francesco d'Assisi. Tra storia e memoria*, 281-292.

9 Text in: *Scripta*, 394-405 and *FA:ED* I: 124-127.

10 Text of the rule is found at: Franciscus Assisiensis, *Regula non bullata*, in *Scripta*, 242-289; Francis of Assisi, *The Earlier Rule*, in *FA:ED* I, 63-86.

11 "Et ubicumque sunt fratres, qui scirent et cognoscerent, se non posse regulam spiritualiter observare, ad suos ministros debeant et possint recurrere."

12 Cf. A. Vauchez, "Tra lettera e spirito," 332. Alfonso Marini's study is excellent as well and concludes that rather than speaking of the "literalism" of Francis one has to speak of his "concreteness": "In fact, Francis had a sense of the concreteness of the Scriptures and of the demands it made upon the believer. Hence, his was certainly an interpretation 'incarnated' into his time and into the spiritual and corporal needs of his contemporaries; no intellectualized allegory, classroom style, but a concreteness even in his spiritual interpretation . . . It is a concreteness that draws him, even as a young man, to rebuild churches and nurse lepers, beyond any literal dictate of Scripture." Alfonso Marini, "'*Vestigia Christi Sequi*' or '*Imitatio Christi*': Two Different Ways of Understanding Francis of Assisi's Gospel Life," translated by Cyprian Rosen, O.F.M. Cap., *GreyfrRev* 11:3 (1997): 331-358, at 351.

13 The very first preaching of Francis is shown to parallel the very first preaching of Jesus (*1 Celano* 23:4; cf. Matt 4:17). Francis also acts very much like Christ when he sends out his disciples two by two (*1 Celano* 29; cf. Mark 6:7; Luke 10:1). When his own preaching is like that of Jesus who "went around to the cities and villages . . . teaching the way of salvation" (*1 Celano* 36:1; cf. Matt 9:35). Francis teaches his disciples to pray, just as Jesus taught his disciples (*1 Celano* 45:1; cf. Luke 11:1; Matt 6:9). While Thomas is speaking of the obedience of creatures to Francis, he relates that once water was even changed to wine for Francis (*1 Celano* 61:6; cf. John 2:9).

14 This and several other examples are found in: Etienne Ledeur, "The Spiritual Tradition," in Edouard Cothenet, Etienne Ledeur, Pierre Adnés, Aimé Solignac, and Bernard Spaapen, *Imitating Christ*, translated by Simone Inkel and Lucy Tinsley, with a preface by John L. Boyle (St. Meinrad: Abbey Press, 1974 (translation of the article *Imitation du Christ* and of the second part of the article *Imitation du Christ [Livre]*, in *Dictionnaire de Spiritualité*, vol. 7:2 [Paris: Beauchesne, 1971], cols. 1536-1601 and 2355-2368), 51.

15 Found in *Regula Clarae* VI:7-9. Text of her Rule is at: Clara Assisiensis, *Regula*, in *Fontes*, 2291-2307; Clare of Assisi, *The Form of Life of Saint Clare*, in

The Lady: Clare of Assisi: Early Documents, edited and translated by Regis J. Armstrong, O.F.M. Cap. (Hyde Park, NY: New City Press, 2006), 108-126. Excerpted text of the *Last Will* can also be found at: Franciscus Assisiensis, *Ultima voluntas ad Claram et sorores*, in *Scripta*, 382.

16 There are already excellent studies on this: Giovanni Iammarrone, "La 'sequela di Cristo' nelle Fonti francescane," *MiscFranc* 82 (1982): 417-461; A. Marini, "Vestigia Christi Sequi" *or* "Imitatio Christi"; Alfonso Marini, "Dalla *sequela* alla *conformitas*. Una ricerca su fonti francescane," in *Franciscana* VII (2005): 69-87. Before these, however, Ledeur had already noticed this important lexical phenomenon in Francis's writings and had drawn valid conclusions from it. See: "The Spiritual Tradition," 50-53.

17 E.g. Mark 2 :14: "And when he was passing by, he saw Levi the son of Alpheus sitting at the receipt of custom; and he said to him: Follow me. And rising up, he followed him" [*et ait illi: Sequere me. Et surgens secutus est eum*] (cf. Matt 9:9; Luke 5 :27); Mark 8:22: "Jesus said to him, 'Follow me, and leave the dead to bury their dead'" [*sequere me, et dimitte mortuos sepelíre mortuos suos*] (cf. Luke 9 :59); Mark 8:34: "And calling the multitude together with his disciples, he said to them: If any man will follow me, let him deny himself, and take up his cross, and follow me" [*si quis vult me sequi, deneget semetípsum: et tollat crucem suam, et sequatur me*] (cf. Matt 16:24; Luke 9:23; John 12:26); John 13:36: "Simon Peter said to him: Lord, where are you going? Jesus answered: Where I go, you can not follow me now; but you shall follow hereafter" [*quo ego vado non potes me modo sequi: sequeris autem postea*], et alia.

18 E.g., 1 Cor 11:1: "Be imitators of me, as I am of Christ" [*imitatores mei estote, sicut et ego Christi*]; 1 Thess 1:6: "And you became imitators of us [*et vos imitatores nostri facti estis*] and of the Lord, for you received the word in much affliction, with joy inspired by the Holy Spirit" (cf. 2 Thess 3:7,9; cf. 1 Cor 4:16), et alia.

19 Cf. Jean-François Godet and George Mailleux, *Opuscula sancti Francisci, Scripta sanctae Clarae. Concordance, Index, Listes de fréquence, Tables comparatives*, Corpus des Sources Franciscaines V (Louvain: Publications du CETEDOC, Université Catholique de Louvain, 1976), 133.

20 *Scripta*, 360.

21 *Testament of Clare* 5: "The Son of God has become for us the Way that our blessed father Francis, His true lover and imitator [*verus amator et imitator ipsius*], has shown and taught us by word and example"; 36: "And, while he lived, our most blessed father Francis, having imitated His footprints [*eius vestigia imitatus*], never either in example or in teaching turned away from this holy poverty that he had chosen for himself and his brothers; 56-57: "I admonish and exhort in the Lord Jesus Christ all my sisters, both those present and those to come, to strive always to imitate the way of holy simplicity, humility and poverty and also the integrity of our holy way of living, as we were taught from the beginning of our conversion by Christ and by our blessed father Francis." Clara Assisiensis, *Testamentum Clarae*, in *Fontes*, 2311-2319; Clare of Assisi, *Testament*, in *The Lady*, 60-65.

22 *Major Legend* XIII:2:3: " . . . quod sicut Christum fuerat imitatus in actibus

vitae, sic conformis ei esse deberet in afflictionibus et doloribus passionis . . ."

23 Théophile Desbonnets, "La Lettre à tous les fidèles de François d'Assise," in *I Frati Minori e il Terzo Ordine. Problemi e discussioni storiografiche*, Atti del XXIII Convegno del Centro di studi sulla spiritualità medievale, 17-20 ottobre 1982 (Todi, 1985), 53-76, at 64-65; cited in A. Marini, *'Sequi' or 'imitatio,'* 353. A more recent study has verified this claim: Silvia Romanelli, "*Sequela*, *imitatio* e *conformitas* in fonti francescane 'non ufficiali,'" in *Franciscana* VII (2005): 89-126, esp. at 113-124. Some examples of the fourteenth-century editor's interventions are as follows. *Mirror of Perfection* 14:1 changes its source (represented for us by *2 Celano* 65:1 / *Assisi Compilation* 27:1), modifying the appellative of Francis, "true friend of God" [*verum summopere amicus Dei*], to "true friend and imitator of Christ" [*verus amicus et imitator Dei*]. Or again, the editor seizes the opportunity at 88:4-9 to elaborate the story of Francis who is on his deathbed asking that the Johannine passage of the Last Supper be read to him (cf. *1 Celano* 110:1-3; *Assisi Compilation* 22:3-9), adding: "Desiring to imitate [*imitari*] his Lord and Master in death, whom he had perfectly imitated in life [*quem in vita sua perfecte fuerat imitatus*], he ordered loaves of bread, etc."; "And it is clear he wished to do this in imitation of Christ [*ad similitudinem Christi*] because he later asked if the day were a Thursday." A significant intervention—though not entirely surprising since *1 Celano* 84:1 had already invented the phrase—is at 43:7-8, where the *sequi* of *Assisi Compilation* 49:8-9 / *2 Celano* 148:16-17 (and originally, 1 Peter 1:21) is changed to *imitari*. In addition to these direct interventions in its source, *Mirror of Perfection* also takes other opportunities to introduce the notion of imitation of Christ by way of addition (e.g., 72:1-3,8; 87:10). The compilation, then, indeed seems to signal a shift in the way of conceiving Francis: from follower to imitator. To this I would only add that an important, slightly earlier, example (and proof of the Spiritual-Franciscan influence on the concept) is to be found in the 1305 *Arbor vitae*. Ubertino of Casale, *The Tree of the Crucified Life of Jesus (Bk. V, Chap. 3-7)*, in *FA:ED* III, 146-203; Latin (non-critical) edition: Ubertino da Casale, *Arbor vitae crucifixae Jesu*, 1485; reprint facsimile, Charles T. David, Monumenta Politica et Philosophica Rariora, Series I:4 (Torino: Bottega d'Erasmo, 1961). Two citations will make the point: "For if we are to talk of the way he lived, who is capable of telling in full how he sought to imitate the closest likeness to the life of Christ? His whole aim, in public and in private, was to reproduce in himself and in others those footprints of Christ which had been covered over and forgotten. And the unique privilege granted the blessed Francis was this: to be the first entitled to transmit to holy Church the life of Jesus, scrupulously in all its aspects, in a communal and durable state through his Order" (Bk. V, Chap. III [1485 edition, 421b, n. 54]); and, "Insofar as it was possible, and allowing for due proportion in certain areas, it was the entire life of the blessed Jesus, his most holy model, that Francis strove to imitate: Jesus' life spent as the price of the redemption of sinners, his daily exemplary conduct, his mirror-like contemplation, the mystery of his doctrinal instruction, his stooping to remedy the maladies of the frail" (Bk. V, Chap. III [p. 430b, n. 22]).

24 "Primo ergo sciendum est quod b.p.n. Franciscus in omnibus suis actibus

fuit Christo conformis." For the text of this work of the second quarter of the fourteenth century, see: *The Deeds of Blessed Francis and His Companions by Ugolino Boniscambi of Montegiorgio*, in *FA:ED* III, 435-565; *Actus beati Francisci et sociorum eius*, nuova edizione postuma di Jacques Cambell con testo dei Fioretti a fronte, a cura di Marino Bigaroni e Giovanni Boccali, Chiesa Nuova 5 (S. Maria degli Angeli—Assisi: Edizioni Porziuncola, 1988); now also in *Fontes*, 2085-2219.

25 "Verissimus servus Dei Franciscus, quia in quibusdam fuit quasi alter Christus datus in mundo, ideo Deus Pater tam felicem hominem in multis Cristo, suo Filio fecit esse conformem, sicut apparuit in sanctorum sociorum sacro collegio, in stigmatum crucis mirando misterio et s. quadragesime continuato ieiunio" (*Acts of Blessed Francis* VI:1-2). Or again: "Falling at his feet, stamped with divine markings, she [Lady Jacoba] received there such consolation, grace and abundance of tears, that just as the Magdalene washed the feet of the Lord with tears her faithful lips were pressing kisses all over the feet of one like another Christ [*quasi alterius Christi*], as she was devoutly crying and embracing them in such a way that the brothers were not able to tear her away from the feet of the saint" (*Acts of Blessed Francis* XVIII:26-7). Cf. Stanislao da Campagnola, *L'Angelo del sesto sigillo e l'"Alter Christus.' Genesi e sviluppo di due temi francescani nei secoli XIII-XIV*, Studi e Ricerche 1 (Roma: Antonianum—Laurentianum, 1971), 203-204.

26 T. Desbonnets, "La Lettre à tous les fidèles," 64-65; cited in A. Marini, "'Sequi' or 'imitatio,'" 353. This general outline seems basically tenable. I would only add a thought as to the origin of imitation language. Why, for example, would a Thomas of Celano think of the word "imitari" in the first place when he was citing the "sequi" of 1 Peter 2:21? The language and concept of imitation had already made an appearance during the early reflections on martyrdom (cf. E. Ledeur, "The Spiritual Tradition," 37-42) and had strong moments of crystallization in certain monastic authors (cf. Ewert Cousins, "The Humanity and the Passion of Christ," in *Christian Spirituality: High Middle Ages and Reformation* [vol. 2], edited by Jill Raitt [New York: Crossroad, 1987], 377-380), but I suspect that it reaches the Franciscan authors immediately through Bernard of Clairvaux. E.g., "All men therefore wish to enjoy you but not to the extent of following your example [*at non ita et imitari*]; they will reign with you but not suffer with you" (*Sermon XXI*, 2; *PL* 183, col. 873); "Only those are temperate who take pains to follow his way of life [*qui eius vitam imitari student*] . . ." (*Sermon XXII*, 11; *PL* 183, col. 883). Writers such as Thomas were certainly familiar with Bernard, while the populace not as much so. I mean to say that I think the language should be attributed immediately to Bernard, though the popularity (and a certain transformation) of the concept, which did not catch on right away, must be attributed to the Minors, who discovered in it the perfect way to make sense of their founder.

27 Leaving aside the three in the *Fragmenta alterius Regulae non bullatae*.

28 "In hoc enim vocati estis, quia et Christus passus est pro nobis, vobis relinquens exemplum, ut sequamini vestigia eius."

29 *Regula non bullata* I:1: "[1]The rule and life of these brothers is this, namely: 'to live in obedience, in chastity, and without anything of their own,' and to follow

the teaching and footprints of our Lord Jesus Christ [*Domini nostri Jesu Christi doctrinam et vestigia sequi*], Who says: [2] If you wish to be perfect, go, sell everything you have and give it to the poor, and you will have treasure in heaven; and come, follow me [*veni, sequere me*]. [3] And: If anyone wishes to come after me, let him deny himself and take up his cross and follow me [*tollat crucem suam et sequatur me*]."

30 "[1] All my brothers: let us pay attention to what the Lord says: Love your enemies and do good to those who hate you [2] for our Lord Jesus Christ, Whose footprints we must follow [*cuius sequi vestigia debemus*], called His betrayer a friend and willingly offered Himself to His executioners. [3] Our friends, therefore, are all those who unjustly inflict upon us distress and anguish, shame and injury, sorrow and punishment, martyrdom and death."

31 Franciscus Assisiensis, *Epistola ad fratrem Leonem*, in *Scripta*, 158-159; Francis of Assisi, *A Letter to Brother Leo*, FA:ED I, 122-123.

32 "Brother Leo . . . in whatever way it seems better to you to please the Lord God and to follow his footprints and poverty [*sequi vestigia et paupertatem suam*], do it with the blessing of the Lord God and my obedience."

33 "[6] And as His Passion was near, He celebrated the Passover with His disciples and, taking bread, gave thanks, blessed and broke it, saying: Take and eat: This is My Body. [7] And taking the cup He said: This is My Blood of the New Covenant which will be poured out for you and for many for the forgiveness of sins. [8] Then He prayed to His Father, saying: Father, if it can be done, let this cup pass from me. [9] And His sweat became as drops of blood falling on the ground. [10] Nevertheless, He placed His will in the will of His Father, saying: Father, let Your will be done; not as I will, but as You will. [11] His Father's will was such that His blessed and glorious Son, Whom He gave to us and Who was born for us, should offer Himself through His own blood as a sacrifice and oblation on the altar of the cross: [12] not for Himself through Whom all things were made, but for our sins, [13] leaving us an example that we might follow His footprints [*relinquens nobis exemplum, ut sequamur vestigia eius*]."

34 "[50]Almighty, eternal, just and merciful God [*Deus*], give us miserable ones the grace to do for You alone what we know you want us to do and always to desire what pleases You. [51] Inwardly cleansed, interiorly enlightened, and inflamed by the fire of the Holy Spirit, may we be able to follow in the footprints of Your beloved Son, our Lord Jesus Christ [*sequi possimus vestigia dilecti Filii tui, Domini nostri Jesu Christi*], [52] and, by Your grace alone, may we make our way to You, Most High, Who live and rule in perfect Trinity and simple Unity, and are glorified God almighty, forever and ever. Amen." Franciscus Assisiensis, *Epistola toti Ordini missa*, in *Scripta*, 210-221; Francis of Assisi, *A Letter to the Entire Order*, in *FA:ED* I, 116-121.

35 "[1]Let all the brothers strive to follow the humility and poverty of our Lord Jesus Christ and let them remember that we should have nothing else in the whole world except, as the Apostle says: having food and clothing, we are content with these."

36 *Last Will for the Poor Ladies*, 1-2: "[1] I, little brother Francis, wish to follow the

life and poverty of our most high Lord Jesus Christ [*volo sequi vitam et paupertatem altissimi Domini nostri Jesu Christi*] and of His most holy Mother and to persevere in this until the end; [2] and I ask of you, my ladies, and I give you my advice that you live always in this most holy life and poverty. And keep careful watch that you never depart from this by reason of the teaching or advice of anyone."

37 "[1] Let all of us, brothers, consider the Good Shepherd Who bore the suffering of the cross to save His sheep. [2] The Lord's sheep followed Him in tribulation and persecution [*secutae fuerunt eum in tribulatione et persecutione*] in shame and hunger, in weakness and temptation, and in other ways; and for these things they received eternal life from the Lord. [3] Therefore, it is a great shame for us, the servants of God, that the saints have accomplished great things and we want only to receive glory and honor by recounting and preaching them."

38 *Regula non bullata* XXII:9: "Now that we have left the world, however, we have nothing else that we must do except be sollicitous to follow the will of the Lord [*sequi voluntatem Domini*] and to please Him"; *Office of the Passion* VII:8: "[8]Take up your bodies and carry His holy cross and follow His most holy commands even to the end"; *Office of the Passion* XV:13: "[13] Take up your bodies and carry His holy cross and follow His most holy commands even to the end."

39 E.g., Eric Doyle and Damian McElrath, "St. Francis of Assisi and the Christocentric Character of Franciscan Life and Doctrine," in *Franciscan Christology*, edited by Damian McElrath (St. Bonaventure, NY: Franciscan Institute, 1980), 1-13, at 1.

40 Cf. Thaddée Matura, O.F.M., *Francis of Assisi: The Message in His Writings*, translated by Paul Barrett, O.F.M. Cap. (St. Bonaventure, NY: Franciscan Institute, 1997), 87.

41 *Regula Clarae* VI:3-4: "Quia divina inspiratione fecistis vos filias et ancillas altissimi summi Regis, Patris caelestis, et Spiritui Sancto vos desponsastis eligendo vivere secundum perfectionem sancti Evangelii, volo et promitto per me et fratres meos semper habere de vobis . . . curam." Cf. Wiesław Block, "La *protoregola* alla luce della Forma vivendi data a Chiara a alle consorelle di S. Damiano," in *La grazia delle origini. Studi in occasione dell'VIII centenario dell'approvazione della prima regola di san Francesco d'Assisi (1209-2009)*, a cura di Paolo Martinelli (Bologna: EDB, 2009), 101-136.

42 O. Schmucki, "The Passion of Christ in the Life of Francis," cited earlier, remains an indispensible resource, despite a few outdated aspects. As usual, Schmucki's exhaustive bibliography is alone something to marvel at, while his systematic treatment of the primary texts saves us much time.

43 E. Cousins, "The Humanity and the Passion of Christ," 383.

44 Bonaventure's 1260 work, *Lignum vitae* (e.g., no. 26), shows the direction (Bonaventure of Bagnoregio, *The Tree of Life*, in *The Works of Bonaventure, Cardinal, Seraphic Doctor and Saint*, vol. 1, *Mystical Opuscula*, translated from the Latin by José de Vinck [Paterson: St. Anthony Guild Press, 1960], 95-144; *Lignum vitae*, in *Doctoris Seraphici Bonaventurae S. R. E. Episcopi Cardinalis Opera Omnia*, edita studio et cura PP. Collegii a S. Bonaventura, Tomus VIII [Quaracchi: Ex Typographia Collegii S. Bonaventurae, 1898], 68-87). Still stronger, and with

more explicit emphasis on stirring the heart's affections, would be a work like that of James of Milan, probably written within the quarter century after Bonaventure's work (*Stimulus Amoris fr. Jacobi Mediolanunsis*, Biblioteca Franciscana Ascetica Medii Aevi IV, edita a PP. Collegii S. Bonaventurae [Quaracchi: Ex Typographia Collegii S. Bonaventurae, 1905]).

45 *2 Letter to the Faithful* 8-12: "[8] Then He prayed to His Father, saying: Father, if it can be done, let this cup pass from me. [9] And His sweat became as drops of blood falling on the ground. [10] Nevertheless, He placed His will in the will of His Father, saying: Father, let Your will be done; not as I will, but as You will. [11] His Father's will was such that His blessed and glorious Son, Whom He gave to us and Who was born for us, should offer Himself through His own blood as a sacrifice and oblation on the altar of the cross: [12] not for Himself through Whom all things were made, but for our sins . . ."

46 O. Schmucki, "The Passion of Christ in the Life of Francis," 22.

47 "[1] All my brothers: let us pay attention to what the Lord says: Love your enemies and do good to those who hate you [2] for our Lord Jesus Christ, Whose footprints we must follow, called His betrayer a friend and willingly offered Himself to His executioners." Cf. O. Schmucki, "The Passion of Christ in the Life of Francis," 24.

48 For introduction to *Office of the Passion* see O. Schmucki, "The Passion of Christ in the Life of Francis," 25-28; Leonhard Lehmann, *Francesco, Maestro di preghiera* (Roma: Istituto Storico Dei Cappuccini, 1993), 123-155; Fernando Uribe, *Orar como Francisco. Notas y sugerencias sobre las oraciones del Santo de Asís*, Colección Karisma 2 (Santiago de Cali: Curso Carisma Misionero Franciscano, 2008), 99-148.

49 Cf. O. Schmucki, "The Passion of Christ in the Life of Francis," 30.

Chapter 14: *PRAISES FOR GOD*, NOTHING OF ONE'S OWN

Having established some foundational layers of Francis's general spiritual portrait, particularly in regard to his subjective way of standing toward Christ and the Gospel, I would like to see how the emerging picture can dovetail with a more direct look at the La Verna event of 1224. In this chapter I will look to *The Praises of God* to be a kind of autobiographical source for us, and I will expound upon the themes that emerge from it by surveying Francis's writings.

I. *The Praises of God*

If there is any source for the stigmata experience of Francis that can be called in some manner a primary, autobiographical one, it would be *The Praises of God.* For, as we have seen, Leo explains that these praises were written by Francis precisely in thanksgiving for the seraph apparition and the impression of the stigmata (*Rubrics of Leo* 5-6). In some manner, then, they should reflect something of Francis's experience, something of his spiritual mindset after the La Verna event. Three things, I suggest, emerge. First, the praises evidence the joy and consolation of the seraph vision. Second, they reveal Francis's reverent consideration of Christ, the meek, Crucified One. Finally, they demonstrate how little Francis was tempted to think of himself after the experience.

I briefly mentioned this piece earlier (when I introduced *The Rubrics of Leo* in Part One) as the prayer of praise found on the flesh side of the *Chartula* of Assisi.[1] Today on the parchment

remain sixteen lines, the last of which is no longer able to be read. Other words and phrases as well are by now illegible, although Attilio Bartoli Langeli has done a masterful job at improving the previous editions. Some early manuscripts, like the fourteenth-century Assisi Cod. 344, fill in the gaps left by impossible readings, and Paolazzi has given convincing reasons to trust the traditional reading also of a seventeenth line, which has apparently been altogether severed from the little paper.[2]

In translation, the prayer could read like this:

> 1 You are holy, Lord God alone, *who works wonders*.
> 2 You are strong, you are great, you are the Most High.
> 3 You are almighty. You, *holy Father*, King of heaven
> 4 and earth. You are three and one, Lord God
> 5 of gods. You are the good, all good, the highest good,
> 6 Lord God living and true. You are love, charity.
> 7 You are wisdom, you are humility, *you are patience*.
> 8 You are beauty, you are security, you are rest.
> 9 You are gladness and joy. You are our hope. You are justice
> 10 and temperance. You are everything, our riches to sufficiency.
> 11 You are beauty, you are meekness,
> 12 *you are protector*. You are our guardian and defender,
> 13 you are strength, you are refuge. You are our hope,
> 14 you are our faith, you are our charity.
> 15 You are [—]. You are all our sweetness, you are
> 16 our eternal life, great and wonderful
> 17 Lord, God Almighty, merciful Savior.[†]

Here I have simply reproduced the text in its diplomatic edition, while others have attempted to add verse divisions that would reflect the content.[3] For my part, I see on the most basic level a two-fold thematic structure: (1) vv. 1-6a: confession of God as he is in himself; (2) vv. 6b-17: confession of God-for-us.

The first part, addressing God as he is in himself, has strong liturgical reminiscences, as some have noted.[4] It is initially addressed to the Father (*Pater sancte*, v. 3), and then continues with a confession of God the Trinity (*Tu es trinus et unus*, v. 4).

In the second part, Francis prays to the economic God. "Patience" (v. 7), for example, is a quality that God exemplifies only in relation to his creatures. Likewise, "security" and "rest" (v. 8-9), "protector," and "guardian" (v. 12), etc. Francis uses *noster* eight times in the last nine verses.

Where the first part of the prayer is addressed to the Father and the Trinity, the second part seems to be largely addressed to Jesus. I say this because certain phrases clearly recall the kenotic activity and sentiments of the Incarnate Son: Francis confesses to God that he is *humilitas* (v. 7), *patientia* (v. 7), and *mansuetudo* (v. 11). This last adjective, for example, calls to mind Jesus who is "meek and humble of heart,"[5] the humble king who fulfilled prophecy by entering Jerusalem riding on an ass,[6] the "meek lamb led to the slaughter" (Jer 11:19).[7] Verse 17 speaks of God as savior.

It would, therefore, be too much to suggest that this prayer (which, it is true, never mentions the name of Jesus) is only addressed to the Father.[8] Sometimes, such a reading is preferred by historians who want to emphasize that Francis's seraph apparition was not necessarily experienced by Francis as an apparition of Christ. I too concluded at the end of Part Two that at the current state of the question it is very difficult to securely base on the extant sources the ideas that Francis had an apparition of a man-seraph (as opposed to a simple seraph), and that his apparition was temporally very close to the appearance of the wounds on his body (as opposed to happening simply during the same retreat on La Verna). But these conclusions I reached need not suggest in any way that Francis had no meditation on Christ during his retreat on La Verna, least of all after the appearance of the wounds on his body.

And yet, it is true that Francis does not mention the wounds of Christ in *The Praises of God.* Nor does he even speak of the anguish and interior suffering of Christ (while he had done so in

Office of the Passion). Nor, in fact, does the word "seraph" appear in the prayer. What experience, then, is Francis truly reflecting in this composition? Can we reasonably say that this prayer expresses anything of the stigmata experience of Francis that I tried to reconstruct in Chapter 12? Should we doubt whether this prayer was really composed in thanksgiving for the *beneficium* of the vision and stigmata?

Paolazzi's commentary on the prayer helps answer these questions by returning to the chronologically earliest written account of the stigmata event, that of *1 Celano*, in an effort to tease out elements of the mystical experience of Francis latent within the prayer. He proceeds by noting an important convergence of *The Praises of God* and *1 Celano*. In *The Praises of God*, Francis's words call to mind not so much the suffering servant that had no "form or comeliness that we should look at him, and no beauty that we should desire him" (Is 53:2), but instead reflect the experience of a more glorious, triumphant God; in this way, while God is indeed "meekness," he is simultaneously "beauty" (v. 11).[9] And this is exactly how Thomas of Celano understood Francis's experience of the seraph: Francis "greatly rejoiced and was thoroughly delighted"[10] by the seraph whose "beauty was beyond comprehension" (*1 Celano* 94:4).[11] For my part, I would add that Thomas of Celano's version not only happily converges with *The Praises of God* but also *The Assisi Compilation*, for the author of *The Assisi Compilation* episode describes how the seraph experience of Francis was the source of profound consolation and joy, such as to last the rest of his life (118:13). Moreover, I mentioned in an earlier note that the *allocutio* of the Seraph mentioned in *Rubrics of Leo* may be translated as "consolation," or "consoling word." It is no surprise, therefore, that Francis is bubbling over with the kind of excitement that pervades *The Praises of God*.

So, the first conclusion regarding our subject is that the

Praises of God seem to betray the mystical experiences of Francis on La Verna. We must say that they overflow with the joy and consolation of the seraph vision and simultaneously show a deep reverence (but clearly not a brooding or melancholic one) for the humble God who has made himself meek and savior, the God who has been crucified—no, it is true that Francis does not use the word, but is it not implied? Indeed, I do not think that before the stigmatization Francis was retracing the details of the historical events of the Passion in his meditation, and that for that reason Jesus Crucified was on his mind and found his way into this prayer. I think, rather, that Francis was pushed beyond himself to a meditation on the humble and wounded Jesus when he looked at the wounds now on his own body. This is a point that I think will become easier to appreciate as my argument unfolds.

The second conclusion is a negative one, namely this: where Francis focuses tremendous attention on the greatness and goodness of God, he focuses not at all on himself, and least of all on his stigmatic marks or probable pain. Leonhard Lehmann explains:

> In the *Praises*, Francis does not treat of himself, but only of the You of God: neither "I" nor "me" ever appear. It is therefore a prayer that is purified of every relationship to the "I"; it is a perfect gift of self, a pure gaze at the other; it is a realization of the mystery of God welcomed with internal fervor, without the taking of positions, without questions, without requests: it is pure praise of God.[12]

This insight is an important one, if we are to understand Francis's subjective experience of the mystical phenomena he lived. I will take it up in a broader way in the next section.

The little autograph prayer of *The Praises of God*, in conclusion, which we have from the stigmatized hand of Francis, clarifies for us that the mystical experiences of La Verna were characterized by a great joy and consolation, a reverent consideration of Christ Crucified,[13] and a striking absence of self-interest or consideration.

II. HAVING NOTHING OF ONE'S OWN; RETURNING GOOD TO GOD

As we have seen in this study, the stigmata of Francis were a "great secret." And this has now been confirmed in some manner by the fact that Francis does not allude to the wounds in his *laudes*. This could raise concerns about the veracity of the stigmata, or at least about whether the experience was subjectively significant to Francis. In fact, the opposite is true: the "secrecy" of Francis that continues in *The Praises of God* finds its *ratio* in certain elements of Francis's religious experience, the understanding of which will move us still further along in painting our portrait of Francis's interior experience.

Cesare Vaiani's studies,[14] which make excellent syntheses of the Poverello's spiritual experience based not on preconceptions but on sound and carefully applied methodology, have shown that all the essential elements of Francis's spirituality finally can be reduced to three; they are like three reference points that pervade all the other moments of his spiritual experience,[15] and are: (1) having the Spirit of the Lord, (which we saw earlier in this chapter, for example, as Francis's solution for the potential pitfall of a literalistic following of the Gospel); (2) living without anything of one's own (*sine proprio*); and (3) returning (*reddere*) to God all good, which belongs to him.[16]

The relevance that Vaiani's synthetic conclusions have for my study, I suggest, is that the latter two elements seem not only to be noticeable in Francis's experience of the stigmata, but to completely pervade it.

We may begin, for example, with Francis's oft-repeated exhortation to return all good to God. Already we have seen how carefully Francis observed the exhortation of Jesus to call no one good but God. Francis must have made extensive meditations on this passage, or experienced the reality of it acutely, because

there emerges in his writings a well-developed expression of it, one that seems to be unique to him.

If anyone does any good, Francis is certain that it is a good that the "Lord says or does through him" (*Dominus operatur per ipsum*), which is the way the phrase occurs and recurs many times in Francis's corpus of writings.[17] And since Francis believes that a servant of God must not have anything of his own anyway,[18] and certainly not anything that does not belong to him or is not attributable to him, then all good must be restored or given back to God by attributing it to him.[19]

This element of Francis's spiritual experience appears so mature and clear, and recurs with such consistent insistence, that it is unimaginable, it seems to me, that Francis would not have experienced the stigmata in its light. When Francis saw wounds on his own body in the form of Christ's own saving ones, he must have seen good things that did not belong to him, and so he "returned" them to God by not appropriating them or drawing attention to himself. That is why he kept the wounds secret, insofar as it was reasonable and human to do so. Thomas of Celano, the first to speak of Francis's great secret and the motivation for it, must not have been far off because his words are in harmony with Francis's:

> Although the servant and friend of the Most High saw himself adorned with such magnificent pearls, like precious stones, and marvelously decorated beyond the glory and honor of all others, still his heart did not grow vain. He did not seek to use this to make himself appealing to anyone in a desire for vainglory. Rather in every way possible he tried to hide these marks, so that human favor would not rob him of the grace given him (*1 Celano* 95:10-11).

It would seem that the "good" of Francis's stigmata were to him little more than a reminder of God's goodness, specifically the goodness of Jesus and his saving cross. That is why *The Praises of God* speak not at all of Francis, but remember God

who became meek and humble, the merciful savior (vv. 7; 11; 17). It is why Francis drew a picture of the salvific event of Golgotha on the other side of the same parchment.

My idea seems also to be supported by and consistent with another theory of Vaiani's, which takes its point of departure from Francis's formulaic exhortation to not just see (*vedere*) the consecrated host on the altar but, through the Spirit, to "see and believe" (*vedere et credere*) "that it is truly the Body and Blood of our Lord Jesus Christ" (*Admonition* I:8-9).[20] Vaiani's suggestion is that this formula of Francis does not apply only to the Eucharist, but is programmatic for Francis's whole spiritual itinerary.[21] Thus, in the *Testament* Francis reinterprets his whole life through a lens where he does not merely *see* each successive stage in his memory, but seems to *see and believe*[22] that each new thing was given to him by the Lord ("Dominus dedit mihi fratri Francisco"), as he states at the transition points of the text (cf. vv. 1; 2; 4; 6; 14; 23; 39). I think Vaiani is correct on this general point. If we apply it to our case, it seems that there is enough reason to legitimately conclude that Francis's own stigmata were for him something like a sign that he tried to avoid merely seeing, instead choosing to see and believe in the thing the sign pointed to, the mystery of salvation. That would be consistent with the portrait of Francis seen through the Writings.

In summary, Francis's experience of his own wounds is one of non-possession, of seeing something good in them, which, given his consistent and articulated tendencies, cannot but lead him immediately back to God, the source of all good.

---

1 As with *The Rubrics of Leo*, I am following the edition of A. Bartoli Langeli, *Gli autografi di frate Francesco e di frate Leone*, 35-41 (now also in *Fontes*, 46-48), but with the emendations of Carlo Paolazzi, *Per gli autografi di frate Francesco: dubbi, verifiche e riconferme*, in *Studi su gli "Scritti" di frate Francesco* (Grottaferrata: Editiones Collegii S. Bonaventurae Ad Claras Aquas, 2006), 101-126, at 118-119, see now also *Scripta*, 112, 114.

2 C. Paolazzi, *Per gli autografi*, 120-125.

†

[1] Tu es sanctus Dominus Deus solus *qui facis mirabilia* [Ps 76:15].
[2] Tu es fortis, Tu es magnus [cf. Ps 85:10], Tu es altis[s]imus.
[3] Tu es omnipotens, Tu *pater san[c]te* [Ioh 17:11], rex celi et
[4] terre [cf. Matth 11:25]. Tu es trinus et unus, Dominus Deus
[5] deorum [cf. Ps 135:2], Tu es bonum omne bonum, summum bonum
[6] Dominus Deus vivus et verus [cf. 1 Thess 1:9]. Tu es amor caritas.
[7] Tu es sapientia, Tu es humilitas, *Tu es pacientia* [Ps 70:5],
[8] Tu es pulcritudo, Tu es securitas. Tu es quie-
[9] tas. Tu es gaudium et letitia, Tu es spes nostra, Tu es iustitia
[10] et temperantia, Tu es omnia, divitia nostra a[d] suf[f] icientiam.
[11] Tu es pulcritudo, Tu es mansuetudo,
[12] *Tu es prote[c]tor* [Ps 30:5], Tu es custos et defensor noster,
[13] Tu es fortitudo [cf. Ps 42:2], Tu es refugium. Tu es spes
[14] nostra, Tu es fides nostra, Tu es caritas
[15] nostra. Tu es [—]. Tu es tota dulcedo nostra. [Tu es
[16] vita eterna nostra, magnus et admirabilis
[17] Dominus, Deus omnipotens, misericors Salvator.]

3 Esser's edition (*Opuscula sancti patris Francisci*, 90-91) divides the text into six verses (at our vv. 1, 2, 4b, 6b, 11, 13c). In addition to these verses, Lehmann sees three major sections delineated by themes: (1) the greatness and the goodness of God, vv. 1-6a; (2) the humility of God: our riches, vv. 6b-10; (3) the strength of God: our security, vv. 11-17 (cf. *Francesco, maestro di preghiera*, 260-274). Paolazzi suggests the following three sections: (1) praise of God the Creator, one and three, highest good, vv. 1-6a; (2) praise of God who is Love, who saves, satisfies, and defends man, vv. 6b-13b; (3) praise of God who is Hope and eternal life, vv. 13c-17 (cf. Carlo Paolazzi, *Lettura degli "Scritti" di Francesco d'Assisi*, 107-112). Uribe's threefold division, with subdivisions, is: (a_a) general opening, v. 1; (a_b) God in himself, vv. 2-5a; (b_a) introductory line, vv. 5b-6a; (b_b) God with us, vv. 6b-15c; (c) closing, vv. 15d-17 (cf. *Orar come Francisco*, 20-22).

4 Cf. C. Paolazzi, *Lettura degli "Scritti,"* 105-106.

Sanctus	*The Praises of God*
Sanctus, Sanctus, **Sanctus Dominus Deus** Sabaoth.	[1] Tu es **sanctus Dominus Deus** solus *qui facis mirabilia*.

Gloria	*The Praises of God*
Quoniam **tu solus Sanctus**, tu **solus Dominus**, **tu solus Altissimus**, Iesu Christe, cum Sancto Spiritu: in gloria Dei Patris. Amen. . . . Domine Deus, **Rex caelestis**, **Deus Pater omnipotens**.	[1] **Tu** es **sanctus dominus** deus **solus** qui facis mirabilia. [2] Tu es fortis. Tu es magnus. **Tu** es **altissimus**. [3] Tu es **omnipotens**. Tu **pater** sancte, **rex celi** et [4] terre. Tu es trinus et unus **Dominus Deus** [5] deorum.

5 " . . . quia mitis sum, et humilis corde" (Matth 11:29).
6 "Dicite filiae Sion: Ecce Rex tuus venit tibi, mansuetus sedens super asinam et pullum filium subiugalis" (Matth 21:5).
7 "Et ego quasi agnus mansuetus, qui portatur ad victimam . . . "
8 Frugoni, for example, seems to go in this direction (*L'invenzione*, 148).
9 C. Paolazzi, *Lettura degli "Scritti,"* 107.
10 "Gaudebat quoque plurimum et vehementius laetabatur . . ."
11 "cuius pulchritudo inaestimabilis erat nimis."
12 L. Lehmann, *Francesco, maestro di preghiera*, 256.
13 Still in Francis's normal manner: it is a consideration of Christ that is inseparably bound up with the Trinity and still seems to focus on the mystery of Christ's humility, subjection, and meekness (therefore less on the outward, physical elements and more on the internal ones).
14 Especially: Cesare Vaiani, *La via di Francesco. Una sintesi della spiritualità francescana a partire dagli* Scritti *di san Francesco*, Presenza di san Francesco 41 (Milano: Edizioni Biblioteca Francescana, 1993, rist. 2001, 2005); "Per una lettura teologica degli Scritti," in Francesco d'Assisi, *Scritti. Testo latino e traduzione italiana*, a cura di A. Cabassi (Padova: Efr—Editrici Francescane, 2002), 73-93; *Teologia e fonti Francescane*, already cited; *Vedere e credere. L'esperienza cristiana di Francesco d'Assisi* (Milano: Glossa, 2000).
15 Cf. C. Vaiani, *Per una lettura*, 91; *Teologia e fonti*, 77-78.
16 This threefold synthesis is the subject of C. Vaiani, *La via di Francesco*.
17 *Admonition* II:3: "For that person eats of the tree of the knowledge of good who makes his will his own and, in this way, exalts himself over the good things the Lord says and does in him [*se exaltat de bonis quae Dominus dicit et operatur in ipso*]." *Admonition* VIII:1-3: "[1] The apostle says: No one can say: Jesus is Lord, except in the Holy Spirit; [2] and: There is not one who does good, not even one. [3] Therefore, whoever envies his brother the good that the Lord says or does in him [*bono quod Dominus dicit et facit in ipso*] incurs a sin of blasphemy because he envies the Most High Himself Who says and does every good thing [*qui dicit et facit omne bonum*]." *Admonition* XII:1-3: "[1] A servant of God can be known to have the Spirit of the Lord in this way: [2] if, when the Lord performs some

good through him [*cum Dominus operatur per ipsum aliquod bonum*], his flesh does not therefore exalt itself, because it is always opposed to every good. [3] Instead he regards himself the more worthless and esteems himself less than all others." *Admonition* XVII:1: "Blessed is that servant who no more exalts himself over the good the Lord says or does through him [*quod Dominus dicit et operatur per ipsum*] than over what He says or does through another." *Admonition* XXI:2: "Woe to that religious who does not hold in his heart the good things the Lord reveals to him [*bona quae Dominus sibi ostendit*] and does not reveal them by his behavior, but, under the guise of a reward, wishes instead to reveal them with his words." *Regula non bullata* XVII:5-6: "[5] In the love that is God, therefore, I beg all my brothers—those who preach, pray, or work, cleric or lay—to strive to humble themselves in everything, [6] not to boast or delight in themselves or inwardly exalt themselves because of the good words and deeds or, for that matter, because of any good that God sometimes says or does or works in and through them [*bono quod Deus facit vel dicit et operatur in eis aliquando et per ipsos*], in keeping with what the Lord says: Do not rejoice because the spirits are subject to you."

18 *Admonition* XI:3: "That servant of God who does not become angry or disturbed at anyone lives correctly, without anything of his own [*recte vivit sine proprio*]." This is in fact the very definition of the friars' way of life: "The rule and life of these brothers is this, namely: to live in obedience, in chastity, and without anything of their own [*sine proprio*], and to follow the teaching and footprints of our Lord Jesus Christ . . ." (*Regula non bullata* I:1; cf. *Regula bullata* I:1).

19 Francis uses the verb *reddere*, which is difficult to render in English with a single word, having in this case the sense of restoring or returning to someone something previously given on loan. *Admonition* VII:4: "And those people are brought to life by the spirit of the divine letter who do not attribute every letter they know, or wish to know, to the body but, by word and example, return them to the most high Lord God to Whom every good belongs [*sed verbo et exemplo reddunt ea altissimo Domino Deo, cuius est omne bonum*]." *Admonition* XI:4: "Blessed is the one for whom nothing remains except for him to return to Caesar what is Caesar's and to God what is God's [*Et beatus est, qui non remanet sibi aliquid reddens quae sunt caesaris caesari, et quae sunt Dei Deo*]." *Admonition* XVIII:2: "Blessed is the servant who returns every good to the Lord God [*Beatus servus, qui omnia bona reddit Domino*] because whoever holds onto something for himself [*qui sibi aliquid retinuerit*] hides the money of his Lord God within himself, and what he thinks he has will be taken away from him." *The Praises to be Said at All the Hours* 11: "All-powerful, most holy, most high, supreme God: all good, supreme good, totally good, You Who alone are good [*qui solus es bonus*], may we give back to You all praise [*tibi reddamus omnem laudem*], all glory, all thanks, all honor, all blessing, and all good." *Regula non bullata* XVII:17-18: "Let us attribute all good to the Lord [*omnia bona Domino . . . reddamus*] God Almighty and Most High, acknowledge that every good is His [*omnia bona ipsius esse recognoscamus*], and thank Him, from Whom all good comes [*a quo bona cuncta procedunt*], for everything. [18] May He, the Almighty and Most High, the only true God, have, be given [*reddantur*], and receive all honor and reverence, all praise and blessing,

all thanks and glory, to Whom all good belongs [*cuius est omne bonum*], He Who alone is good [*qui solus est bonus*]."

20 See C. Vaiani, *Vedere e credere*; and C. Vaiani, *Teologia e fonti*, 72-73.

21 C. Vaiani, *Teologia e fonti*, 72.

22 Vaiani does not mean that Francis in fact uses this formula in *Testament*, but only that the concept seems to show itself.

Chapter 15: **RESOLUTION OF A "VERY GRAVE TEMPTATION"**

It remains to locate Francis's stigmata experience in the more general emotional and spiritual context of those months in which he received them. I would like to note first how this period seems to have been characterized by a kind of grave temptation, and, second, how the La Verna experience apparently was the occasion of its resolution.

I. The Great Temptation of Francis

Some years ago, Grado Giovanni Merlo drew attention to the fact that the *Mirror of Perfection* groups the stigmata experience of La Verna with a great trial that had begun for Francis when he was staying at St. Mary of the Angels, the trial described as a two-year *gravissima tentatio* (*Mirror of Perfection* 99:1).[1] The precise nature of this temptation is not revealed, and scholarly arguments concerning it have ranged the gamut,[2] but at least one thing is clear: the temptation affected Francis such that "he frequently withdrew from the company of the brothers because he was unable to be his usual joyful self" (*Mirror of Perfection* 99:2).[3] It is a point reemphasized in the little stigmata-related addendum:

> Likewise, at the time he received on his body the stigmata of the Lord on the holy mountain of La Verna, he suffered so many temptations and afflictions from the devil that he was unable to appear his usual joyful self [*quod non poterat se laetum ostendere*]. He said to his companion: "If the brothers knew how many trials and how great are the afflictions the demons cause me, there would not be one of them who would not be moved to pity and compassion for me" (*Mirror of Perfection* 99:6-7).

And not only do we see that his trials prevent him from being joyful around his brothers, but there seems to be the additional point that the friars lack compassion for him.

We are not permitted to imagine that these struggles Francis is having with certain confreres are attributed to him by later friars with a polemical intent, because not even the first and official *vita* could cover them over, even if the details are left vague. *1 Celano*, Bk. II covers the last two years of Francis's life, which, while not coinciding exactly with the two-year trial, certainly overlaps with part of it. And where we might expect the hagiographer to smooth out the rough edges, instead we see traces of a real Francis with real struggles, mostly of an interpersonal nature. One such indication comes in fact at the end of a passage we have seen several times, the one about Francis's great secret. After explaining that Francis rarely, if ever, revealed his secret to anyone, Thomas goes on to describe in a surprisingly frank manner how Francis suffered from a certain distrust of people in general because of the dishonesty of a few. "For, he had met some people who agreed with him outwardly but inwardly disagreed, applauding him to his face but laughing behind his back" (*1 Celano* 96:5).[4] It could be argued from the immediate context that these people are not friars, but I think they probably are, based on what is found in the succeeding sections. The paragraph on the great secret closes a brief chapter (III), which is followed by two other brief chapters, one on the illnesses of Francis (IV), the other an encomium to Hugolino (V). The chapter there following is the pertinent one, and it treats of the "four pillars" who cared for Francis in his last two years (*1 Celano* 102). The curious thing about this section is that the "four pillars" are as if contrasted with another group, one much less pleasing to Francis, those "he saw rushing for positions of authority" (*1 Celano* 104:1).[5] Francis suffers (*"dolebat,"* v.6) because of these brothers, and grieves (*"lamentabatur,"* v. 7) their behavior. So, Francis

is specifically struggling because certain friars are too interested in governance and/or pastoral positions (*"magisterii regimina"*; *"gerere curam aliorum,"* vv. 1, 2), which to him means that these friars are abandoning what they had originally chosen, the way of simplicity.[6]

This is already enough information to give us the key for unlocking the meaning of another source, the dictated writing of Francis, *On True and Perfect Joy.*[7] This is a source that has received renewed attention in recent years,[8] especially as it is now clear that we have a primitive version of it that nullifies the one in *Acts of Blessed Francis* VII and *Fioretti* VIII, which had flattened the original meaning of the work. In *True Joy,* Francis dictates a two-part lesson concerning "what true joy is." The first part answers the question negatively, explaining what true joy is not: it is not all the Masters of Paris hypothetically entering the Order; nor would it be the arrival in the Order of prelates, bishops, or kings; neither is it the friars converting all the non-believers; nor even would it be Francis being used by God to work miracles or heal the sick. Instead, positively, true joy is described in a kind of parabolic anecdote in which Francis is the protagonist. It is a story of Francis arriving at St. Mary of the Angels—the heart of the Order—in the dead of night, after a terrible night of cold travel and inconvenience, only to find the porter unwilling to let him in. Conversation ensues:

> [9] "Who are you?" "Brother Francis," I answer. [10] "Go away!" he says. "This is not a decent hour to be wandering about! You may not come in!" [11] When I insist, he replies: "Go away! You are simple and stupid! [*Vade, tu es unus simplex et idiota*] Don't come back to us again! There are many of us here like you—we don't need you!" [12] I stand again at the door and say: "For the love of God, take me in tonight!" [13] And he replies: "I will not! [14] Go to the Crosiers' place and ask there!" [15] I tell you this: If I had patience and did not become upset, true joy, as well as true virtue and the salvation of my soul, would consist in this [*Dico*

> *tibi quod si patientiam habuero et non fuero motus, quod in hoc est vera laetitia et vera virtus et salus animae*]."

This lesson, which scholars agree is indeed traceable to Francis, is very interesting and has strong confirmatory value for what we have seen thus far. For, we again see Francis as one wary of ambition in the Order, for true joy does not consist in this. Also, Francis's simplicity—the quality he was lamenting the ambitious friars to have lost in *1 Celano* 104:6—is explained by the porter to be unnecessary and superfluous. Finally, Francis knows that true joy (*"vera laetitia"*) would consist in patiently bearing this situation, which here seems to be a self-exhortation, in light of this two-year period where Francis in fact did not always succeed in showing true joy to his confreres (*"non poterat eis se ostendere laetum," Mirror of Perfection* 99:2, 6).

If we take the data emerging from these sources and return to our primary ones for historical knowledge of the stigmata, we find some important convergences. I refer particularly to *Assisi Compilation* 118 and *1 Celano* 91-96.

Assisi Compilation 118:15-17, for example, now finds its relevance. After the narrator describes the seraph that would appear to Francis and the ensuing consolations, he explains how Francis also had terrible demonic trials while on La Verna:

> [15] And, although he had many consolations in that cell, demons also gave him many trials at night, as he himself told his companion. [16] That is why he once said: "If the brothers knew how many trials the demons cause me, there would not be one of them who would not have great pity and compassion for me." [17] As a result, as he often said to his companions, he was unable by himself to satisfy the brothers or sometimes to show them the friendliness that the brothers desired [*non poterat de se satisfacere fratribus et ostendere illis aliquando familiaritatem sicut fratres desiderabant*].

So, as stated elsewhere, this period of retreat on La Verna is associated with a period in which, first, Francis is suffering because

the brothers do not offer compassion and, second, Francis fails to show the brothers the friendly attention they desire.

And, in my thinking, this is also precisely the type of thing Thomas of Celano is aware of when he is writing his own account of the days on La Verna. For, in addition to the things I have mentioned so far from *1 Celano*, Bk. II concerning Francis's fraternal struggles, there are other relevant elements just preceding the stigmatization. Thomas's Francis goes to La Verna for various related motives: (1) to seek "a place of rest and secret solitude [*secretum solitudinis*]" (*1 Celano* 91:1); (2) "to know what in him and about him was or could be most acceptable to the Eternal King . . . to know in what manner . . . he would be able to cling more perfectly to the Lord God" (91:4-5); and (3) to "bring to complete fulfillment what he had earlier simply and devotedly begun [*simpliciter et devote inceperat*]" (92:7). And I do not think it is by chance that Thomas presents this last point in the context of Francis's prostrated, Gethsemane-like prayer, the prayer of discernment answered by the triple-opening of the Gospel book to the Passion prediction narratives.

Accordingly, it seems to me that, taken together, *The Assisi Compilation* and *1 Celano* offer glimpses of a Francis who is suffering and struggling interiorly during the La Verna retreat. This Francis is so tormented that he cannot be joyful with or friendly to the friars. He therefore seeks rest, a period of "secret solitude." During this time of retreat, Francis is preoccupied with the simple plan of the beginning of the Order because he is displeased with those abandoning the original plan for a more ambitious one. That displeasure is what is taking his joy away, and that is why he goes to La Verna seeking resolution.

II. Resolution of the Temptation

1. Resolution in the Sources

Merlo says that Francis's struggle drives him into a place of solitude, that in this very solitude is the struggle resolved, and that this resolution is somehow bound up with the stigmata.[9] He cites the fact that after the La Verna event there are no longer evidences of Francis being tormented. In the *Testament*, for example, although Francis is certainly very firm on his opinions about the direction the Order should go, he nevertheless does not show signs of being disturbed or of lacking peace and joy. I think Merlo is right: the vision of the seraph and the reception of the stigmata are indeed a turning point in Francis's interior life, especially in regards to the so-called grave temptation.

While *Assisi Compilation* 118 does not give much information on the context of the struggle, it certainly describes resolution, characterizing it by the many consolations Francis received, above all from the vision of the seraph. In the mind of the companion-narrator of *The Assisi Compilation*, this consolatory aspect is really the most salient characteristic of La Verna.

The Rubrics of Leo state the same: after the impression of the stigmata and the consoling words of the seraph, Francis bubbles over with thanksgiving, says Leo, and consequently writes the *Praises of God*.

As for those praises, one can easily see catharsis there also. Paolazzi points out that while Francis emphasizes in *The Praises of God* certain objective aspects of the God he has come to know through his mystical experience (e.g., humility, patience, beauty), he also divulges his subjective experience of those objective aspects;[10] and the specific subjective aspects are revelatory of resolution and catharsis: God is security, rest, joy, happiness.

2. Experience of Resolution in Encounter with Christ

Whatever meaning God intended for Francis's stigmata to have for his contemporaries or for us, they were for Francis, before anything else, a unique encounter with the Christ who brings meaning to human lives.

On La Verna, Francis had a two-fold encounter with God, which in a very particular manner addressed his very particular situation. It was a difficult situation. He had begun his mountain-top retreat laboring with an ugly joylessness, one which he had suffered for quite some time. All that changed on La Verna.

First, he encountered the majesty of God through a vision of and a conversation with a celestial creature, a seraph.

Second, he encountered the meek and humble Christ, who had been led like a lamb to the slaughter, who had even borne wounds on his hands, feet, and side. We do not know that Francis had a vision of Christ like he had had of the seraph, but we are certain that he could not have experienced this reality more concretely, since every time he looked at his own hands and feet and side, he encountered it anew.

The former moment seems to have been enough to break the spell and lift his spirits; in fact, he enjoyed consolations from it the rest of his days, said his companion. The latter moment gave him the will to bear with patience and joy the difficulties that were besetting him. With the grace of the first moment, he felt the love and care of God for him, and it brought him back to himself. But in the second moment, Francis had a renewed but entirely unique encounter with Christ "who suffered for you, leaving you an example, that you should follow in his footsteps" (1 Peter 2:21). That is to say, through the stigmatization Francis relearned in a decisive and unforgettable way that, if faithful to his deepest vocation (follower of Christ), he would sometimes, like now, inevitably be led down difficult paths. From this moment forward, though the struggle may not have ceased,

Francis would always have a concrete way to see that this vocation imbued the struggle with meaning, which is why he could never again allow himself to lapse into a joyless self-pity.

III. Conclusion to Part Three

Francis of Assisi, then, is not the caricature sometimes portrayed who wanted to practice a literalistic observation of the Gospel, but rather someone who wanted to practice the whole Gospel rigorously. If he practiced anything literally it was because he saw deeply into the meaning of the letter and clung to it tenaciously. To imagine him, therefore, as one who would think to simply mimic the external patterns of the life of Jesus is to imagine not the real Francis at all. But Francis did badly want to follow wherever the footsteps of Jesus might lead. Certainly Francis considered the earthly life of Jesus daily, and he devoted an entire Office to the part of the earthly life that was filled with anguish. He knew that this Jesus he was following suffered.

And it turned out that Francis, in his following, in his receiving what "the Lord gave him" and his brothers, suffered too. Since Francis listened to what the Lord had for him and accepted what "no one else but the Lord showed him," he had to face conflict with those who did not see what he received or accept what he was given.

Still, he followed the Lord up the mountain of La Verna, carrying the cross of his many interior burdens. And God, who had given him each thing he needed every step along the way was faithful. The Lord not only consoled him, but consoled him in a tremendous way. Francis sings out his thanksgiving for this consolation in his *Praises*, looking to God and not himself, in gratitude and in a renewed wonder for the mystery of the Cross, which he could now contemplate in an unheard of and humbling way by looking at the wounds of Christ present on his own body.

1 G. Merlo, "Le stimmate e la 'grande tentazione,'" 139-142. The episode appears in *Assisi Compilation* 63 in a slightly more primitive form, the main difference being the addendum about La Verna in *Mirror of Perfection*. When Thomas of Celano uses the story (*2 Celano* 115) he does not know that addition.

2 Somehow I think Sabatier comes the closest when he resigns himself to the fact that the nature of the struggle remains a "secret of history" (P. Sabatier, *Life of Francis*, 248).

3 " . . . quod a consortio fratrum se multoties subtrahebat, quia non poterat eis se ostendere laetum, sicut consueverat."

4 "Invenerat enim aliquos sibi exterius concordantes et interius dissidentes, applaudentes coram, irridentes retro . . . "

5 "Videbat enim multos ad magisterii regimina convolare . . ." The Italian editors translate "magisterii regimina" with the provocative "cattedre degli insegnamenti" ("teaching chairs," *Fonti Francescane*, 320; no. 501), in an interpretation that I suspect may be a bit preemptory, but certainly gives pause for thought, especially in light of *True Joy*, which we will look at presently.

6 "It hurt him that some had abandoned their early deeds and, in the midst of new discoveries, had forgotten their original simplicity. That is why he grieved over those who now sank to the level of what was low and cheap, although they once had striven for higher things with all their desire" (*1 Celano* 104:6-7).

7 Franciscus Assisiensis, *De vera et perfecta laetitia* [=*True Joy*], in *Scripta*, 416-418; Francis of Assisi, *True and Perfect Joy*, in *FA:ED* I, 166-167.

8 E.g., Giovanni Miccoli, "A Christian Experience between Gospel and Institution," translated by Paul Barrett, O.F.M. Cap., *GreyfrRev* 11:2 (1997): 113-141, at 118-120, 139-141; G. Merlo, "Le stimmate e la 'grande tentazione,'" 133-138; C. Vaiani, *Teologia e fonti*, 126-171.

9 G. Merlo, "Le stimmate e la 'grande tentazione,'" 140-141.

10 Cf. C. Paolazzi, *Lettura degli "Scritti,"* 110.

GENERAL CONCLUSION

It is risky to write a book or article on the stigmata of Francis, since there are already so many. Yet it has seemed to me so important as to warrant the effort. It has seemed important not to allow the historical debate to fizzle out just yet. It has seemed important to draw the historical debate into its healthiest domain, that of theology.

To achieve my goal I had to begin with a lengthy historical study of the early written sources that treat the topic, engaging directly the historiography of recent decades.

In assessing that debate I found so much that was good. Chiara Frugoni, for example, has helped us to see the gradual evolution of both the La Verna story and the portrait of the stigmatic Francis, which is important if we are going to make better hypotheses about the empirical event at their origin. I also must say, now that my own hypothesis has been fully developed, that some of her other intuitions would seem to stand largely vindicated (even if the way she arrived at them or the conclusions she drew from them would not always be in accord with my own approach and conclusions). I am thinking of her insistence that the accounts of the seraph appearance and the stigmatization were not at their origin so intertwined. And does it not also seem that she was right to suggest that the La Verna story as Francis first experienced and recounted it was more about the resolution of interior trials than about external conformity to Christ?

But Frugoni's idea that we can peel off layer after evolutionary layer of the stigmatization story, only to eventually discover that behind it all is nothing more than the exaggerated tale of

Elias or someone else, has to be reassessed. That was successfully shown when Giovanni Miccoli explained that the unified witness of the sources establishes the "fact" of the stigmata.

But even with this last theory, there is room for reconsideration. Miccoli had said that the weight of the unified witness only extends to the fact of the stigmata, and not also to their supernatural origin. My effort, though, was to show that reliable witnesses attest to the fact that Francis, for his part, believed the wounds to be from God. For example, a careful reading of Thomas of Celano's first legend shows that, among the special companions Francis had with him on La Verna, one was a special confidant for the mystical experiences of those days. Moreover, it seems to me that the simple annotations of Leo on the *Chartula* are equally valuable testimony to the understanding of Francis, who apparently explained that he was moved to give thanks for a two-fold grace, the seraph and the stigmata. Meanwhile, I did not come across any information that would weaken the basic value of these testimonies, and so I take them at face value.

The key for rectifying the idea of the invention of the seraph was twofold. Primarily, it was necessary to establish for the first time the *terminus ante quem* of the annotations of Leo. Philological analysis proved that *The Rubrics of Leo* were written before the *Florilegium* (therefore, at least before August of 1246). That testimony, therefore, cannot be called a conflation of the data given in *Assisi Compilation* 118 and *MS Little* 154. Least of all can it be called a borrowing of the *Major Legend* of Bonaventure. So, when it speaks of Francis giving thanks for the vision and conversation with the seraph, it speaks with authority. That authority comes from the independence of the testimony (proven by how it differs from *1 Celano*) and by the identity of the author, who was one of the four special companions with Francis during the days in question (and even writes his recollections on a little parchment that had been given to him then and

there). The theory of the invention of the seraph lost credibility, secondarily, with my analysis of *Assisi Compilation* 118, which I believe to have shown preserves in some ways a version of the La Verna story more primitive than that of *1 Celano*; this is really the only explanation for how a retelling of the La Verna event in 1246 could remain so uninfluenced by the official vita.

I also had to take a moment to consider some other doubts about the stigmatization of Francis, which have been around for about a century or so, but had in recent years received a fresh expression in an article by Richard Trexler. I actually think, as a matter of fact, that his attempt to explain Francis's stigmata by situating them in the context of physical mortification practices of the Middle Ages was probably the best effort yet made by those who look for a natural explanation for the phenomenon. It afforded me the opportunity to look objectively into the documentary dossier of Francis in order to ask if this theory may be a tenable one. Nowhere, though, could I find even a single foothold from which to begin the climb towards a solution like Trexler's. Next, his attempt to reread *The Letter of Elias* as not in fact announcing miraculous stigmata also seemed weak after my analysis. And the old conspiracy theory about the hiding of Francis's non-stigmatized body proved to be scintillating but unfounded.

By the time I finished discussing the historiographical debate, I found that we can be confident about the nature and value of the documentary sources for Francis's stigmata, understanding the place that each source holds. In addition to making sense of the Leonine sources, I was able to make fairly confident assertions even concerning the witnesses for each aspect of Thomas's narrative. I was also able to shore up our sense of historical certainty about the basic facts of the La Verna event when I showed the essential convergence of the narratives of *1 Celano* and *Assisi Compilation* 118.

All this created the possibility of proposing a historical reconstruction of the La Verna days of September 1224. Basically, Francis went to La Verna to seek rest and solitude and peace. He prayed to God, and the answer to his prayer took a twofold form, extravagant and unusual: a beautiful seraph appeared to him and five wounds appeared on his body.

When I was finally able to move into the more spiritual-theological part of my paper (Part Three), I realized that we will never be able to uncover the core meaning of these historical events until we understand how they were woven into the fabric of the concrete and unrepeatable life, personality, vocation, and situation of the little man, Francis.

It is crucial, for example, to know and understand that Francis's struggle in those days was tremendous. The famously joyful Poverello could find no manner of joy. The normally charismatic and gregarious natural leader felt driven into solitude and isolation.

Likewise, it is essential to comprehend that Francis had never thought to pick and choose aspects of the life of Christ to dress himself up in, but rather had chosen something that I would say is much harder because there is far less control in it: he had chosen, simply, to *follow*. Francis chose to move forward step-by-step in the footprints of the Lord, which I say is dangerous, because who can know where it will lead?

When we understand these sorts of things, we begin to enter, perhaps for the first time, into the real experience of Francis on La Verna.

Now it seems clear that the gratuitous in-breaking of God into Francis's heart in those days was first an encounter with the concrete solicitude of God for him and his vocation. Before La Verna meant to Francis a physical conformity with Christ or participation in Christ's cross, it was the extraordinary, unmerited, and very particular care of God for him and for his vocation.

La Verna was God loving the man, Francis. La Verna was God holding precious the mission of the man, Francis.

This point is emphasized especially by the form this solicitude took. First, Francis was consoled by the seraph. Its beauty shook him free from the ugliness of his solitude and brooding, probably reminding him of his earlier reasons for joy.

Second, the wounds that appeared on his body were not his own: they were the wounds of the meek and humble Christ who had been unjustly led like a lamb to the slaughter, but who bore them without bitterness. As Francis was often astounded when he thought of the poverty and earthly wants to which Jesus subjected himself, this concept must have all the more taken his breath away. And in this moment the experience was acute because Francis realized that in his brooding and joylessness he was failing in his fundamental vocation to follow Christ wherever he might lead, including down this concrete and particular path of struggle.

But all that changed when Francis, in an extraordinary way, experienced God as "patience" and "hope" and "protector" and "guardian" and "strength" and "refuge," as he wrote in thanksgiving. Francis experienced in that moment not only that God loved him, but that God loved the vocation he had given him and wanted to preserve it and protect it and renew it.

Thus, the wounds were indeed a seal of approval, as was claimed by Franciscan writers almost from the very beginning. But they were not, first and foremost, the approval those writers described. They were not, for example, primarily the divine seal that asserted Francis to be perfectly conformed to Christ. Nor were they, above all, a divine stamp of approval on the Order that the Assisian founded. Rather, the wounds were a seal of approval on the basic *propositum* of Francis, to follow in the footsteps of Christ, wherever they may lead.

Francis probably never understood why the brothers were

leaving behind their original simplicity and choosing ambition instead. But after God broke through his melancholy and shattered the fetters of his joylessness, his attention was no longer on the affront that this was to him as the founder, but only on the wounds of the Lord, whom he had promised to follow anywhere. His attention shifted away from himself to the "beautiful" and "meek" and "humble" Lamb, who "is gladness and joy," who is "all our sweetness," who is "Lord God Almighty, merciful Savior."

Normally, the resolutions to the struggles of life will not come in visions or other extraordinary phenomena. Such things are always to be considered *gratia gratis data*, graces freely given, not for their own sake but for the service of the truly essential thing, the life of grace. But when they do occur in the lives of the exemplary Christians given to history for the instruction of the rest of us, they should do for us exactly what the La Verna experience did for Francis: direct our attention back to the heart of the Christian life, the *sequi vestigia eius*.

BIBLIOGRAPHY

Medieval Works and Tools

Actus beati Francisci et sociorum eius. Nuova edizione postuma di Jacques Cambell con testo dei Fioretti a fronte. A cura di Marino Bigaroni e Giovanni Boccali. Chiesa Nuova 5. S. Maria degli Angeli—Assisi: Edizioni Porziuncola, 1988. Now also in *Fontes Franciscani,* 2085-2219.

Analecta Franciscana sive Chronica aliaque varia documenta ad historiam Fratrum Minorum spectantia. Edita a Patribus Collegii S. Bonaventurae. XV tomi. Ad Claras Aquas (Quaracchi): Ex Typographia Collegii S. Bonaventurae, 1926-1941.

Annales Minorum seu trium Ordinum a S. Francisco institutorum. Auctore A. R. P. Luca Waddingo Hiberno. Editio tertia edita a patribus collegii s. Bonaventurae. Ad Claras Aquas (Quaracchi), XXXII tomi, 1931-1964.

Anonimo della Porziuncola. *Speculum perfectionis status fratris Minoris.* A cura di Daniele Solvi. Edizione Nazionale dei Testi Mediolatini 12. Firenze: SISMEL, 2006.

The Assisi Compilation. In *FA:ED* II, 118-230.

Athanasius. *The Life of Antony.* In *Athanasius: The Life of Antony and The Letter to Marcellinus,* 29-99. Translated and introduced by Robert C. Gregg. New York: Paulist Press, 1980.

The Beginning or Founding of the Order and the Deeds of Those Lesser Brothers Who Were the First Companions of Blessed Francis in Religion (The Anonymous of Perugia) by John of Perugia. In *FA:ED* II, 34-58.

Beguin, Pierre. *Actus beati Francisci et sociorum eius. Concordance, Index, Listes de fréquence.* Corpus des Sources Franciscaines VI. Louvain-la-Neuve: Publications du CETEDOC, Université Catholique de Louvain, 1987.

Biblia sacra vulgatae editionis. Sixti V Pontificis Maximi iussu recognita et Clementis VIII auctoritate edita. Milano: Edizioni San Paolo, 2003.

Bihl, Michael. "Statuta generalia Ordinis edita in capitula generalibus celebratis Narbonae an. 1260, Assisii an. 1279 atque Parisiis an. 1292." *ArchFrancHist* 34 (1941): 13-94; 284-358.

Bonaventura de Balneoregio. *Legenda maior S. Francisci*. In *Analecta Franciscana* X, 555-652. Now also in: *Fontes Franciscani*, 777-961.

___. *Legenda minor S. Francisci*. In *Analecta Franciscana* X, 653-678. Now also in: *Fontes Francescani*, 965-1013.

Bonaventure of Bagnoregio, *Itinerarium mentis in Deum*, Works of St. Bonaventure II, Latin text from the Quaracchi Edition, New English Translation by Zachary Hayes, O.F.M., Introduction and Commentary by Philotheus Boehner, O.F.M., Franciscan Institute Publications, St. Bonaventure, New York, 2002.

A Book of the Praises of Saint Francis by Bernard of Besse. In *FA:ED* III, 31-74.

Bullarium franciscanum romanorum pontificum. Constitutiones, epistolas, ac diplomata continens tribus ordinibus minorum, clarissarum, et poenitentium a Seraphico Patriarcha Sancto Francisco institutis concessa. Studio et labore fr. Joannis Hyacinthi Sbaraleae. Tomus I (ab Honorio III ad Innocentium IV). Roma: Typis Sacrae Congregationis de Propaganda Fide, 1759.

Chronica Fratris Jordani. Editit, notis et commentario illustravit H. Boehmer. Collection d'etudes et de documents sur l'histoire religieuse et littéraire du Moyen-âge, Tomus VI. Paris: Librairie Fishbacher, 1908.

Chronica XXIV generalium Ordinis Minorum. Cum pluribus appendicibus inter quas excellit hucusque ineditus *Liber de laudibus s. Francisci fr. Bernardi a Bessa*. Analecta Franciscana III. Ad Claras Aquas (Quaracchi): Ex Typographia Collegii S. Bonaventurae, 1897.

The Chronicle of Brother Jordan of Giano. In *XIIIth Century Chronicles*, 1-78. Translated from the Latin by Placid Hermann O.F.M.. With Introduction and Notes by Marie-Therese Laureilhe. Chicago: Franciscan Herald Press, 1961.

The Chronicle of Brother Salimbene degli Adami: Selections. In *XIIIth Century Chronicles*, 193-290. Translated from the Latin by Placid Hermann O.F.M. With Introduction and Notes by Marie-Therese Laureilhe. Chicago: Franciscan Herald Press, Chicago, 1961

The Chronicle of Brother Thomas of Eccleston. The Coming of the Friars Minor to England. In *XIIIth Century Chronicles*, 79-191. Translated

from the Latin by Placid Hermann O.F.M. With Introduction and Notes by Marie-Therese Laureilhe. Chicago: Franciscan Herald Press, Chicago, 1961.

Chronicle of Salimbene de Adam. Edited by Joseph L. Baird. Binghamton: Medieval and Renaissance Texts and Studies, 1986.

Clara Assisiensis. *Regula*. In *Fontes Franciscani*, 2291-2307. A cura di E. Menestò, S. Brufani. S. Maria degli Angeli—Assisi: Edizioni Porziuncola, 1995.

"Compilatio Assisiensis" dagli scritti di fra Leone e Compagni su s. Francesco d'Assisi. Dal Ms. 1046 di Perugia. II edizione integrale riveduta e corretta con versione italiana a fronte e varianti. A cura di Marino Bigaroni. Chiesa Nuova 2. S. Maria degli Angeli—Assisi: Edizioni Porziuncola, 1992.

Die Constitutionen des Prediger-Ordens vom Jahre 1228. In *Archiv für Litteratur- und Kirchengeschichte des Mittelalters* I, 193-227. Herausgegeben von Heinrich Denifle, Franz Ehrle. Berlin: Weidmannsche Buchhandlung, 1885.

Declaratio fratris Ubertini de Casale et sociorum eius contra falsitates datas per fratrem Raymundum procuratem et Bonagratiam de Pergamo. In *Zur Vorgeschichte des Concils von Vienne*, 162-195. Herausgegeben von Heinrich Denifle, Franz Ehrle.. Archiv für Litteratur- und Kirchengeschichte des Mittelalters III. Berlin: Weidmannsche Buchhandlung, 1887.

The Deeds of Blessed Francis and His Companions by Ugolino Boniscambi of Montegiorgio. In *FA:ED* III, 435-565.

Delle Sacre Sante Istimate di Santo Francesco e delle loro considerazioni. In *I Fioretti di San Francesco*, 183-254. A cura di P. Benvenuto Bughetti. Ad Claras Aquas (Quaracchi): Ex Typographia Collegii S. Bonaventurae, 1926. Now also in *Fonti Francescane*, 1233-1272 (nos. 1896-1957).

Delorme, Ferdinand-Marie (ed.). "Diffinitiones' capituli generalis O.F.M. Narbonensis (1260)." *ArchFrancHist* 3 (1910): 491-504.

Desbonnets, Théophile. "Legenda trium Sociorum. Edition critique." *ArchFrancHist* 67 (1974): 38-144, text at 89-144. Now also in: *Fontes Franciscani*, 1373-1445. A cura di E. Menestò, S. Brufani. S. Maria degli Angeli—Assisi: Edizioni Porziuncola, 1995.

Di Fonzo, Lorenzo. "L'Anonimo Perugino tra le Fonti Francescane del Sec. XIII. Rapporti Letterari e Testo Critico." *MiscFranc* 72

(1972): 117-483, text at 435-465. Now also in: *Fontes Franciscani*, 1311-1351.

The Divine Office of Saint Francis by Julian of Speyer and Others. In *FA:ED* I, 327-345.

Doctoris seraphici S. Bonaventurae opuscula varia ad theologiam mysticam et res Ordinis Fratrum Minorum spectantia. Opera Omnia VIII. Edita a Patribus Collegii S. Bonaventurae. Ad Claras Aquas (Quaracchi): Ex Typographia Collegii S. Bonaventurae, 1898.

Epistola encyclica de transitu S. Francisci a Fr. Helia tunc Ordinis vicario generali ad omnes provincias ordinis missa. In *Analecta Franciscana* X, 525-528. Now also in: *Fontes Franciscani*, 253-255.

Fontes Franciscani. A cura di Enrico Menestò, Stefano Brufani, Giuseppe Cremascoli, Emore Paoli, Luigi Pellegrini, Stanislao da Campagnola. Apparati di Giovanni M. Boccali. S. Maria degli Angeli—Assisi: Edizioni Porziuncola, 1995.

Fonti Francescane. Nuova edizione. Scritti e biografie di san Francesco d'Assisi. Cronache e altre testimonianze del primo secolo francescano. Scritti e biografie di santa Chiara d'Assisi. Testi normativi dell'Ordine Francescano Secolare, 27-217. A cura di Ernesto Caroli. Padova: Efr—Editrici Francescane, 2004.

Francis of Assisi. *A Letter to a Minister*. In *FA:ED* I, 97-98.

___. *The Admonitions*. In *FA:ED* I, 128-137.

___. *Earlier Exhortation to the Brothers and Sisters of Penance (The First Version of the Letter of the Faithful)*. In *FA:ED* I, 41-44.

___. *Later Admonition and Exhortation to the Brothers and Sisters of Penance (Second Version of the Letter of the Faithful)*. In *FA:ED* I, 45-51.

___. *A Letter to Brother Leo*. In *FA:ED* I, 122-123.

___. *The Office of the Passion*. In *FA:ED* I, *The Saint*, 139-157.

___. *The Testament*. In *FA:ED* I, 124-127.

___. *True and Perfect Joy*. In *FA:ED* I, 166-167.

Francis of Assisi: Early Documents. Vol. 1, *The Saint* [=*FA:ED* I]. Edited by Regis J. Armstrong, J. A. Wayne Hellmann, and William J. Short. Hyde Park, NY: New City Press, 1999.

Francis of Assisi: Early Documents. Vol. 2, *The Founder* [=*FA:ED* II]. Edited by Regis J. Armstrong, J. A. Wayne Hellmann, and William J. Short. Hyde Park, NY: New City Press, 2000.

Francis of Assisi: Early Documents. Vol. 3, *The Prophet* [=*FA:ED* III]. Edited by Regis J. Armstrong, J. A. Wayne Hellmann, and William J. Short. Hyde Park, NY: New City Press, 2001.

Francisci Assisiensis, *Scripta* [=*Scripta*]. Critice edidit Carolus Paolazzi, Carlo OFM. Spicilegium Bonaventurianum XXXVI. Grottaferrata (Roma): Editiones Collegii S. Bonaventurae ad Claras Aquas, 2009.

Franciscus Assisiensis. *Admonitiones*. In *Scripta*, 352-377.

___. *De vera et perfecta letitia*. In *Scripta*, 416-418.

___. *Epistola ad Fideles* I. In *Scripta*, 174-179.

___. *Epistola ad Fideles* II. In *Scripta*, 186-201.

___. *Epistola ad fratrem Leonem*. In *Scripta*, 158-159.

___. *Epistola ad quendam Ministrum*. In *Scripta*, 164-167.

___. *Laudes Dei Altissimi*. In *Scripta*, 112-115.

___. *Officium Passionis Domini*. In *Scripta*, 70-107.

___. *Regula bullata*. In *Scripta*, 322-339.

___. *Regula non bullata*. In *Scripta*, 242-289.

___. *Testamentum*. In *Scripta*, 394-405.

___. *Ultima voluntas ad Claram et sorores*. In *Scripta*, 382.

The Goad of Divine Love by St. Bonaventure. London: R. & T. Washbourne, 1906 (Douai translation of 1642, re-edited by W. A. Phillipson).

Godet, Jean-François, George Mailleux. *Legenda trium sociorum, Anonymus Perusinus, Fr. Juliani de Spira Vita sancti Francisci, Sacrum commercium s. Francisci cum domina paupertate. Concordance, Index, Listes de fréquence, Tables comparatives*. Corpus des Sources Franciscaines III. Louvain-la-Neuve: Publications du CETEDOC, Université Catholique de Louvain, 1976.

___. *Opuscula sancti Francisci, Scripta sanctae Clarae. Concordance, Index, Listes de fréquence, Tables comparatives*. Corpus des Sources Franciscaines V. Louvain-la-Neuve: Publications du CETEDOC, Université Catholique de Louvain, 1976.

Godet, Jean-François. *Legenda seu Compilatio Perusina, Speculum Perfectionis. Concordance, Index, Listes de fréquence, Tables comparatives*. Corpus des Sources Franciscaines IV. Louvain-la-Neuve: Publications du CETEDOC, Université Catholique de Louvain, 1978.

___. *Sancti Bonaventurae Legendae maior et minor sancti Francisci. Concordance, Index, Listes de fréquence, Tables comparatives*. Corpus des

Sources Franciscaines II. Louvain-la-Neuve: Publications du CETEDOC, Université Catholique de Louvain, 1975.

Grundmann, Herbert. "Die Bulle ‚Quo Elongati' Papst Gregors IX." *ArchFrancHist* 54 (1961): 3-25.

Henrici Abrincensis. *Legenda s. Francisci versificata.* In *Analecta Franciscana* X, 405-521. Now also in: *Fontes Franciscani,* 1131-1242.

Iulianus de Spira. *Officium rhythmicum S. Francisci.* In *Analecta Franciscana* X, 375-388. Now also in: *Fontes Franciscani,* 1105-1121.

___. *Vita S. Francisci.* In *Analecta Franciscana* X, 333-371. Now also in: *Fontes Franciscani,* 1025-1095.

The Kinship of Saint Francis by Arnald of Sarrant. In *FA:ED* III, 678-733.

Legenda liturgica antiqua ordinis fratrum praedicatorum. In *Analecta Franciscana* X, 694-719.

The Legend for Use in the Choir by Thomas of Celano. In *FA:ED* I, 319-326.

The Legend of the Three Companions. In *FA:ED* II, 66-110.

Legendae S. Francisci Assisiensis saeculis XIII et XIV conscriptae ad codicum fidem recensitae a patribus collegii. Analecta Franciscana X. Ad Claras Aquas (Quaracchi): Ex Typographia Collegii S. Bonaventurae, 1941.

A Letter on the Passing of Saint Francis Attributed to Elias of Assisi. In *FA:ED* II, 489-491.

Liber chronicarum sive tribulationum di Frate Angelo Clareno. Edizione a cura di P. Giovanni Boccali, ofm. Con introduzione di Felice Accrocca. Traduzione italiana a fronte di P. Marino Bigaroni, ofm. Chiesa Nuova 8. S. Maria degli Angeli—Assisi, Edizioni Porziuncola, 1998.

The Life of Marie d'Oignies by Cardinal Jacques de Vitry. 2nd edition. Translated with introduction and notes by Margot H. King. Toronto: Peregrina Publishing, 1989.

A Life of Saint Francis by an Anonymous Monk of a German Monastery. In *FA:ED* III, 837-871.

The Life of Saint Francis by Julian of Speyer. In *FA:ED* I, 368-420.

The Life of Saint Francis by Thomas of Celano. In *FA:ED* I, 180-308.

Life of St. Anthony "Assidua" by a Contemporary Franciscan. Introduced by Vergilio Gamboso, O.F.M. Conv. Translated by Bernard Przewozny, O.F.M. Conv. Padova: Messaggero di Sant'Antonio Editrice, 2006.

Little, A. G. "Definitiones capitulorum generalium Ordinis fratrum minorum." *ArchFrancHist* 7 (1914): 676-682.

The Little Flowers of Saint Francis (A Translation and Re-editing of The Deeds of Saint Francis and His Companions by an Anonymous). In *FA:ED* III, 566-658.

The Little Flowers of Saint Francis: First Complete Edition, An Entirely New Version with Twenty Additional Chapters, also The Considerations on the Holy Stigmata, The Life and Sayings of Brother Giles. A modern English translation from the Latin and the Italian. Introduction, Notes and Biographical Sketches by Raphael Brown, Franciscan Tertiary. Garden City, NY: Image Books, 1958.

Mailleux, George. *Thesaurus Celanensis. Vita prima, Legenda ad usum chori, Vita secunda, Tractatus de miraculis, Legenda sanctae Clarae virginis. Concordance, Index, Listes de fréquence, Tables comparatives*. Corpus des Sources Franciscaines I. Louvain-la-Neuve: Publications du CETEDOC, Université Catholique de Louvain, 1974.

The Major Legend of Saint Francis by Bonaventure of Bagnoregio. In *FA:ED* II, 525-683.

The Minor Legend of Saint Francis by Bonaventure of Bagnoregio. In *FA:ED* II, 684-717.

Mira circa nos of Gregory IX. In *FA:ED* I, 565-569.

A Mirror of the Perfection of the Status *of a Lesser Brother (The Sabatier Edition)*. In *FA:ED* III, 253-372.

A Mirror of the Perfection, Rule, Profession, Life, and True Calling of a Lesser Brother (The Lemmens Edition). In *FA:ED* III, 214-252.

Opuscula Sancti Patris Francisci Assisiensis. Denuo edidit iuxta codices mss. Caietanus Esser. Biblioteca Franciscana Ascetica Medii Aevi XII. Grottaferrata: Editiones Collegii S. Bonaventurae Ad Claras Aquas, 1978.

Quo elongati of Gregory IX. In *FA:ED* I, 570-575.

The Remembrance of the Desire of a Soul (The Second Life of Saint Francis) by Thomas of Celano. In *FA:ED* II, 239-393.

The Sacred Exchange between Saint Francis and Lady Poverty. In *FA:ED* I, 529-554.

Salimbene de Adam da Parma. *Cronica*. Due volumi. Testo latino a cura di Giuseppe Scalia. Traduzione di Berardo Rossi. Prefazione di Luigi Malerba. Parma: Monte Università Parma Editore, 2007.

Scripta Leonis, Rufini et Angeli, Sociorum S. Francisci: The Writings of Leo, Rufino and Angelo, Companions of St. Francis. Edited and translated

by Rosalind B. Brooke. Oxford Medieval Texts. Oxford: Clarendon Press, 1970. Reprinted with corrections, 1990.

Speculum perfectionis (minus). Introduzione di Raoul Manselli. Testo latino, versione italiana a fronte e note, a cura di Marino Bigaroni, ofm. Chiesa Nuova 3. S. Maria degli Angeli—Assisi: Edizioni Porziuncola, 1983.

Le Speculum perfectionis ou Mémoires de frère Léon sur la seconde partie de la vie de Saint François d'Assise. Tome 1. Texte Latin, Résultant de la comparaison des onze meilleurs manuscrits connus jusqu'ici, avec l'indication de toutes les variantes fournies par eux, et d'un grand nombre d'autres, provenant des documents secondaires, préparé par Paul Sabatier. Manchester: The University Press, 1928. (First edition: *Speculum Perfectionis seu S. Francisci Assisiensis Legenda Antiquissima, Auctore Fratre Leone.* Collection de Documents pour L'Histoire Religieuse et Littéraire du Moyen Âge 1. Paris: Librairie Fishbacher, Paris, 1898.) Now also in *Fontes Franciscani*, 1849-2053.

Stimulus Amoris fr. Jacobi Mediolanunsis—Canticum paperi fr. Ioannis Peckam. Biblioteca Franciscana Ascetica Medii Aevi IV. Edita a PP. Collegii S. Bonaventurae. Ad Claras Aquas (Quaracchi): Ex Typographia Collegii S. Bonaventurae, 1905.

Sulpicius Severus. *De vita Beati Martini, Liber unus.* In *PL* 20, col. 159-176.

___. *Epistola III. Ad Bassulam socrum suam (Quomodo beatus Martinus ex hac vita ad immortalem transierit).* In *PL* 20, col. 181-184.

___. *The Life of Saint Martin, Bishop and Confessor.* In *The Fathers of the Church* VII, 101-140. Translated by Bernard M. Peebles. New York: Fathers of the Church, 1949.

Thomas de Celano. *Legenda ad usum chori.* In *Analecta Franciscana* X, 118-126; 720-721. Now also in: *Fontes Franciscani*, 427-439.

___. *Tractatus de miraculis B. Francisci.* In *Analecta Franciscana* X, 269-330. Now also in: *Fontes Franciscani*, 643-754.

___. *Vita prima S. Francisci.* In *Analecta Franciscana* X, 3-115. Now also in: *Fontes Franciscani*, 275-424.

___. *Vita secunda S. Francisci.* In *Analecta Franciscana* X, 127-268. Now also in: *Fontes Franciscani*, 443-639.

Tractatus fr. Thomae vulgo dicti de Eccleston de adventu Fratrum Minorum in Angliam. Edidit notis et commentario illustravit Andrew G. Little.

Collection d'etudes et de documents sur l'histoire religieuse et littéraire du Moyen-âge. Tomus VII. Paris: Librairie Fishbacher, 1909.

The Treatise on the Miracles of Saint Francis by Thomas of Celano. In *FA:ED* II, 399-468.

Ubertino da Casale. *Arbor vitae crucifixae Jesu,* 1485. Reprint, Charles T. David. Monumenta Politica et Philosophica Rariora, Series I, 4. Torino: Bottega d'Erasmo, 1961.

___. *The Tree of the Crucified Life of Jesus (Book V, Chap. 3-7).* In *FA:ED* III, 146-203.

An Umbrian Choir Legend. In *FA:ED* II, 473-482.

The Versified Life of Saint Francis by Henri D'Avranches. In *FA:ED* I, 428-520.

Vita prima di S. Antonio, o "Assidua" (c. 1232). Introduzione, testo critico, versione italiana e note a cura di Vergilio Gamboso. Fonti Agiografiche Antoniane 1. Padova: Messaggero, 1981.

Walter Daniel. *The Life of Ailred of Rievaulx.* Translated from the Latin with introduction and notes by F. M. Powicke. Oxford: Clarendon, 1951; reprint. 1978.

Modern works

Accocca, Felice. *"Alter apostolus." Per una rilettura della Vita beati Francisci.* In *La leggenda di un santo di nome Francesco. Tommaso da Celano e la* Vita beati Francisci, 143-260. Istituto teologico San Bernardino—Verona Settimana di studi francescani, 31 agosto—6 settembre 1997 (2). Milano: Edizioni Biblioteca Francescana, 1999.

___. "Due diverse redazioni del Memoriale in desiderio animae di Tommaso da Celano? Una discussione da riprendere." *CollFranc* 74 (2004): 5-22.

___. "Le due redazioni del Memoriale nel desiderio dell'anima di Tommaso da Celano." *FrateFr* 72 (2006): 153-186.

___. "Un'inedita e incompleta trascrizione del Ms. Little ad opera di Paul Sabatier." *ArchFrancHist* 90 (1997): 587-590.

___. "Is the 'Encyclical Letter of Brother Elias on the Transitus of St. Francis' Apocryphal?" Translated by Robert Stewart. *GreyfrRev* 13, supplement (1999): 18-64. (Original: "Un apocrifo la 'lettera enciclica di frate Elia sul transito di S. Francesco'?" *CollFranc* 65 [1995]: 473-509.)

___. "La lettera (o le lettere) di frate Elia sul transito di san Francesco." *FrateFr* 69 (2003): 503-520.

___. "La *Vita beati Francisci* di Tommaso da Celano. Un'opera elevata e complessa." *FrateFr* 70 (2004): 485-505.

___. *"Viveva ad Assisi un uomo di nome Francesco." Un'introduzione alle fonti biografiche di san Francesco.* Padova: Edizioni Messaggero, 2005.

Angelic Spirituality: Medieval Perspectives on the Ways of Angels. Translated and introduced by Steven Chase. Preface by Ewert H. Cousins. The Classics of Western Spirituality. New York: Paulist Press, 2002.

Aumann, Jordan. *Spiritual Theology.* Huntington: Our Sunday Visitor, 1980.

Barone, Giulia. "Brother Elias Revisited." Translated by Giles Bello. *GreyfrRev* 13, Supplement (1999): 1-18. (Original: "Frate Elia. Suggestioni da una rilettura." In *I Compagni di Francesco e la prima generazione Minoritica*, 61-80. Atti del XIX convegno internazionale della S.I.S.F. e del C.I.S.F. Assisi, 17-19 ottobre 1991. Spoleto: Centro Italiano di Studi sull'Alto Medioevo, 1992.)

___. *Da frate Elia agli Spirituali.* Milano: Edizioni Biblioteca Francescana, 1999.

Bartoli Langeli Attilio, Carlo Paolazzi, Giulia Barone, e Luigi Pellegrini. "Paleografia, filologia e storia a servizio di Tommaso da Celano: la *Legenda Umbra.*" *FrateFr* 74:2 (2008): 571-603.

Bartoli Langeli, Attilio. *Gli autografi di frate Francesco e di frate Leone.* Corpus Christianorum Autographa Medii Aeui V. Turnhout: Brepols, 2002.

___. "Gli scritti da Francesco. L'autografo di un 'illiteratus.'" In *Frate Francesco d'Assisi*, 101-159. Atti del XXI convengo internazionale. Assisi, 14-16 ottobre, 1993. Spoleto: Centro Italiano di Studi sull'Alto Medioevo, 1994.

Bihl, Michael. "De S. Francisci Legenda ad usum chori auctore Fr. Thoma Celanensi iuxta novum codicem Senensem." *ArchFrancHist* 26 (1933): 343-389.

___. "De stigmatibus s. Francisci Assisiensis (Occasione recentis cuiusdam libri)." *ArchFrancHist* 3 (1910): 393-432.

___. "Die Stigmata des hl. Franz von Assisi." *Historisches Jahrbuch der Görres-Gesellschaft* 28 (1907): 529-550.

Block, Wiesław, O.F.M. Cap., "La *protoregola* alla luce della *Forma vivendi* data a Chiara a alle consorelle di S. Damiano." In *La grazia*

delle origini. Studi in occasione dell'VIII centenario dell'approvazione della prima regola di san Francesco d'Assisi (1209-2009), 101-136. A cura di Paolo Martinelli. Bologna: EDB, 2009.

Bortolussi, Liviana. "Le stigmate di San Francesco nel dibattiti del '900." Dissertatio ad Lauream, Pontificia Universitas Antonianum, 2010.

Bösch, Paul. "Opinationes de stigmatibus Francisci. Annotationes ad quaestionem disputatam." *CollFranc* 76 (2006): 561-565.

___. *Franz von Assisi—neuer Christus. Die Geschichte einer Verklärung.* Düsseldorf: Patmos Verlag, 2005.

Brooke, Rosalind B. *Early Franciscan Government: Elias to Bonaventure.* Cambridge Studies in Medieval Thought—New Series 7. Cambridge: Cambridge University Press, 1959; first paperback edition, 2004.

___. *The Image of St Francis: Responses to Sainthood in the Thirteenth Century.* Cambridge: Cambridge University Press, 2006.

Constable, Giles. "The Ideal of the Imitation of Christ." In *Three Studies in Medieval Religious and Social Thought*, 145-248. Cambridge: Cambridge University Press, 1995.

Cooper, Donal. "'In loco tutissimo et firmissimo': The Tomb of St. Francis in History, Legend and Art." In *The Art of the Franciscan Order in Italy*, 1-37. Edited by William R. Cook. Leiden: Brill, 2005.

Cousins, Ewert. "The Humanity and the Passion of Christ." In *Christian Spirituality: High Middle Ages and Reformation.* Vol. II, 375-391. Edited by Jill Raitt in collaboration with Bernard McGinn and John Meyendorff. New York: Crossroad, 1987.

Cusato, Michael. "Of Snakes and Angels: The Mystical Experience behind the Stigmatization Narrative of 1 Celano." In *The Stigmata of Francis of Assisi: New Studies, New Perspectives*, 29-74. St. Bonaventure, NY: Franciscan Institute Publications, 2006.

D'Alessandro, Anna. "Chiara Frugoni, *Vita di un uomo: Francesco d'Assisi* (Recensione)." *Antonianum* LXXI (1996): 581-586.

___. "Il Medieoevo tra storia e santità. Sulle tracce dell'uomo Francesco" (Chronica: 10 maggio 1996 presentazione del libro: Chiara Frugoni, *Vita di un uomo: Francesco d'Assisi*, riportando integralmente il testo del intervento di F. Iozzelli, p. 610-619). *Antonianum* LXXI (1996): 604-619.

Dalarun, Jacques. "The Great Secret of Francis." In *The Stigmata of Francis of Assisi: New Studies, New Perspectives*, 9-26. St. Bonaventure,

NY: Franciscan Institute Publications, 2006.

___. *The Misadventure of Francis of Assisi: Towards a Historical Use of the Franciscan Legends*. Translated by Edward Hagman, O.F.M. Cap. St. Bonaventure, NY: Franciscan Institute, 2002. (Original: *La Malavventura di Francesco d'Assisi. Per un uso storico delle leggende francescane*. Milano: Biblioteca Francescana, 1996.)

___. "Tractatus de miraculis beati Francisci: un manuscrit, un texte, un mot." In *Retour aux sources. Textes, études et documents d'histoire médiévale offerts a Michel Parisse*, 601-612. Paris: Editions A&J Picard, 2004.

___. *Vers une résolution de la question franciscaine. La* Légende ombrienne *de Thomas de Celano*. Paris: Fayard, 2007.

Doyle, Eric and Damian McElrath. "St. Francis of Assisi and the Christocentric Character of Franciscan Life and Doctrine." In *Franciscan Christology*, 1-13. Edited by Damian McElrath. St. Bonaventure, NY: Franciscan Institute, 1980.

Englebert, Omer. *Saint Francis of Assisi: A Biography*. A new translation by Eve Marie Cooper. Second English edition revised and augmented by Ignatius Brady, O.F.M. and Raphael Brown, with introduction, appendices, and comprehensive bibliography covering modern research. Chicago: Franciscan Herald Press, 1965.

Faure, Philippe. "Vie et mort du séraphin de saint François d'Assise." *Revue Mabillon* 62 (1990): 143-177.

Frugoni, Chiara. "Saint Francis, a Saint in Progress." In *Saints: Studies in Hagiography*, 161-190. Edited by Sandro Sticca. Binghamton: Medieval and Renaissance Texts and Studies, 1996.

___. *Francesco e l'invenzione delle stimmate: Una storia per parole e immagini fino a Bonaventura e Giotto*. Torino: Einaudi, 1993.

___. *Francis of Assisi A Life*. Translated by John Bowden. New York: Continuum, 1995. (Original: *Vita di un uomo. Francesco d'Assisi*. Torino: Einaudi, 1995.)

Gatti, Isidoro. *La tomba di s. Francesco nei secoli*. Il Miracolo di Assisi 6. Assisi: Casa Editrice Francescana, 1983.

Gieben, Servus. "Recensione [of Frugoni, Francesco e l'invenzione delle stimmate, 1993]." *CollFranc* 65 (1995): 279-281.

Gratien de Paris. *The Foundation and the Evolution of the Friars Minor in the Thirteenth Century: A History*. 3 vols.. Translated by Stephen Paul Laliberté. printed privately. (Original: *Histoire de la fondation*

et de l'évolution de l'ordre des Frères Mineurs au XIIIe siècle. Paris: Librairie Saint-François d'Assise, 1926-1928; 2nd edition: Bibliotheca Seraphico-Cappuccina 29. Con bibliografia ampliata. A cura di M. D'Alatri, S. Gieben. Roma: Istituto Storico dei Cappuccini, 1982.)

Grau, Englebert. "Thomas of Celano: Life and Work." Translated by Xavier John Seubert. *GreyfrRev* 8:2 (1994): 177-201. (Original, 1989.)

Grundmann, Herbert. *Religious Movements in the Middle Ages. The Historical Links between Heresy, the Mendicant Orders, and the Women's Religious Movement in the Twelfth and Thirteenth Century, with the Historical Foundations of German Mysticism*. Translated by Steven Rowan. With an introduction by Robert. E. Lerner. Notre Dame: University of Notre Dame Press, 1995. (German 1st edition: 1935. German 2nd edition: 1960.)

Hampe Karl. "*Altes und Neues über die Stigmatisation des hl. Franz von Assisi*." *Archiv für Kulturgeschichte* 8 (1910): 257-290.

___. "Die frühesten Stigmatisationen und der hl. Franz von Assisi." *Internationale Wochenschrift für Wissenschaft, Kunst und Technik* 4 (1910): 1485-1494.

___. "Die Wundmale des hl. Franz von Assisi." *Historische Zeitschrift* 96 (1906): 385-402.

Heffernan, Thomas. *Sacred Biography: Saints and their Biographers in the Middle Ages*. Oxford: Oxford University Press, 1988.

Hellmann, J. A. Wayne. "The Seraph in the Legends of Thomas of Celano and St. Bonaventure: The Victorine Transition." In *Bonaventuriana. Miscellanea in onore di Jacques Guy Brougerol, ofm*, 347-356. A cura di Francisco de Asís Chavero Blanco. Roma: Edizioni Antonianum, 1988.

___. "The Seraph in Thomas of Celano's Vita Prima." In *That Others May Know and Love: Essays in Honor of Zachary Hayes, OFM, Franciscan Educator, Scholar*, 23-41. Edited by Michael F. Cusato, O.F.M. and F. Edward Coughlin, O.F.M. St. Bonaventure, NY: The Franciscan Institute, 1997.

Iammarrone, Giovanni, *La cristologia francescana. Impulsi per il presente*, Studi Francescani 1. Padova: Edizioni Messaggero, 1997.

___. "La 'sequela di Cristo' nelle Fonti francescane." *MiscFranc* 82 (1982): 417-461.

Lapsanski, Duane. "The Autographs on the 'Chartula' of St. Francis of

Assisi." *ArchFrancHist* 67 (1974): 18-37.

Lazzeri, Zeffirino. "Le stimate di s. Francesco in un libro recente." *La Verna* VIII (1910): 100-105; 209-213; 279-285.

Ledeur, Etienne. "The Spiritual Tradition." In Edouard Cothenet, Etienne Ledeur, Pierre Adnés, Aimé Solignac, and Bernard Spaapen, *Imitating Christ*. Translated by Simone Inkel and Lucy Tinsley. With a preface by John L. Boyle. St. Meinrad: Abbey Press, 1974. (Translation of the article *Imitation du Christ* and of the second part of the article *Imitation du Christ [Livre]*. In *Dictionnaire de Spiritualité*. Vol. 7:2 [Paris: Beauchesne, 1971], cols. 1536-1601 and 2355-2368.)

Lehmann, Leonhard. *Francesco, Maestro di preghiera*. Bibliotheca Ascetico-Mystica 5. Roma: Istituto Storico Dei Cappuccini, 1993. (Revised translation of *Franziskus—Meister des Gebets*. Werl, 1989).

Little, Andrew George. *Description of a Franciscan Manuscript, formerly in the Phillipps Library, now in the possession of A. G. Little*, in Collectanea Franciscana, vol. I, 9-113. British Society of Franciscan Studies 5. Ediderunt A. G. Little, M. R. James, H. M. Bannister. Aberdonia: Typis Academicis, 1914.

Lunghi, Elvio. "La morte di san Francesco alla Porziuncola e la scoperta delle stimmate nei dipinti del XIII secolo." In *Il fatto delle stimmate di S. Francesco*, 49-72. Atti della tavola rotonda tenuta alla Porziuncola di Assisi il 17 settembre 1996. Assisi: Edizioni Porziuncola, 1997.

Magro, Pasquale. "Tomba di san Francesco." In *Dizionario francescano. Spiritualità*, col. 2065-2086; 2598. A cura di Ernesto Caroli. 2ª edizione riveduta e ampliata. Padova: Edizioni Messaggero, 1995 (ristampa 2002).

Manselli, Raoul. "Un giorno alla Verna: san Francesco e frate Leone." In *Francesco e i suoi compagni*, 303-313. Bibliotheca Seraphico-Capuccina 46. Roma: Istituto Storico Dei Cappuccini, 1995. (Originally found in *FrateFr* 50 [1983]: 161-171.)

___. *San Francesco d'Assisi*. Editio maior. Introduzione di Marco Bartoli. Epilogo di Edith Pásztor. Milano: Edizioni San Paolo, 2002.

___. *St. Francis of Assisi*. Translated by Paul Duggan. Chicago: Franciscan Herald Press, 1988. (Original first edition: Roma, 1980.)

___. "We Who Were With Him: A Contribution to the Franciscan Question." Translated by Edward Hagman, O.F.M. Cap. Edited by Regis Armstrong and Ingrid Peterson. *GreyfrRev* 14, Supplement (2000): 1-196. (Original, 1980.)

Marianeschi, Paolo Maria. *Il problema scientifico della stimmatizzazione somatica*. In *Il fatto delle stimmate di S. Francesco*, 73-87. Atti della tavola rotonda tenuta alla Porziuncola di Assisi il 17 settembre 1996. Assisi: Edizioni Porziuncola, 1997.

Marini, Alfonso. "Dalla *sequela* alla *conformitas*. Una ricerca su fonti francescane." *Franciscana* VII (2005): 69-87.

___. "'*Vestigia Christi Sequi*' or '*Imitatio Christi*': Two Different Ways of Understanding Francis of Assisi's Gospel Life." Translated by Cyprian Rosen, O.F.M. Cap. *GreyfrRev* 11:3 (1997): 331-358. (Original: '*Vestigia Christi sequi*' o '*imitatio Christi*.' Due differenti modi di intendere la vita evangelica di Francesco d'Assisi." *CollFranc* 64 [1994]: 89-119.)

Marrou, Henri I. *The Meaning of History*. Translated by Robert J. Olsen. Montreal: Palm, 1966. (Original: *De la connaissance historique*. Paris: Éditions du Seuil, 1954.)

Matura, Thaddée. "Sequela Christi." In *Dizionario francescano. Spiritualità*, col. 1883-1891. A cura di Ernesto Caroli. 2[a] edizione riveduta e ampliata. Padova: Edizioni Messaggero, 1995 (ristampa 2002).

Menestò, Enrico. *Leone e i compagni di Assisi*. In *I compagni di Francesco e la prima generazione minoritica*, 33-58. Atti del XIX convegno internazionale. Assisi, 17-19 ottobre 1991. Spoleto: Centro Italiano di Studi sull'Alto Medioevo, 1992.

Merkt, Josef. *Die Wundmale des Heiligen Franziskus von Assisi*. Beiträge zur Kulturgeschichte des Mittelalters und der Renaissance. Herausgegeben von Walter Goetz. Heft 5. Leipzig: B. G. Teubner, 1910.

Merlo, Grado Giovanni. "Le stimmate e la 'grande tentazione.'" In *Intorno a frate Francesco. Quattro studi*, 131-156. Presenza di san Francesco 39. Milano: Edizioni Biblioteca Francescana, 1993.

Miccoli, Giovanni. "A Christian Experience between Gospel and Institution." Translated by Paul Barrett, O.F.M. Cap. *GreyfrRev* 11:2 (1997): 113-141. (Original, "Un'esperienza cristiana tra vangelo e istituzione." In *Dalla "sequela Christi" di Francesco d'Assisi all'apologia della povertà*. Atti del XVIII convegno internazionale, Assisi, ottobre 18-20 1990. Spoleto: Centro Italiano di Studi sull'Alto Medioevo, 1992.)

___. "Considerazioni sulle stimmate." In *Il fatto delle stimmate di S. Francesco*, 13-39. Atti della tavola rotonda tenuta alla Porziuncola di Assisi il 17 settembre 1996. Assisi: Edizioni Porziuncola, 1997. (Later republished in *Franciscana* 1 [1999]: 101-121.)

___. "Francis of Assisi's Christian Proposal." Translated by Edward Hagman, O.F.M. Cap. *GreyfrRev* 3:2 (1989): 127-172. (Original: "La proposta cristiana di Francesco d'Assisi." *Studi Medievali* 24 [1983]: 17-76.)

Michetti, Raimondo. *Francesco d'Assisi e il paradosso della* minoritas. *La* Vita beati Francisci *di Tommaso da Celano*. Nuovi Studi Storici 66. Roma: Istituto Storico Italiano per il Medio Evo, 2004.

Moioli, Giovanni. "Esperienza cristiana." In *Nuovo dizionario di spiritualità*, 536-542. A cura di Stefano De Fiores e Tullo Goffi. 7ª edizione. Milano: Edizioni San Paolo, 1999.

___. *L'esperienza spirituale. Lezioni introduttive*. A cura di Claudio Stercal del Centro Giovanni Moioli. Contemplatio 6. Milano: Glossa, 1992, rist. 2006.

___. "Teologia spirituale." In *Dizionario teologico interdisciplinare*. Vol. 1, 36-66. Torino: Marietti, 1977.

___. "Teologia spirituale." In *Nuovo dizionario di spiritualità*, 1597-1609. A cura di Stefano De Fiores e Tullo Goffi. 7ª edizione. Milano: Edizioni San Paolo, 1999.

Moorman, John R. H. *The Sources for the Life of S. Francis of Assisi*. With a foreword by A. G. Little. Manchester: Manchester University Press, 1940 (reprint 1966).

Paolazzi, Carlo. "Francis and His Use of Scribes: A Puzzle to be Solved." Translated by Edward Hagman, O.F.M. Cap. *GreyfrRev* 18:3 (2004): 323-341. (Original: "Gli 'Scritti' tra Francesco e i suoi scrivani: un nodo da sciogliere." In *Studi su gli "Scritti" di frate Francesco*, 81-99. Prefazione di Aldo Menichetti. Spicilegium Bonaventurianum XXXV. Grottaferrata: Editiones Collegii S. Bonaventurae Ad Claras Aquas, 2006.)

___. "Francesco in Cammino. Testimonianza Cristiana e *'Lodi di Dio Altissimo*.'" Absorbeat 9. Villa Verucchio: Pazzini Editore, 2003.

___. *Lettura degli "Scritti" di Francesco d'Assisi*. 2ª edizione. Milano: Edizioni Biblioteca Francescana, 2002.

___. "Per gli autografi di frate Francesco: dubbi, verifiche e riconferme." In *Studi su gli "Scritti" di frate Francesco*, 101-126. Prefazione di Aldo Menichetti. Spicilegium Bonaventurianum XXXV. Grottaferrata: Editiones Collegii S. Bonaventurae Ad Claras Aquas, 2006.

___. "Il rendimento di grazie per le stimmate: Le 'Lodi di Dio Altissimo.'" In *La contemplazione del Cristo Crocifisso*, 87-96. Quaderni di

Spiritualità, Incontri di spiritualità francescana, 19-24 agosto 1991. La Verna: Santuario della Verna, 1992.

Pazzelli, Raffaele. "Penitenza, mortificazione." In *Dizionario francescano. Spiritualità*, col. 1147-1471; 2501-2504. A cura di Ernesto Caroli. 2ª edizione riveduta e ampliata. Padova: Edizioni Messaggero, 1995 (ristampa 2002).

Pellegrini, Luigi. "La raccolta dei testi francescani del codice assisano 338. Un manoscritto composito e miscellaneo." In *Frate Francesco e i suoi agiografi*, 371-423. Saggi 8. S. Maria degli Angeli—Assisi: Edizioni Porziuncola, 2004.

Poulenc, Jérôme. "Conformità." In *Dizionario francescano. Spiritualità*, col. 239-246. A cura di Ernesto Caroli. 2ª edizione riveduta e ampliata. Padova: Edizioni Messaggero, 1995 (ristampa 2002).

Pozzi, Giovanni. "San Francesco 'di seconda mano.'" In *Verba domini mei. Gli* Opuscula *di Francesco d'Assisi a 25 anni dalla edizione di Kajetan Esser, ofm*, 279-327. Atti del Convegno internazionale. Roma, 10-12 aprile 2002. A cura di Alvaro Cacciotti. Roma: PAA—Edizioni Antonianum, 2003.

___. "Lo stile di san Francesco." In *Italia medioevale e umanistica* 41 (2000): 7-72.

Prinzivalli, Emanuela. "A Saint to Be Read: Francis of Assisi in the Hagiographic Sources." Translated by Edward Hagman, O.F.M. Cap. *GreyfrRev* 15:3 (2001): 253-298. (Original: "Un Santo da leggere: Francesco d'Assisi nel percorso delle fonti agiografiche." In *Francesco d'Assisi e il primo secolo di storia francescana*, 71-116. Torino: Einaudi, 1997.)

Romanelli, Silvia. "*Sequela*, *imitatio* e *conformitas* in fonti francescane 'non ufficiali.'" *Franciscana* VII (2005): 89-126.

Rusconi, Roberto. "Attraversando Francesco." *Cristianesimo nella storia* 16 (1995): 599-625.

___. "Francesco d'Assisi, santo (Francesco di Pietro di Bernadone)." In *Dizionario biografico degli Italiani*, vol. 49, 664-678. A cura di Alberto Maria Ghisalberti. Roma: Istituto della Enciclopedia Italiana, 1997.

___. *Francis of Assisi in the Sources and Writings*. Translated from the Italian by Nancy Celaschi, OSF. St. Bonaventure, NY: Franciscan Institute, 2008. (Original: *Francesco d'Assisi nelle fonti e negli scritti*. Padova: Efr—Editrici Francescane, 2002.)

Sabatier, Paul. *The Life of St. Francis of Assisi.* Translated by Louise Seymour Houghton. New York: Charles Scribner, 1894.

Schmucki, Octavian. "The Illnesses of Saint Francis of Assisi before His Stigmatization." *GreyfrRev* 4 (1990): 31-61. (Original: "Le malattie di Francesco durante gli ultimi anni della sua vita." In *Francesco d'Assisi e francescanesimo dal 1216 al 1226*, 315-362. Atti del IV Convegno Internazionale della S.I.S.F. Assisi, 15-17 ottobre 1976. Rimini: Maggioli Editore, 1977.)

___. "Infermità, malattia, malato, salute, assistenza ai malati." In *Dizionario francescano. Spiritualità*, col. 827-872; 2413-2417. A cura di Ernesto Caroli. 2ª edizione riveduta e ampliata. Padova: Edizioni Messaggero, 1995 (ristampa 2002).

___. "The Mysticism of St. Francis in the Light of His Writings." Translated by Ignatius McCormick, O.F.M. Cap. *GreyfrRev* 3 (1989): 241-266. (Original: "Zur Mystik des hl. Franziskus von Assisi im Lichte seiner 'Schriften.'" In *Abendlandische Mystik in Mittelalter*, 241-268. Stuttgart, 1986.)

___. "The Passion of Christ in the Life of St. Francis of Assisi: A Comparative Study of the Sources in the Light of Devotion to the Passion Practiced in His Time." Translated by Ignatius McCormick, O.F.M. Cap. *GreyfrRev* 4, Supplement (1990). (Original: "Das Leiden Christi im Leben des hl. Franziskus von Assisi: Eine Quellenvergleichende Untersuchung im Lichte der Zeitgenössischen Passionsfrömmigkeit." *CollFranc* 30 [1960]: 5-30; 129-145; 241-263; 353-397.)

___. *The Stigmata of St. Francis of Assisi.* Translated by C. F. Connors. St. Bonaventure, NY: The Franciscan Institute, 1991. (Translated from the author's 1988 revision of "De Sancti Francisci Assisiensis stigmatum susceptione: Disquisitio historico-critica luce testimoniorum saeculi XIII." *CollFranc* 33 [1963]: 210-66, 392-422; 34 [1964]: 241-338.)

Short, William J. "Francis, the 'New' Saint in the Tradition of Christian Hagiography." In *Francis of Assisi: History, Hagiography, and Hermeneutics in the Early Documents*, 153-163. Edited by Jay M. Hammond. Hyde Park, NY: New City Press, 2004.

Southern, Robert, W. *Saint Anselm and His Biographer: A Study of Monastic Life and Thought 1059-c. 1130.* Birbeck Lectures, 1959. Cambridge: Cambridge University Press, 1963.

Stanislao da Campagnola. *L'Angelo del sesto sigillo e l'"Alter Christus.' Genesi*

e sviluppo di due temi francescani nei secoli XIII-XIV. Studi e Ricerche 1. Roma: Antonianum—Laurentianum, 1971.

___. "Il 'fatto' delle stimmate nelle fonti documentarie." In *Il fatto delle stimmate di S. Francesco*, 41-48. Atti della tavola rotonda tenuta alla Porziuncola di Assisi il 17 settembre 1996. Assisi: Edizioni Porziuncola, 1997.

___. "L''invenzione' delle stimmate di Francesco. Una storia per ipotesi da Frate Elia a san Bonaventura." *Commentari d'arte* I/2 (1995): 21-34.

Tamassia, Nino. *Saint Francis of Assisi and His Legend*. Translated by Lonsdale Ragg. London: T. Fisher Unwin, 1910. (Original: *S. Francesco d'Assisi e la sua leggenda*. Padova—Verona: Ed. Tip. Fratelli Ducker, 1906.)

Trexler, Richard C. "The Stigmatized Body of Francis of Assisi. Conceived, Processed, Disappeared." In *Frömmigkeit im Mittelalter. Politisch-soziale Kontexte, visuelle Praxis, körperliche Ausdrucksformen*, 463-497. Hrsg. Klaus Schreiner. München: Wilhelm Fink Verlag, 2002.

Uribe, Fernando. *Il Francesco di Bonaventura: Lettura della* Leggenda Maggiore. S. Maria degli Angeli—Assisi: Edizioni Porziuncola, 2003.

___. *Introduzione alle fonti agiografiche di san Francesco e santa Chiara d'Assisi (secc. XIII-XIV)*. Traduzione dell'edizione spagnola rivista ed ampliata. Saggi 7. S. Maria degli Angeli—Assisi: Edizioni Porziuncola, 2002. (Original: *Introducción a las hagiografías de san Francisco y santa Clara de Asís [siglos XIII y XIV]*. Madrid-Murcia: Publicaciones Instituto Teológico Franciscano, 1999.)

___. *Orar como Francisco. Notas y sugerencias sobre las oraciones del Santo de Asís*. Colección Karisma 2. Santiago de Cali: Curso Carisma Misionero Franciscano, 2008.

Vaiani, Cesare. "Per una lettura teologica degli Scritti." In Francesco d'Assisi, *Scritti. Testo latino e traduzione italiana*, 73-94. A cura di A. Cabassi. Padova: Efr—Editrici Francescane, 2002.

___. *Teologia e fonti Francescane. Indicazioni di metodo*. Presenza di san Francesco 46. Milano: Edizioni Biblioteca Francescana, 2006.

___. *Vedere e credere. L'esperienza cristiana di Francesco d'Assisi*. Sapientia 2. Milano: Glossa, 2000 (rist. 2007).

___. *La via di Francesco. Una sintesi della spiritualità francescana a partire dagli* Scritti *di san Francesco*. Presenza di san Francesco 41. Milano: Edizioni Biblioteca Francescana, 1993 (rist. 2001, 2005).

Van Dijk, Stephen. "The Breviary of Saint Francis." *Franciscan Studies* 9 (1949): 13-40.

Van Dooren, Kees. "The Stigmatization of St. Francis, Fact or Fiction?" In *Verum, pulchrum et bonum. Miscellanea di studi offerti a Servus Gieben in occasione del suo 80° compleanno*, 155-183. A cura di Y. Teklemariam. Roma: Istituto Storico dei Cappuccini, 2006.

Vauchez, André. "Autour de la stigmatisation de saint François : une histoire de textes et d'images." *Revue Mabillon* 66 (1994): 270-274. (Now also in: *Francesco d'Assisi e gli Ordini mendicanti*, 73-79. Saggi 10. S. Maria degli Angeli—Assisi: Edizioni Porziuncola, 2005.)

___. "Francesco d'Assisi e il vangelo tra lettera e spirito." *FrateFr* 74 (2008): 325-338.

___. *Francesco d'Assisi. Tra storia e memoria*. Edizione italiana a cura di Grado Giovanni Merlo. Torino: Giulio Einaudi Editore, 2010. (Original: *François d'Assise. Entre histoire et mémorie*. Paris: Librairie Arthème Fayard, 2009.)

___. *Sainthood in the Later Middle Ages*. Translated by Jean Birrell. Cambridge: Cambridge University Press, 1997; paperback edition, 2005. (Original: *La sainteté en Occident aux derniers siècles du Moyen Age*. Rome: Ecole française de Rome, 1988.)

___. *The Spirituality of the Medieval West: The Eighth to the Twelfth Century*. Translated by Colette Friedlander. Kalamazoo: Cistercian Press, 1993. (French 1st edition: 1975; French 2nd edition: 1994; Italian 3rd edition: 2006.)

___. "The Stigmata of St. Francis and Its Medieval Detractors." Translated by Edward Hagman, O.F.M. Cap. *GreyfrRev*13 (1999): 61-89. (Original: "Les stigmates de saint François et leurs détracteurs dans les derniers siècles du Moyen Âge." *Mélanges d'archéologie et d'histoire* 80 [1968]: 595-625.)

Von Hase, Karl August. *Franz von Assisi: Ein Heiligenbild*. Leipzig: Breitkopf und Härtel, 1856.

Zerbi, Pietro. "'L'ultimo sigillo'" (Par. XI, 107). Tendenze della recente storiografia italiana sul tema delle stigmate di s. Francesco." *Rivista di storia della chiesa in Italia* 48 (1994): 7-42.

INDEX